Spanning The Century

The Story of an Ordinary Man in Extraordinary Circumstances

Spanning The Century

The Story of an Ordinary Man
in Extraordinary Circumstances

by

TONY HARE

The Memoir Club

© Tony Hare 2002

First published in 2002 by
The Memoir Club
Whitworth Hall
Spennymoor
County Durham

All rights reserved.
Unauthorised duplication
contravenes existing laws.

British Library Cataloguing in
Publication Data.
A catalogue record for this book
is available from the
British Library.

ISBN: 1 84104 046 0

Typeset by George Wishart & Associates, Whitley Bay.
Printed by Bookcraft (Bath) Ltd.

To the family who have always been ready with their support

Contents

Illustrations ix
Acknowledgements xi

Part I: My Life

Chapter 1	The 'Moravian Gate'	3
Chapter 2	Born 'in Between'	5
Chapter 3	Early Memories	10
Chapter 4	Vienna 1920	13
Chapter 5	The Clock	19
Chapter 6	Lessons and the Beginning of School	24
Chapter 7	The Prussian Cure	27
Chapter 8	Lausanne, Dunkerque and Paris	31
Chapter 9	Life at College	37
Chapter 10	Travelling	43
Chapter 11	Textile Apprentice – Brno	49
Chapter 12	National Service	53
Chapter 13	Contrasts	62
Chapter 14	Permission to Leave	70
Chapter 15	Final Destination England	81
Chapter 16	Yorkshire	87
Chapter 17	Early Days of the War	95
Chapter 18	British Forces	103
Chapter 19	Problems of Nationality	110
Chapter 20	Joint American/British Unit	117

Chapter 21	Interrogation	120
Chapter 22	Yugoslavia	130
Chapter 23	A Historical Perspective	138
Chapter 24	Preparation for War Crime Trials, and Return to Czechoslovakia	148
Chapter 25	Back to Civvy Street	162
Chapter 26	The Gurdjieff Society and my Family	173

Part II: Hebrew Study

Introduction		191
Chapter 1	Looking for my Roots	199
Chapter 2	The Connection Between Hebrew Grammar and Thinking	202
Chapter 3	The Cycle of the Week and the Year	210
Chapter 4	The Idea of Covenant in the Hebrew Tradition	227
Chapter 5	Sacrifices and Offerings	232
Chapter 6	The Ten Sephirot – The Tree of Life	238
Epilogue		242
Bibliography		244

Illustrations

Grandfather Adolph Haas	6
Trading licence for Adolph Haas and his brother Julius	7
My great-uncle Isidor who wove the trousers	8
My grandfather K&K Kommerzialrat Moritz Löffler at Karlovy Vary-Karlsbad	9
Myself aged 4	14
My mother	21
My father	23
The family council and their children	44
The team of foremen and designers in the firm of Eduard Ernst Essler, Brno-Obřany	50
As Officer Cadet in the 2nd Siberian Dragoons	56
Being promoted 'in the field'	59
The Germans march in	65
My parents and myself just before departure	73
Certificate of good conduct	75
Health and vaccination certificates	76
Sailing 13 May 1939	78
On board the *St Louis*	79
The little boats with our relatives	82
Mr & Mrs Churchill and Sarah Churchill	98
As an officer in the Home Guard	100
Certification of compassionate leave	154
Movement order	156

Jean at the time of our meeting 175
Our wedding photograph 179
John's wife Giselle with their children 184
John and Deborah 185
John Hare 15 December 1957 – 7 September 1998 186
All the present family except three grandchildren from Sydney 187
The synagogue in Olomouc 194

Acknowledgements

I would like especially to thank my daughter Deborah and my son-in-law Miles who gave freely their time and effort during all the processes of converting the early hand written drafts into a technically accomplished form.

PART I

My Life

Chapter 1

The 'Moravian Gate'

In the middle of the nineteenth century my great grandfather acquired a brewery in a little hamlet called Týnec. The nearest sizeable village was called Hranice which means border, and it was given this name because it divides the river system of the river Oder flowing north through to the plains of Silesia and Poland into the Baltic, and the river Morava flowing south into the Danube and eventually into the Black Sea. It was also the gap between the Sudeten Mountains reaching the height of nearly 2,000 metres in the west which formed a wooded barrier around Northern Moravia and Bohemia, and the system of the Carpathian Mountains to the east which swung in a long arch dividing Slovakia, Ruthenia, Austria, Hungary and the rest of south east Europe from the plains of Poland, the Ukraine, and Russia to the north.

This 'Moravian Gate' thus formed the only easy access route between the plains of north eastern Europe and Asia on the one hand and the Danube basin in the south. Then when thousands of years ago the pressure of population from the area of Lake Van started, the attraction of this route from the cold and often marshy plains of the north east to the particularly fertile areas of Moravia, Bohemia and the Danube became obvious.

The earliest arrivals who left some traceable marks were the Celts who came about 2,500 years ago and in excavations in southern Moravia delicate artefacts have shown what a high civilisation this must been. It was only when I came to Wales that I realised that some ways of expression and even some grammatical forms used in local dialects of both Czech and German must have had Celtic connections.

The Celts were followed by some Germanic tribes around the beginning of the Christian era followed by the Czechs in the first and second century AD.

As the new invaders arrived they pushed the earlier population out of the fertile plains into the surrounding mountain area. In modern times, therefore, the Czechs lived mainly in the centre of the country whilst the so called Sudeten-Germans were in the mountain areas near the border.

Moravia is between Bohemia in the west and Slovakia in the east. Going from west to east a gradual change of temperament becomes clear: more easy going and slower. The dialect also changes gradually. The name Bohemia requires some explanation. It is the Latin name of the country. As Latin was the official language of government until the seventeenth century this name was used in all official and international communications and when the King of Bohemia became the senior elector of the Emperor of the 'German' Empire the world did not know that the natives, namely the Czechs, called this country 'Čechy'. So it was that the world discovered only in 1918, when Czechoslovakia was created, that a country and nation of this name existed, and even twenty years later the British Prime Minister Chamberlain was unaware that he was talking about one of the oldest and most powerful kingdoms of Central Europe and the former Austro Hungarian Empire, when he referred to 'the small and foreign people of the east for whom it was not worth going to war'.

The Germans used the word Böhmen for this country, which is derived from the Latin. The King of Bohemia was also Margrave of Moravia and ruled over parts of Silesia.

When Czechoslovakia was divided in 1993 the Czechs started to talk about the 'Czech Lands' meaning Bohemia and the administrative county of Moravsko-Slesko which is the former Moravia and the part of Silesia which remained under Czech rule in 1945, i.e. not in Poland or Germany.

Christianity arrived in Moravia first from Constantinople in the east, up the Danube valley, and later from Rome in the west. The Romans conquered the area and until the building of motorways the road system was built by the Romans. It is quite possible that the first Jews arrived in the area following the Romans as traders, although the earliest known settlements are in the tenth century.

Now that I look back at more than three-quarters of a century of my life I realise that this place of birth of mine at the meeting of so many crossroads connects with the pattern of my life. It is our area that is always 'in between', between north and south, between east and west, between Slav and German, and the more I am trying to find out who I am, the more I find myself 'in between'.

CHAPTER 2

Born 'in Between'

My GREAT-GREAT-GRANDFATHER on my father's side was described to me as a teacher in a small Jewish ghetto-community in central Moravia called Holešov. As there was no secular education in those communities I must assume that he must have taught in a yeshiva, a Jewish religious school. My great-grandfather Abraham who was born in the year of the battle of Waterloo left the ghetto in 1848, when Jews were allowed to live outside the specific Jewish communities. Up to that time the family would have spoken Yiddish and would have known Hebrew as the sacred language.

Until then Jews had only used their Jewish names, the secular authorities had no records and no surnames were used. On leaving the ghetto the use of surnames became necessary and Jews had to apply 'to the Emperor' to use a specific name. My family was given permission to use the name Haas. This name I bore until 1947. I was living in Yorkshire at the time where in the local dialect h's are often dropped and it was indicated to me that I was embarrassing for the girls at the other end of the telephone. So I translated my name to Hare. As I am the only one of my family who has survived the holocaust the old name has now completely disappeared.

On leaving the ghetto Abraham Haas became a distiller and made sufficient money to buy the brewery in Týnec mentioned earlier. In our sitting room was a little painting of him standing very proudly before our aspidistra type plant, his pockets bulging, which my father said was because they contained the money for the purchase.

He founded the firm of A. Haas' Söhne and for the next four generations the eldest son always had a name beginning with A. The firm became eventually one of the most important maltsters for the brewery industry, shipping more than a thousand 'wagons' (10,000 tons) of malt per season to South America apart from exports to Europe and other parts of the world.

The Hana region of central Moravia, called after a small tributary of the river Morava, produced the best barley in the world for brewing lager beers. Until the late 1930s when conditioning of whole buildings, i.e. controlling temperature and humidity, became a practical possibility it was impossible to make malt in subtropical or tropical countries and the Hana region with its capital Olomouc produced and shipped a very large proportion of the malt for

Grandfather Adolph Haas.

Gemeinderat der königl. Hauptstadt Olmütz

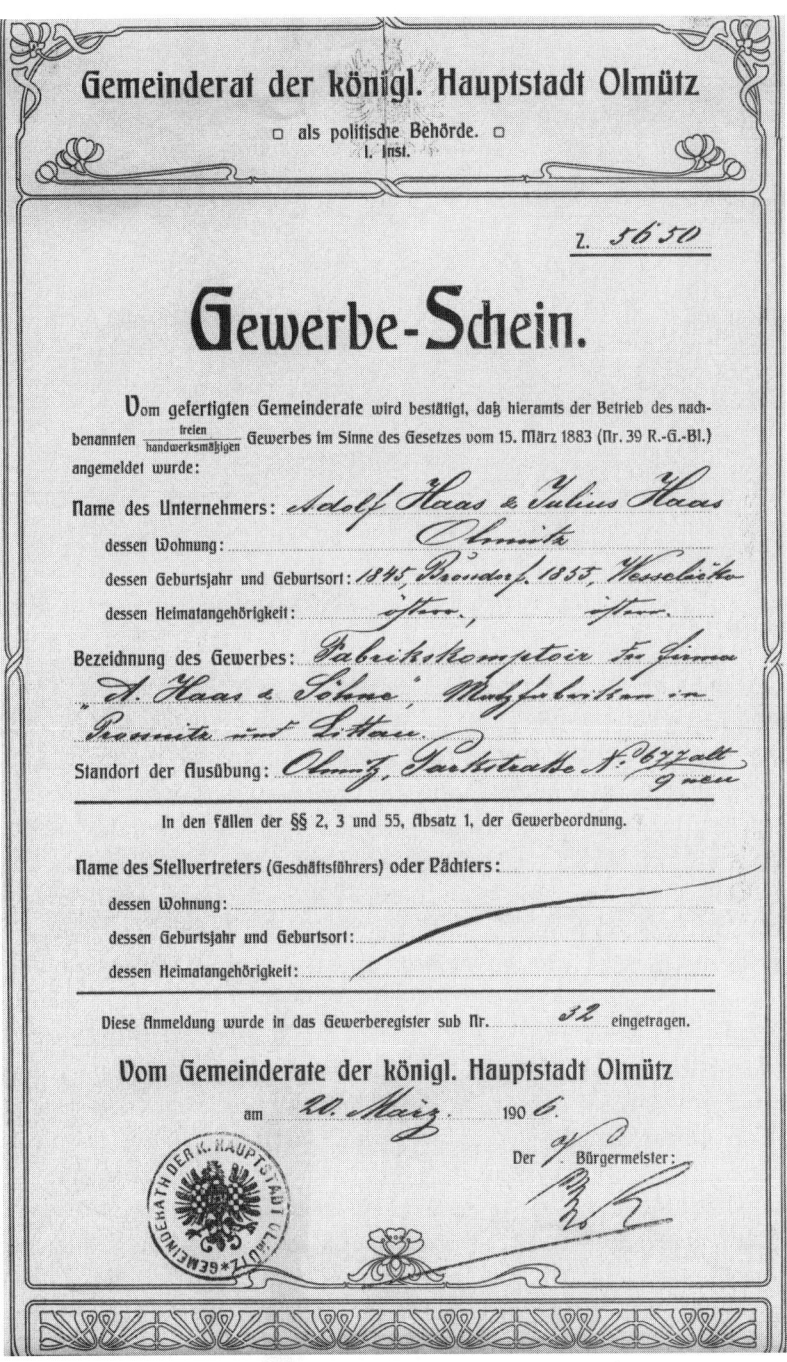

□ als politische Behörde. □
I. Inst.

Z. 5650

Gewerbe-Schein.

Vom gefertigten Gemeinderate wird bestätigt, daß hieramts der Betrieb des nachbenannten freien/handwerksmäßigen Gewerbes im Sinne des Gesetzes vom 15. März 1883 (Nr. 39 R.-G.-Bl.) angemeldet wurde:

Name des Unternehmers: *Adolf Haas & Julius Haas*

dessen Wohnung: *Olmütz*

dessen Geburtsjahr und Geburtsort: *1845 Proßnitz, 1855 Wesselitz*

dessen Heimatangehörigkeit: *österr., österr.*

Bezeichnung des Gewerbes: *Fabrikskomptoir der Firma "A. Haas & Söhne", Mützfabriken in Proßnitz und Littau.*

Standort der Ausübung: *Olmütz, Parkstraße N. 677 alt 9 neu*

In den Fällen der §§ 2, 3 und 55, Absatz 1, der Gewerbeordnung.

Name des Stellvertreters (Geschäftsführers) oder Pächters:

dessen Wohnung:

dessen Geburtsjahr und Geburtsort:

dessen Heimatangehörigkeit:

Diese Anmeldung wurde in das Gewerberegister sub Nr. *32* eingetragen.

Vom Gemeinderate der königl. Hauptstadt Olmütz
am *20. März* 1906.

Der Bürgermeister:

Trading licence for Adolph Haas and his brother Julius.

My great-uncle Isidor who wove the trousers (seated second from left).

beers made in most hot countries in the world, as well as many of the high class German beers.

This industry was almost completely Jewish owned so that the combination of the holocaust and the impossibility of trade with the west in the period immediately after the communist take-over practically wiped out this industry in its traditional form.

My mother's family came from southern Moravia where one of my great-uncles owned a woollen mill and the family was very proud of the fact that he got a very large order for weaving cloth for the red trousers of the army of the Emperor Maximilian of Mexico, who was a member of the Habsburg family, who also reigned in Austria-Hungary. But alas, he was decapitated by the people and the order was never delivered. The Hungarian monarchy had to take over all these red trousers which were then used in many Austrian cavalry regiments. When the monarchy fell to pieces in 1918 the 'successor states' had to take over the stocks. The Czechoslovakian army had to take over so many red trousers that when I joined the Czech cavalry in 1937 I still wore 'my great-uncle's trousers'.

My grandfather became a cloth merchant in Brno, the capital of Moravia, and the business became so important that he was awarded the honour of Commercial Counsellor to his Imperial and Royal Majesty the Emperor Francis Joseph (K.u.K. Kommerzialrat). I suppose this was equivalent to some award in the British honours list.

Third from the right: my maternal grandfather Moritz Löffler K&K (Kaiser und Königlicher) Kommerzialrat (Imperial and Royal Commercial Adviser to his Majesty). Taking the waters with his friends at their annual visit to the most famous Czech spa Karlovy Vary-Karlsbad.

In view of the rise of Jews in the world of commerce and international trade Yiddish had been replaced by German in the use of the business world whilst in the factories and in the household Czech was used as an everyday language.

I was born during the early part of the First World War. My father served as Lieutenant in the K&K army and my mother's brother was a lieutenant stationed in the now infamous Sarajevo at the outbreak of the war. My father's sister was married to a German Jew who had achieved the unusual honour for a Jew of receiving an Iron Cross for bravery as a sergeant major in the Prussian army.

All very Imperial and Royal and German. At the same time my nanny was Czech and Czech was the first language I spoke as a small child. One of my earliest memories is of making red, white and blue paper flowers to decorate the balcony of the flat for the return of the first legionaries of the Czechoslovak Republican Army. And so I grew up feeling myself a Czech Republican born into a family of Imperial and Royal Austro-Hungarians, all this of course in a Jewish framework. Can one be more 'in between'?

CHAPTER 3

Early Memories

ONE OF MY EARLIEST memories is going with my nanny to get some milk which must have been a very scarce commodity in the latter part of World War One. It entailed a tram ride past the municipal cemetery. It must have been the Catholic saint's day of All Saints when it was a tradition for people to visit the graves of their family and take a wreath of flowers, often chrysanthemums which were very colourful. For this occasion the trams were equipped with special metal bars and hooks along both sides as well as the front and rear of the carriage. This moving flower show and the procedure of fixing the wreath which occurred at each tram stop and finally the dismantling of all this when we reached the cemetery and the re-emergence of the large red and white eagle, the town's emblem, on the side of the tram was undoubtedly a major event in my life. Even the long walk to the farm where the can that the nurse had brought was filled with milk and all this journey back again did not dim the glory of this event.

Another very important moment was a walk to the nearby airfield when I saw my first aeroplane from a short distance. I had often seen aeroplanes in the sky and I was very exercised by the question: how would they be on the ground? Would they simply lie on the ground or would they somehow stand up? I was not at all prepared for the shock of seeing such a large structure standing on wheels and a structure which was many times my own size before my eyes even reached the body of the plane. It was so entirely different from those 'little' things in the air that I used to see every day.

The occasion of this visit must have been a commemoration for some airmen and soldiers fired a volley into the air. The shock of this sudden noise, and the men pointing the rifles into the sky, somehow seemed particularly evil. Perhaps this was the origin of my dislike of any ceremonial or festivity which involves loud bangs, including fireworks. Strangely enough, this has never extended to actual 'noises of war' although I probably have the normal dose of fear, and dislike of bombs and shells.

In the summer of 1918 my father was given an administrative job not far from the town of Bielsko, then Austrian Galizia, now part of Poland. He came to fetch us from the place we stayed at, which had the picturesque name of Zigeunerwald (gypsy forest), with a carriage and horses. I was allowed to sit next to the driver and even to hold the reins. My clearest memory of this afternoon is the combination of the smell of the horses and that of the horse blankets in the damp air of the woods on a warm sunny summer's afternoon.

Another series of events were the visits of Uncle Gustav. He was a brother of my grandfather who had a place in Opava, a town in what was then Austrian Silesia, for making malt extract. What was important for me was that he made sweets from this malt extract which came in tiny red boxes. He never came to visit us without bringing a supply of these cherished little boxes. So when I heard that Uncle Gustav was coming I spent a long time at the window waiting for him to come round the corner. I cannot visualise Uncle Gustav's face, but only the little red boxes and his hand handing them to me.

'Theatre of War.' I heard a lot of discussion of the 'Theatre of War' and I was given maps which, I was told, showed the Russian 'Theatre of War'. They were large maps in different colours, big enough to put my toy soldiers on and 'fight' all the battles I had heard about. I pictured that the 'real' war was fought on a big field where grown-ups performed in a similar way as I moved my toy soldiers, according to some rules which I could not yet understand, but that according to these theatre performances the fate of the countries was somehow decided and the 'front line' was moved forward or backward. When I later discovered that people did no such thing but devastated whole countries and killed each other, I was very surprised at the stupidity of these grown ups and that none of them had even thought of my solution of these matters which seemed such common sense to me.

The first visible sign for me of the end of the war was that all the sentry boxes which had been black and yellow were re-painted red, white and blue, and that the soldiers suddenly had khaki uniforms instead of blue/grey ones, and what I considered particularly important was that the shiny uniform buttons had disappeared and that they were now black and quite plain. I suppose there had been no possibility of impressing them with the Czech Lion instead of the Austrian Double Eagle. This change of Double Eagle to Lion was done however on all the official buildings.

There were also a lot of parades with lovely colourful uniforms of new or previously oppressed youth organisations, somewhat similar to Boy Scouts and Girl Guides, and all the beautiful national costumes which in the Hana region were particularly colourful. There were of course also all the new flags on all the buildings.

These were the impressions of a little boy of what to all the loyal subjects of his Imperial and Royal Majesty the Emperor Charles, who had only recently succeeded the Emperor Francis Joseph, was the utter collapse of their known world. The Habsburgs who had reigned for nearly eight hundred years had suddenly disappeared and their empire was divided into some half dozen 'successor states'. It was only twenty years later, when the turmoil preceding the Second World War became plain, that I realised how great had been the shock for the people who had grown up under that order.

For the Czechs this event was a liberation of many centuries of oppression, so that they now could use their language freely and educate their children in schools in their own language. Under the leadership of an important philosopher, Thomas G. Masaryk, this led to the establishment of a tolerant democratic state with a remarkable constitution. But more of this later.

As in most countries the end of a four year war when no building had taken place, meant a severe housing shortage. The government or local council therefore decided that families who had more space than they required had to make some space available for the homeless. We had a three room flat, with kitchen, bathroom and servants' room, to which had been added another two rooms from the block next door which also had another kitchen and all the service rooms. As our family only consisted of my parents and me plus a cook and a maid, it was decided that we had to let off one kitchen and one room. This could easily be done as we had two entrance doors; so Mr Kostka, the bricklayer who lived in the basement of one of the houses, was instructed to build a single brick wall partition and a couple could move into that part. My father always referred to this man as 'the Bolshevik and his wife'. I was very curious as to what a 'Bolshevik' looked like. Fortunately the partition wall had only risen to just over three feet when 'the Bolshevik and his wife' arrived and I could not only see him enter but also heard him explain very politely who he was. My disappointment was immense. He looked just like any other man. He did not even have a beard, was quite small in stature and obviously well mannered and polite, not at all like the revolutionary my father had described. Perhaps this has coloured my attitude to Bolsheviks for the rest of my life and could have given me the first inkling that even my father's statements might have to be looked at with some suspicion.

CHAPTER 4

Vienna 1920

By the beginning of 1920 general trade conditions in Czechoslovakia had improved to such an extent that it was possible to resume export trade and my father was able to undertake a trip to South America to re-establish the sale of malt to the various countries in that continent who required this commodity for making lager beers. Until modern refrigeration made it possible to alter the temperature in a whole factory it was impossible to produce malt in a tropical or sub-tropical climate. Even in Europe this could only be done in the period from October to about April as it was necessary to let the barley be grown slowly enough to allow for the correct transformation in the grain from starch to sugar. The main markets were Argentina, Uruguay and Brazil. In the spring of that year my father went to visit these countries and it proved possible to re-establish the export of about 10,000 tons of malt per annum, which is the equivalent of one thousand railway wagons.

In our days of jet travel and instant communications it is difficult to realise that in those days the journey by sea took six weeks and although wireless-telegraphy existed on board ship communications were only possible over short distances and in practice detailed communications had to wait until it was possible to write a letter on arrival after the six week journey, so that it took twelve weeks from leaving Europe until one had news of the arrival.

Although life in Czechoslovakia seemed pretty stable it was different in Eastern Europe. The border between Poland and the Soviet Union, still in a state of revolution, was not yet stabilised. It was in that year that the Polish forces assisted by British forces under General Alexander and a French contingent were engaged in pushing the border further east and the outcome of this campaign was still in doubt.

My mother's brother and sister lived in Vienna at that time and my mother decided she wanted to be with her family during this period of nearly eight months whilst my father was away. She took some rooms in the Hotel Hübner, which was just opposite the former Imperial Palace in Schönbrunn, and I spent the spring and early summer of that year being taken daily into the park of the palace which was now open to the public. In spite of the unemployment, economic hardship and general poverty in that community and particularly in Vienna which had once been the administrative capital of an empire of nearly

Myself aged 4.

seventy million people and was now the capital of a country of about eight million, most former imperial palaces and parks continued to be kept in the best possible order. This fact was brought home to me when I visited the Hofburg, the town residence of the emperors, in about 1965. The man in charge of winding the clocks was still employed and explained to the visitors that he was still winding every clock in the palace just as he had done in the days of the emperor.

In the same way all the flower beds in the park of Schönbrunn were kept just as in former days and I remember in particular the tulips in the spring followed by constantly changing displays of whatever flowers were in season.

Particularly exciting treats were lunches at a restaurant called the Hof Stüberl, which to me seemed the supreme luxury, and I felt almost as if I had been invited by the Emperor personally. The word Hof means court (i.e. imperial court) and Stüberl literally a small room (*Stube*) but as the Austrians use diminutives, as the Slavs do, it is better translated as 'intimate'. If I were to describe it today, I would simply say it was like a stage set of the period of the turn of the century: red flock wallpaper, gilded wall candle holders, recently electrified, baroque tables and chairs and waiters who genuinely still came from that period. As inflation in Austria was very much higher than in Czechoslovakia such luxuries were more affordable than in normal times.

In order to look after me on my visits to the park and when my mother went out, a new governess was engaged, Slečna Levová. This means Miss Lion, and indeed a lion she was; she kept me in order in every respect and also acted as a pre-school instructor. She was a Czech who had lived in Vienna for several years. Her German was more perfect than that of the 'natives' and her Czech had just the right accent and vocabulary that was required. The 'vocabulary' was particularly important at that time. As higher education in Czech was rather restricted in the days of the monarchy, the intelligentsia had to finish their education either in German schools or abroad, which meant largely in French speaking countries. The Czech language of that period therefore used a lot of German or French loan words. When the Independent Czech state was established, and even before that when it was seen as an achievable aim, this was considered bad form and the language had to be 'purified'. This was done by either inventing or constructing new words from Czech roots or if this was impossible, to borrow them from the big Slav brother, the Russian. Miss Levová had just the right 'vocabulary'.

Whilst in Vienna my mother made contact with followers of Rudolf Steiner, and she became an ardent follower of this movement from then on. As a boy I did not appreciate the change that gradually took place in her and which I now attribute to that influence. It became obvious to me at the time of Hitler's occupation in 1939, and the description I received of her behaviour in the concentration camp in Teresín in 1941, where she helped as a nurse, further confirmed this to me.

In those days in 1921 I was sometimes taken along when experiments in some kind of 'special magnetism' took place. The person conducting the experiment asked the person whom he had selected for the demonstration to sit on a chair and close his eyes. He would then, without telling him what he was trying, induce him to lift his arms or feet, or move them sideways. This was done by moving his hands over the person demonstrated on without touching them. I was never told why or how this was done but I saw people lift their arms and move in various ways. It was apparently considered that children were particularly useful for these experiments as they were less prejudiced and would not know what they should do. So I was often used as a 'guinea pig'. I cannot remember how, but I soon found a way of guessing what was expected of me and performed in a way which delighted the man who was conducting these experiments. On some days I did not want to do the 'right' things, and then no experiment worked. The leader of these experiments who, if I remember rightly, was addressed as 'Ingenieur Tetter' was described to me as a very important man who knew a great deal and could cure a great many ills. This proved to be an unfortunate description of this 'superman' because when during that period I had a bad cold, he looked at me and advised my mother, probably quite rightly, to call a doctor. However, the fact that he could not 'cure' me and that it was so easy to mislead him during the 'experiment' left me with grave doubts, from this age of five onwards, about people with 'extraordinary' powers.

As my father was due to return from South America in the autumn of that year it was decided to spend the summer in Germany so that we could conveniently meet him when his ship docked in Hamburg. The place chosen was a seaside resort on the Baltic coast called Warnemünde. It was there that I saw the sea for the first time in my life and was able to play in the marvellous soft sand which to a child born in the centre of the continent was an extraordinary event. I imagine that this was also the first time that my 'Miss Lion' saw the coast as she insisted that I wore galoshes on the beach, so that I would not 'catch cold' on the wet sand. This aroused the anger of my grandmother, who had joined us for that holiday. These two had taken an immediate dislike to each other, and this was only the first of many battles that followed, very much to my delight as it proved very easy to exploit this situation and get my own way, between these two opposing forces.

One of the very exciting things during that summer was to watch the ferry loading and unloading. It linked Warnemünde with Denmark and the feeling that there was another coast on the other side of this immense water was very thrilling and allowed my imagination to wander and have the first inkling of a great unknown across the water. This feeling linked later with a description my father gave me to my question: 'What is an Englishman?' The answer was: 'It is a man who sits on deck of a ship, smokes a pipe, sails all the oceans, and rules the world.' Even today I cannot think of a better way of explaining to a little boy the meaning of Imperial Britain. It certainly coloured my view of this country when I arrived here a refugee many years later.

But back to the ferry. It was so large that a whole railway train could be driven on board, and railway wagons were the biggest moving objects I had ever seen. This was proof to me that the sea was superior to land.

A very clear memory of this summer is also my first experience of anti-Semitism. We had booked a table at some café where I assume my mother was known. Together with the 'reserved' notice was a piece of paper with an anti-Semitic poem mentioning my mother by name. I have no idea what the paper said or whether the content was really insulting or whether it was just a joke in bad taste, but my mother's reaction to this and the grave and upset faces of the other grown-ups present made it quite clear that something frightening had happened. This emotion and the word anti-Semitism remained linked for me from then on. The name Hitler was then still completely unknown.

At the end of this summer we went to Hamburg to await the arrival of the *Capolonio*, a liner of the HAPAG (Hamburg Amerikalinie). There were very exciting trips in little motor boats on the Alster, a river which forms lakes: the Aussen and Binnen Alster. I think this was the first time I travelled on water. I also remember sitting in a well known café and restaurant, the Alster Eck, and watching these little boats coming and going. I was taken on sight-seeing tours around the town and the harbour and saw the large ocean liners and big freighters and the innumerable cranes. I was also shown the 'Czech Harbour' in Hamburg, which was an important 'free port' arranged in the treaty of Versailles, and was the only possibility for land-locked Czechoslovakia to send or receive goods from the 'outer world'.

The river Elbe (*Labe* in Czech) flows from Bohemia through Saxony and central Germany through Hamburg and into the North Sea at Altona, at the estuary of the Elbe. The river is navigable from the confluence of the Vltava (Moldau) and the Elbe north of Prague, and played an important part in the shipment of bulk cargo such as coal, grain, iron ore and bulky machinery. Apart from the possibility of duty free shipments this was also important because it was the only way Czechoslovakia could control the cost of freight as otherwise the country could have been held to ransom by foreign shipping or railways.

The *Hanse-Stadt* Hamburg has always been talked about in our family and at various important moments in my life I have found myself in that town. The Hanse or Hanseatic League (the word means Association or League) started as an association of merchants in the thirteenth century mainly in towns along the Baltic and eastern North Sea coast. It included Hamburg, Lübeck, Rostock, Danzig (Polish Gdansk) and Riga (the capital of Latvia). When, as a student in about 1930, I read a history of the Hansa, which described how for five or six centuries these towns endeavoured and at times succeeded in putting national and political matters into the background and putting commercial and human problems first, I guessed what a far-seeing effort it had been. At times it had been possible for all these various peoples, Germans, Poles, Latvians, Russians etc., to live and trade together. It is said that the Hansa association at times kept a relationship as far away as Brugge in the west and Novgorod in the east, as well as with the main trade routes across the seas. Wars and nationalist hatreds always interrupted these efforts and in my lifetime hardly anything was left except perhaps a certain tolerance amongst the citizens of Hamburg which could perhaps even be discerned during the Nazi period.

When, at the beginning of the twentieth century, my grandfather decided that his son needed some experience of world trade he equipped him with a minimum amount of money and sent him to Hamburg with the instruction: 'When you have lost this money without going bankrupt come back home and you will be able to run the family business.' My father's trade then was mainly with India, much of it via London. It happened exactly as my grandfather had predicted and when my father returned home around 1908 he became a partner in the family business, was found a wife and settled down. Marriages in Jewish families were not left to chance in those days. They were carefully prepared, and although there was no compulsion, love at first sight was not required and the number of successful marriages was extremely high. So my parents got married in 1910 and lived successfully together until Hitler's henchmen ended it all in the gas chambers of Auschwitz (Osvěčín) in 1942.

One of the first major innovations my father had to undertake was to organise and increase the trade with South America and he set off on a trip to Argentina, Uruguay and Brazil in a ship of the HAPAG sailing from Hamburg, about 1911. The fascinating detail he told me about was that there was as yet no wireless telegraphy on board and when two ships met at sea they signalled to each other by flags.

In 1921 however wireless telegraphy already existed and when we went to meet my father it was possible to know in advance when the ship would arrive which was considered a great technical success. Unfortunately this new information did not cover the tides and when the ship reached Altona there was low tide and the passengers disembarked and proceeded by train to Hamburg. This was a great disappointment for me as instead of seeing this large ship dock I had to meet my father from a train. The only redeeming feature was that I was allowed to stay up till 11 p.m. in spite of Miss Levová's predictions that this would be an absolute disaster for my health.

The next time Hamburg played a part in my life was in 1939 when I got out of Hitler's clutches again on one of the ships of the HAPAG. I visited Hamburg frequently during my period in the forces and left Hamburg on my way to my demobilisation in Hull. This time it was not a HAPAG cruise liner but on one of those wartime 'utility constructions'.

When I took over the export management of a group of companies I was then working for, my first visit to Germany was to appoint an agent in Hamburg. This time I came by air. For the next ten years Hamburg appeared regularly on my itinerary. I was then nearly fifty-five so my visits to Hamburg covered just about half a century.

CHAPTER 5

The Clock

During my father's absence in South America my grandmother decided to cheer my mother up by buying her a particularly nice birthday present. It was a beautiful antique Biedermeier clock. My mother decided that one could only do this clock justice by having a room which was an appropriate background and so she decided to acquire gradually a Biedermeier drawing room. The Biedermeier style was described to me as derived from 'Baroque' but simpler, and as my mother always used to say 'in much better taste'. It was very a fashionable style of furniture in the early part of the nineteenth century, when the Napoleonic Empire had collapsed, and the Austrian chancellor Metternich, during the Congress of Vienna (1812-15), very cleverly influenced the whole organisation of Europe for the following decades. He lavishly entertained all the heads of governments and their relatives and whilst they enjoyed themselves and danced to the early Strauss waltzes he got them to sign the treaties which would give the largest possible influence to the Austro-Hungarian monarchy. The comfortable style of the Biedermeier furniture allowed them to be relaxed and at the same time allowed the ladies to display their beautiful dresses to the best advantage.

I cannot vouch for the historical accuracy of this story, but I can certainly confirm that our Biedermeier sitting room had these qualities.

My mother found a restorer who knew where to acquire old pieces and restore them, keeping to the correct style. There was a relatively easy supply of such pieces about, because owing to the revolution of 1918 and the following inflation, many people who had formerly been well off were now living on or below the breadline. This applied particularly to the former civil servants of the large Austro-Hungarian Empire, for whom there was now no work whatever. Even in the 'good old days' these families had more good taste than money, so that a fair amount of antique furniture that had once seen better days came on to the market. So one bargain after another appeared and for years my mother and the cook and the maid and sometimes Miss Lev were busy making petitpoint covers in silk for the settee and armchairs until a perfect Biedermeier drawing room was complete. My father used to describe the original clock as the most expensive present (for him) he had ever received.

These silk tapestries were considered far too valuable to be left uncovered, so some rather expensive covers were made to protect them. But even these covers were considered too valuable for little boys to sit on and a cheaper cover was made for use when I and my friends were allowed into the room.

A strict regime started from then on. When no guests were present the ordinary covers were used. When friends or guests of 'lesser' importance came, the top covers were removed and when 'special' guests came or on important family occasions the tapestries in all their beauty were revealed.

In the end Hitler's henchmen took the whole lot with the exception of a glass showcase which our neighbours had rescued, which they offered to return to me when I visited Czechoslovakia in 1946.

I have mentioned that my mother and the servants did the embroidery and it is very difficult to imagine today the lifestyle that was possible for a middle class family in Czechoslovakia in the 1920s. We were by no means rich. The five-room apartment consisted of a three-room (not three bedrooms) flat to which two rooms from the neighbouring house had been added, which meant that there were two kitchens, two toilets, two servants' bedrooms and two bathrooms. One of the servants' rooms had been used to enlarge the main bathroom and the entrance hall and the servants' kitchen converted into a bedroom. The second kitchen, servants' room and servants' bathroom formed the then servants' area. There was my parents' bedroom, my bed-sitting room, a dining room, the already mentioned antique sitting room and a room which was called the 'gentleman's' room, possibly best translated as the 'study'. It had a large desk, very heavy leather armchairs and settee and a very large bookcase.

The family consisted of my parents and me and required the services of a cook, a chambermaid and a nanny or governess On wash days a washerwoman came.

There were of course no labour saving devices. We had no car and were a good mile away from any public transport. Horse drawn carriages (*fiaker*) were only used for journeys to the railway station for the summer holidays. Taxis were purely for my father for special business trips.

All shopping was therefore done on foot. After breakfast (about 8 a.m.) the cook would set out to purchase the day's food. There were no refrigerators, no tins, no prepared packets or sauces. All ingredients were purchased separately, pounded, mixed and ground or blended. The coal fire was started in the cooking range about ten o'clock for the meal at about one o'clock. After everything in the kitchen was cleared and polished, by about three, both the cook and the maid were free to do any mending or sewing and apart from the petitpoint stitching already mentioned, crochet curtains were made as well as all kinds of mats and tablecloths. The evening meal was usually at about 6 p.m., a one- or at most

My mother.

two-course affair and at about 7.30 p.m. both the cook and the maid came to say ceremoniously 'Good night' and withdrew to their own quarters.

This apparently feudal lifestyle, however, took place in a very socialist controlled community. Our cook was the steward of the Domestic Servants Union and as their living area was rather larger than standard, union meetings were often held in our servants' quarters. Wages were not high by Western standards, the equivalent of about £2.00 per month. Working conditions were fairly strictly controlled. The actual working hours could not exceed forty-eight per week and any work after 8 p.m. had to be paid at overtime rate. In typical Czech (Bohemian) fashion this overtime was rarely paid by the employer but it was a habit that guests at any dinner party gave tips that would exceed the sum that would have been paid for the required overtime. So all servants were particularly nice to any guest and everybody was happy. All domestic servants had to be given a half day off on Sunday and Bank Holidays so the Sunday evening meal was traditionally cold charcuterie and making the hot drink for this was the only cooking I remember my mother doing in these years. In addition the servants had to have one afternoon off per week, and any time required for union meetings. There was one week of paid holiday per year. As our holidays were usually about six weeks, of which my father spent about two to three weeks with us, this constituted no problem.

Both the cook Mili, or Milka (our abbreviation of Emily), and Minna, the maid, had been with us ever since I could remember, certainly before 1918. Milka, who was the daughter of a farmer in an ethnically Czech village just outside Olomouc, left us in the mid 1930s in order to get married to a farmer in her native village. Minna came from a village near the town of Litovel, where one of our malting places was. It was an ethnically mixed village and they were basically German speaking, by which I mean that they spoke the local dialect which contained a mixture of Czech words which did not exist in proper German and their pronunciation would sound 'Czech' to any real German. The Czechs in the area in turn spoke Czech with a dialect which contained a lot of German words given a 'Czech' pronunciation. In fact if somebody spoke a proper fluent Czech you knew he was an ethnic German who had learnt Czech at school, and vice versa. This of course did not apply to the 'intelligentsia'. Both languages were taught in all schools after 1918 so that gradually an equivalent of a King's English gained ascendancy and after 1945 a lot of words based on Russian roots came into the language. But in the days when I was a small boy no such development had yet reached the villages in the area, and when Minna took me for a visit to her parents I heard her address her father as *Fotr* (derived from the German *Vater*) and there were other German words pronounced as if they were Czech or had Czech roots with a Germanic ending.

Minna's father was a joiner and I still remember the enjoyment of sitting in the wood shavings listening to the sound of the plane and watching the rhythm of the old man working. My admiration of joinery led later to my father hiring a joiner to teach me the use of tools and I was allowed to build shelves for storing apples and a footstool for my father. After this my father decided that the need for my learning crafts was satisfied and this tuition was ended. The idea of doing some useful work around the house (now called DIY) was considered almost criminal. When the crocheted curtains were washed and starched, which happened twice a year, a man was called to nail them onto the boards which had been fixed to the windows. On one occasion I decided this was a job I could very well do myself. But just as I had started my father happened to come home. He was horrified; he made me stop at once and gave me a long lecture about the severity of my misdeed: how did I imagine this poor man would live, if I deprived him of his trade! In fact I ended with a picture that the whole structure of the world would come to an end if people did such dreadful deeds and I do not remember ever doing any 'curtain' work until I was about to get married after the Second World

My father.

War and my wife made me paint the bathroom walls. I still remember her patience with me and her utter amazement at the fact that I had never held a paintbrush in my hand.

CHAPTER 6

Lessons and the Beginning of School

But I am rather jumping ahead with my story. After our return from Hamburg with my father a strict regime started for me. Miss Lion was preparing me for school in the following year, teaching me 'proper' table manners, and last but not least teaching me 'proper' Czech as distinct from the language mixture which, with great disdain, was called '*Küchel-Behmisch*'. This expression is derived from the German word *Küche* and a mispronounced Viennese diminutive which would have been *Kücherl*, and *Behmisch* is the mispronounced German for *Böhmisch* meaning Czech, but used in this phrase had the derogatory meaning of a person who spoke the lowest kind of language.

So I began to learn proper Czech. and Miss Lev concentrated very much on fairy tales, which I learned from books with lovely illustrations. As I later discovered, the Czech folklore is one of the most important parts of Czech literature and had survived orally for a long period of time. It was then written down in the nineteenth century when the oppression of the Czech language was relaxed and schools other than primary schools could again use the language of the country.

Up to the latter part of the sixteenth century all higher education was in Latin and it was only as a result of the Reformation with the translation of the Bible into the vernacular that higher secondary and higher education in the vernacular was introduced. In the area where I lived the first Czech language grammar school was started by Jan Amos Komenský (Comenius), at the beginning of the seventeenth century. Komenský was not only a very important educationalist but was also the founder of the Moravian Church, which was a re-statement of the earliest Husite Protestantism. Although the number of members of this church was never very large the spiritual influence of this teaching in Moravia became dominant and remained so certainly until 1946 when I visited the area. With its stress on tolerance and humanity, I believe that its influence on Thomas G. Masaryk, philosopher/writer and founder-President of the Czechoslovak Republic, was quite considerable. Masaryk grew up in Hodonín at the southern end of the Hana district whilst the grammar school mentioned earlier was in Přerov, a town about 30 km further north. Komenský later established the centre of his church in Fulneck, a town about another 30 km north east. As the Protestant forces were being defeated in the later part of the Thirty Year war Komenský had to flee. He first went to the Protestant Netherlands and after the treaty of Utrecht (1648) he came to England where he started schools according to his educational principles; first in the West Country and later near Pudsey in Yorkshire where a settlement and school called Fulneck survives to this day and where our eldest son was educated.

I do not think Miss Lev realised any of the deeper meaning of the stories she was reading to me. She seemed mainly concerned with the fact that they were well written in literary Czech. I remember particularly one story which was a kind of 'King Lear' story where the third daughter wished for the king to have salt, and how all the cattle died and people became ill when the country had no salt. In early times in the middle of the continent, rock-salt was the only source and there were indeed no salt mines in the traditional territory of the kingdom of Bohemia. It made a deep impression on me that survival could depend on such an unimportant looking commodity, more important than gold, silver or jewels.

The following year it was time for me to go to school, so this pre-school training ended.

It was decided to send me to a German language school, because German was a world language and as my father was convinced that I would follow in his footsteps and take over the family firm I would have to be able to deal in the major world languages, whilst Czech could only be used within the country and Czech would in any case be taught in all schools including German language schools from the age of six onwards.

There was a teachers training college just one block away from our block of flats and I was therefore enrolled in the primary school there. The tuition there happened in the following way: there were rather large classrooms with a lower part for 24 to 30 primary school children and seats for about 24 teacher trainees raised as in a lecture hall behind them. The teaching was done by 'Professors', i.e. teachers with full Doctor degrees trained in the latest methods of education. Demonstrations were given by the 'Professor' followed by the trainees teaching us in the way they had just learned, being carefully and politely corrected if they made any mistakes. The primary school children thus got very much more attention as this system required a continuous assessment of the result of any lecture. Every subject was taken by a Professor specialising in it and its method of instruction. One hour of Czech language instruction each day was included in the curriculum as were two hours per week of religious education which was denominational and was taken by a clergyman of the particular religion, which in this case meant mainly Catholic, Lutheran and Jewish. The clergyman or priests were paid for this tuition by the state and therefore came under the Ministry of Education for the curriculum although I believe that this control was rather minimal.

Nearly all schools in the country were state schools with a national curriculum which made it possible for children to continue their education in any other town if the parents had to move. Primary school education had been compulsory for a very long time and grammar schools started in 1848 and existed in sufficient numbers so that most children capable of this form of education could be accommodated. Olomouc was a town of 60,000 inhabitants and had in the 1920s one Czech classical grammar school, one German classical grammar school, two Czech and one German *Real-gymnasia* (a mixed technical and classical grammar school) and one Czech technical grammar school, thus six grammar schools, one per 10,000 of the population. In addition there was one Czech and one German 'Commercial Academy', a kind of senior commercial college with a matric qualifying for university entry.

To compare it with Britain: in the 1950s in Huddersfield there were two grammar schools for a population of 120,000. According to the headmaster of the primary school our son went to, this enabled just ten per cent of the children capable of grammar school education to enter such a school.

Whilst pure numbers are not the only criterion for the educational question I feel that the almost complete disregard of making a grammar school level of education available to the large percentage capable of it is the central problem rather than methods of selection or any other details discussed continuously over the years in Britain.

Primary schools in Czechoslovakia were entirely free, and secondary education had nominal school fees of about one pound per term. Children of below average income not only did not have to pay this but also received a grant for books and aids. University education had to be paid for, but again relief was given where students could not afford the fees.

The biggest drawback of the Czech system, I think, was its rigidity and the fact that you had to have a 'pass' in practically all subjects before you could advance to the next year. Even one 'fail' in a compulsory subject meant that you had to repeat the whole year. As the marks were largely based on continuous assessment, a certain flexibility was given to the masters, so that only a relatively small minority suffered from the basically rigid system.

When I was twelve and thirteen years old my father sent me to various courses in Switzerland and France. At the age of seven or eight I went to a school in Berlin for about six months. I served in both the Czechoslovak and the British Forces for a total period of about five years and I had to deal with the education of my own children from the mid fifties to the seventies. I feel that this has given me a rather unusual insight into different educational systems and whilst generalisations in such matters are always dangerous I have come to the conclusion that the system under which I was educated and the quality of the teachers that I met, trained by the methods I have described, were somewhere near the top of education systems I have encountered.

Chapter 7

The Prussian Cure

As an educator Miss Lev turned out to be excellent, but as a disciplinarian she was somewhat extreme. One of her principles was that any food served to me had to be eaten up. I was given food that was 'good for me'. Particularly memorable for me was spinach. This was served in a dish which had a double bottom which could be filled with hot water. There were occasions when the dish had to be re-filled with hot water, before the picture on the bottom of the dish appeared and the spinach could be considered as eaten. The result of all this food was that my weight increased very rapidly and physical exercise was rather neglected and my natural tendency for colds and bronchitis led to more and more pampering which made the general situation only worse. One of the local doctors suggested a Professor Czerny in Berlin who was apparently famous for curing bronchitis and similar diseases. This famous Professor took one look at me and pronounced in the typical severe Prussian dialect: 'This young man has been given far too many eggs, and too much butter and cake to eat. He needs little food and firm military type treatment.'

It so happened that I had an uncle in Berlin who had been a sergeant major in the Prussian Army in the First World War and had received an Iron Cross for bravery and toughness. He volunteered to give me the appropriate treatment. I was given an attic in his very large house, and enrolled in a local school a reasonably long way away, so that I had to walk a fair distance every morning. My aunt, who was my father's sister and given to rather soft treatment, was given strict instructions to refrain from any pampering. When my first attack of bronchitis appeared, I was sent to school as long as I did not have any high fever. Within a very short time, these attacks ceased and I became a normal healthy boy. As Germany at that time was in the throes of terrible inflation food was extremely short and sometimes unobtainable so that it was an easy matter to reduce my weight to normal proportions.

I stayed in Berlin for a period of about six or seven months which for a boy of seven is quite a long time, and seem to have adjusted to the new way of life without much difficulty. Certain episodes stand out particularly clearly: I was given 39 million Marks to take to school to pay for a copy book and a few weeks later my uncle bought me a shoebox full of one billion Mark notes to play with. I think I acquired then an understanding of what inflation can mean and could from then on understand the German fear of inflation particularly when this happened again in 1945. Very soon after my arrival at school a French boy in my class was bullied and beaten up and as a Czech my turn was to be next. To my surprise one of the biggest and toughest boys in the class appeared and assured me that he was my friend and that he would defend me, and indeed proceeded to do so. I had never noticed this boy before or spoken to him, and do not remember him at all apart from these occasions when he came so effectively to my defence. This happening became a pattern in my life and whenever I found myself in a corresponding situation the biggest or most powerful person appeared in my defence, in many different sets of circumstances and different sets of people. I never had to defend myself physically; it was always done for me.

There were occasions when I had to travel from the suburb where we lived towards the centre of the city and on these tram rides I was always accompanied by the chauffeur's son, who was several years older than me and whom I considered to be already 'a man of the world'. He explained to me amongst many other things the details of the treaty of Versailles, and how Germany had been forced to restrict its army to 100,000 men. He proceeded to tell me that Germany had overcome this handicap by having another 30,000 men in Russia where they were trained in all the modern methods of warfare including such weapons as were forbidden by the treaty of Versailles. By rotating these men in Russia the whole army was fully trained.

In 1945 I interrogated a German Air Force Officer, who had fought with the 'Blue Division' in Spain in about 1936, who had been trained in Russia in 1923 by the Reichswehr and who confirmed all the details my young friend had told me during our tram rides in 1923/4.

In the spring of 1924 it was considered that my health was sufficiently restored and I could return home and start the summer term in a boys school at home. This school was on top of a hill in the old part of the town and I was now considered old enough to walk by myself. This walk took me past a building where you could see a Swedish cannon ball which became lodged in the wall of a building at the time of the Thirty Year War, the war of reformation. It also led past a number of baroque buildings: the theological seminary and a Jesuit church and monastery in the same style. For me the most important part of this walk was that it took me past the market stalls where on certain feast days 'Turkish honey' was sold. This 'Turkish honey' was in large blocks and men in white coats, sometimes wearing the Turkish fez, would hack off some of this delicious commodity with a big knife and wrap it into a piece of paper in portions costing 50 hellers or one crown (1*d*. or 2*d*.), praising their wares in wonderful rhymes. We wandered from stall to stall watching carefully which one might possibly give you a bit more for your penny before making this weighty decision. This was then consumed slowly on the way home, with the result that I was told off firstly for being late and secondly for having no appetite for my supper.

I was now considered old enough not to require a nanny and was allowed to play with my school friends and go out with them, as long as I was back at mealtimes. It was considered very important that the family always had all meals together. I do not remember questions of danger in going out by myself. It must have been considered absolutely safe and all the perils that parents have to worry about today concerning the safety of their children were never mentioned.

After four years of primary school I passed my entrance exam to grammar school, which was in the same block as my first school had been, just about five minutes from my home.

There were three kinds of grammar school. First was the Classical grammar school where Latin was taught from the age of ten and Greek from the age of thirteen. Mathematics and science subjects were of lesser importance, and Matriculation taken after eight years.

The second type was called 'Real' school where the stress was on mathematics and science subjects as well as modern languages, with Matriculation after seven years

The third type, the 'Real Gymnasium' was a mixture of the two. Latin was taught from the age of ten as well as at least a third modern language from the age of thirteen. Czech and German were compulsory in all schools from the age of ten. A fourth modern language was optional. Mathematics and technical subjects were less important than in the second type but were also taught. I went to this third type of school, taking English as a third modern language.

English was particularly easy for me as I had already learned to speak some English although I had never written it. When I was about eight or nine years old some acquaintance of my parents who was a manufacturer of wire bird cages had given hospitality to an out of work ship's engineer from Belfast. This Mr Fieldhouse had to find some means of earning a livelihood and so he was engaged to take me for walks on some afternoons and teach me English.

The only words he knew in Czech were about bird cages, otherwise he spoke neither Czech nor German. It was thus a marvellous opportunity for me to learn the language in a natural way as a small child would learn. Mr Fieldhouse was very high in my esteem because he could not only make my toy steam engine work properly, but could also explain to me all about safety valves, steam pressure etc. Disaster struck when my father returned from a long business trip and realised that I had during his absence learned English with an Irish accent and poor Mr Fieldhouse was immediately dismissed. The Irish accent has long ago been lost but I was left with a strange association between Belfast, steam engines and bird cages for the rest of my life.

One conversation with Mr Fieldhouse has remained very clearly in my mind and has even gained some importance over the years because it illustrates the power of preconceived ideas and how we build up quite imaginary views and pictures. On one of our walks we passed a newly erected administrative building of the Czechoslovak Railways which was a huge construction of five or six stories which stretched over two or three blocks. I had been brought up with the idea that everything in Britain must be bigger and better than in our country, so I said to Mr Fieldhouse, 'I expect this is nearly as big as buildings in which you live in your country.' Mr Fieldhouse looked at me in absolute amazement and after a long pause said, 'Oh no, we don't have such vast buildings; we live in little houses.' And he proceeded to describe to me the average English suburban house. I still remember the shock of this revelation.

The only subject that caused me some difficulty during the next few years of my grammar school was Latin. One of the teachers of the school who did not take me in any subject was engaged to coach me in Latin. He was Professor Kořínek, which means 'little root' in Czech, and he was a very small man, probably not much more than 5ft 2ins. I remember very little about the Latin except that I did scrape through in the final exams, but I recollect a great deal about his stories covering his experiences in Russia where he spent several years as prisoner of war. Like most Czech prisoners he moved to the east of Siberia and spent a long time around Lake Bajkal. He described in detail how in winter the railway lines were laid on the ice so that the trains could travel across the lake instead of around it, thus saving a lot of time and mileage. Before the spring the lines were taken up again. This was the first time that I heard about life in the eastern part of the Russian Empire, which at that time was almost unknown to most western and central Europeans. Hearing about and meeting people who had lived in that part of the world runs like a thread through my life from then on.

CHAPTER 8

Lausanne, Dunkerque and Paris

WHEN I HAD FINISHED the first four years of my grammar school, before entering on the second stage of secondary education which entailed more specialisation, my father sent me to a school in Lausanne to learn French and also to give me a taste of the way of life in Western Europe. This Lycée Jacquard in Lausanne, Pully was a private school run by three brothers, which was not so much orientated to give a lot of academic knowledge as to teach children from various countries and backgrounds the values of the culture of French speaking Switzerland and by doing a lot of sport kept them out of mischief without too rigid a discipline. A number of the students were there because their parents were abroad on temporary jobs where education facilities were difficult: civil servants serving in the colonies who sent their children to boarding schools for the same reasons as British civil servants sent their children to public schools, or parents who considered that a Swiss education would give their sons a wider outlook on life than they could obtain at home.

This meant that there were children from a great variety of countries and I remember in particular English, US, Puerto Ricans, Argentineans, Spanish, Italians, Germans, Czechs and Hungarians.

Any language teaching in the ordinary sense was therefore impossible and all lessons were purely in French so you had to pick up the language as best you could. In the playground and in your various 'off duty' activities you could use any language possible and I think I learned quite a bit of English in that period. I also remember the extraordinary experience of hearing a boy from Cincinnati, Ohio talking to a boy from Texas in very broken French and declaring that it was easier than understanding their respective local dialects. There were of course also some local Swiss children and some from the neighbouring districts of France.

I suppose that you had to learn the language more or less like a small child acquires his mother tongue, which meant that you learned a lot about the way of thinking and the attitudes of that part of the country, something that we weren't quite aware of at the time.

Perhaps this can best be illustrated by two little incidents which happened many years later. In the early 1960s, just before jet travel started, I flew from London to Milan on a relatively slow propeller plane which flew fairly low over the Lake of Geneva. I sat next to an English lady who had been educated in Geneva. I described it as the Léman, the normal name used in Lausanne, and she rather emotionally corrected me that this was the Lac de Genève. We got into quite an argument until we each realised that we had both taken the emotional attitude of our childhood and a good laugh restored the peace.

The second incident took place in the mid 60s when I visited Lausanne on business for the first time after thirty-five years. On a journey from the hotel to the station the taxi driver told me about the plan to pull down a series of buildings which housed a well known café which I knew from my student days. I heard myself, to my own surprise, showing a very emotional reaction, which caused the taxi driver to consider me as a 'local'.

When I returned home after this period at the Lycée Jacquard I realised that I had not mastered French grammar but it was only many years later that I realised the importance of the start of my 'Swiss soul' which prevented me having the same 'parochial' attitudes as before.

The following year I was sent onto a course organised by the university of Lille. There was a contingent of about fifteen people from Czechoslovakia supervised by a professor from Prague, some thirty boys and girls from France, mostly from the Northern Region, and about sixty from England, a girls' school from Preston and a boys' school from Liverpool. We stayed for about two weeks in Calais. The highlight of this stay was a reception for us by the Mayor of Calais in the Town Hall. After that we were moved to Dunkerque and the boys stayed at the Collège Jean Bart, which was very near the main square, the Place Jean Bart which had a famous clock which played whole tunes every hour and minor performances in between. It took quite a few nights before I learned to sleep through these recitals. The washing facilities were somewhat primitive and there was only cold water. This reduced the enthusiasm for washing somewhat but the leaders in this respect were some of the French boys who wore vests with long sleeves which they only removed once a week when a new clean vest was put on which was preceded by a great effort to remove the dirt mark that had appeared on the lower arm where the vest ended. Strangely enough this procedure was greatly admired by the boys of other nationalities who wore no such vests and felt obliged to wash all over.

The girls were staying at a Lycée Lamartine which was about ten minutes walk away and most of the lessons and lectures were for both sexes together so that we had to walk to the girls' lycée every morning. This walk took us through some streets near the harbour area and it was there that I saw coloured people for the first time in my life. Up to that time I had only read about blacks in stories like *Uncle Tom's Cabin*, or seen pictures or illustrations. It had never occurred to me that their hair could also go white in old age and I remember stepping off the narrow pavement to let an old man with white hair pass because he had such a patriarchal bearing.

The lectures were very varied and interesting and without realising it after a few weeks I could more or less understand what was being said. Apart from literature and poetry we learned a lot about French institutions, parliamentary and political organisation and many things of ordinary French life.

In the afternoons when the weather was good we went to the beach at Malo les Bains which was a short tram ride away. One detail of the situation in France at that time (1931) stands out particularly in my memory. The tram had to cross a canal which was part of the harbour area. The bridge had been destroyed during the First World War and we were told that the Germans had to build a new bridge adjacent to it, but the French had to lay the new lines for the tram. The old rails had however not been taken up but, at the spot where the new rails had to take a new direction, some points had been put in. These points had later broken or somehow defied human control and every third time or so the tram started to career on to the old line towards the water. There was some frantic braking and fortunately the tram always stopped before plunging into the canal. There were no overhead wires so all able bodied passengers got out and pushed the tram back on to the proper line. If my memory is correct this procedure continued most of the summer. Whether the points were finally mended or whether I was just lucky that nothing went wrong on later rides I cannot say.

One of the big events that summer was a visit to Paris, in particular to the 'Exposition Coloniale' where all parts of the French Empire were represented and many temples or other important buildings were reproduced, which gave me a very good picture of the size and variety of that Empire. I was particularly impressed by Indo-China, an area which has become tragically familiar in the post Second World War period. The rest of my Paris visit was very typically 'tourist' style and I think I saw just enough not to have to be a 'tourist' again but could go and see what interested me on later visits.

The other big event was a visit to London, which was made possible by one of my teachers at this course who was an officer in the French Forces and who invited me on an outing which was for officers and their families. I thus went with the Officiers de la Reserve de la 1ière, Region de Lille, and arrived at St Pancras which was covered in French flags and where a military band played the Marseillaise. All the tourist guides on the various coaches which took us all over the 'sights' were of course French, so I saw London very much through French eyes.

One of the English experiences was the English breakfast which impressed me greatly and I now realise what agonies our cook must have suffered when I came home and wanted an 'English breakfast' and she could never get it right.

This period was also the time of my first girlfriends, very innocent affairs with holding hands and some furtive kisses. Perhaps more important was that it gave me the opportunity of learning to write love letters in English to Joyce Mary Edwards from Cardiff and to a girl from Soissons, Aisne in French, whose name I have forgotten. Although my French at that time was much better than my English I found it much easier to write the ones in English. I think this is because in English one can always remain vague and uncommitted whilst French is a very clear and logical language and everything had a right way of saying it.

This period in Western Europe with the visits to both Paris and London, the contact with the world outside the provincial town where we lived, brought some difficulties with most of my friends who in the usual way mocked everything that was different. I soon learnt not to say too much and things quietened down and no serious problems arose.

I was now in a college called a 'Commercial Academy'. A direct comparison with an English school is difficult to make. It was a four year course for students who had successfully completed four years of grammar school. All the basic education had to have been completed and the students were being prepared to pass a 'master degree' in the 'craft' of running a commercial enterprise. In all countries that at some time in history were part of the Habsburg Empire, the legal principle existed that anybody who undertook any type of commercial, trade or technical enterprise had to have the necessary apprenticeship and test of a 'master degree' or equivalent higher education. From my later experience I think that this was an excellent principle. It reduced the possibilities of 'cowboys' carrying out a trade or business they did not understand, and increased quality in every sphere of life. This principle is applied in all countries that were once part of the Austro/Hungarian Empire, the Netherlands, Belgium, and I believe Spain. The drawback of course is that the exceptionally talented entrepreneur has more difficulty in establishing himself.

This type of college was often owned by the local Chamber of Commerce or a trade organisation and the curriculum was adjusted, at least to a certain extent, to the trade in the area.

An important subject which at first did not have much to do with the rest of the curriculum was called 'Knowledge of Merchandise' and was a mixture of physics, chemistry and technology and dealt with the processes applied in all industries in the area. We thus had to learn at least in very general outline about the processes and machinery used in the textile industry, paper making, iron and steel production, mining, the production of beet sugar and the principles of forestry, to give just some examples.

The approach to certain subjects was also somewhat different from the one I encountered later in other countries.

Geography: we had to learn the basic geological formation of a country, its position on the globe and its prevailing winds. From that we had to work out the likely climate and the products which might be grown there, and what raw materials for industry and energy sources might be available. Having given some thought to what might be possible we were then told what actually took place and the role that country in fact played. I never remember having to memorise names of towns, heights of mountains or other details of this kind which one can look up so easily.

History: the emphasis was on what was going on at a given period in all important countries. For instance the time of the French Revolution: what was the background for this situation in France; why was Napoleon at first welcome as liberator in the various kingdoms, dukedoms etc in Germany; what went on in Britain at the same time, how did this affect America?

The attempt was to give you a global view of life at a certain period. The names of emperors and kings, the dates when they ruled and their various moral or immoral affairs were only of secondary interest, and the real causes were usually described as spiritual or economic.

Modern languages were taught with the specific aim of being able to communicate both verbally and in writing with foreign customers which meant that it was important to write grammatically correct letters using phrases acceptable in those countries and to speak with a pronunciation intelligible to those foreigners. Thus in the early 1930s we used gramophone records developed by the University of Grenoble to learn the right sound.

I do not think this aim was completely realised but when I later encountered the teaching of languages that my own children received in both state and public schools in this country I could not even discern such an aim or a corresponding intention. Perhaps I was particularly lucky in my education and our children rather less so.

As the main aim of this 'Commercial Academy' was to prepare students for the qualification of being a 'master' in the 'craft' of running a business or trade there was of course quite an emphasis on learning commercial law and I was told that the knowledge required was equal to that required for this subject for a degree in law. Whether this is true or not I cannot know. I have certainly found during nearly forty years of executive positions that I did not have any difficulty in the legal problems one has to deal with in the commercial world.

Book keeping, now called accountancy, had to be mastered to be able to organise a system of records and draw a balance sheet for any 'private' company.

The teaching of economics was understood in the widest sense and dealt with the philosophical as well as with the economic background from the growth of empires onwards in general terms and from Adam Smith to Karl Marx in specific terms. This sort of enquiry of course also led to the question of whether Marxism was the ultimate economic answer or whether the economists who dealt with other possibilities had anything really new to offer.

For me these questions became important after my visit to France during the winter 1931/2. The collapse of the New York stock exchange had taken place in 1929. This brought about the collapse of Western economies, the beginning of mass unemployment and when the pound left the gold standard on Yom Kippur 1931 (the holiest day of the Jewish year) my father lost about one million of Czech crowns in one day as all export contracts had always been made in pounds sterling, the most important and most stable currency in the world. In a very practical way I experienced that the things I had considered stable and basic were perhaps not quite what they had seemed up to now. The situation in Germany was also going from bad to worse, Nazism was on the increase and constant clashes between communists and National Socialists became frequent occurrences.

Chapter 9

Life at College

It happened that I read a book about the Turkish atrocities against the Armenians after World War One, which for reasons that I did not analyse at the time, touched me very much. It was called *The 40 days of Musa Dag* and was by a German/Jewish writer called Franz Werfel. A book by F. Osbourne which gave the latest theories of how our universe had come about and how it was changing increased this feeling in me that perhaps nothing was stable.

There was a lot of talk then about Einstein's Theory of Relativity and Freud's psycho-analysis, neither of which I could understand but which were always discussed by the 'grown-ups' whom I admired, with such gravity and conviction that I was left with the uneasy feeling that they perhaps did not know either.

Then there were the occasional remarks by my mother which came from Steiner's *Antroposophy* which seemed to counteract a great number of other views. I envied some of my friends who always knew what was right and what was wrong, what was good and what was bad, and what 'one had to do or not to do'. I was mostly left 'in between', seeing more than one point of view.

One occasion that took place during the winter of 1931/2 has remained very clearly in my mind. We were asked to write an essay, and although I have forgotten the actual title, it seemed to me to be the question: 'If you were asked to create the best organisation of society and economics, how would you do it?' I filled quite a number of pages giving various details of the economic theories we had learned, thus showing that I had dutifully absorbed the curriculum, but then surprised myself with a conclusion which I had not expected myself. I cannot remember the words I used and whether I in fact expressed what had suddenly come to me. What I tried to say was that no purely economic solution was possible unless behind it there was an acceptance of religious principles based on the age-old laws. This conclusion was really surprising to me because up to that time I had thought of myself as a thorough socialist and had considered 'religion' as something to be done on certain days of the year, because it was 'the done thing', and certainly not something that could lead to a more just society. I cannot say why this essay has stayed so clear in my memory as it does not seem to have changed any of my behaviour at the time nor do I remember any discussions with my friends about it.

It was during this year that my parents began to treat us as nearly grown up and we were allowed more freedom. Pocket money was increased to allow for occasional visits to the pictures. Theatre, plays and opera were considered 'educational' and were willingly paid for by my parents in addition to the pocket money. Most entertainment was fairly cheap by English standards. A visit to the pictures would be about 2 to 3 crowns (about 4*d*. to 6*d*.), a visit to the theatre about 5 Kcs (Czechoslovak crowns), about 10*d*., and when the Viennese Burg Theatre was visiting, Kcs 6. A coffee in the coffee house was Kcs 1.10 (just over 2*d*.) and for that the waiter would also bring you any newspaper you wished to read including foreign periodicals like *Illustrated London News* and papers like *Punch* or the German or French equivalent. The waiter also brought fresh cold water several times. When you left an hour or more later and you felt generous and gave a tip of 20 hellers (about one farthing) this was remembered and when you came next time you were addressed one rank higher than before. If you had previously been addressed just as Herr (Mr) and then the name, you were now addressed as Herr Doctor, and in later years and when the tip had increased the address could then be Herr Professor, but that I reached only very rarely. It was quite obvious that nobody assumed that you held such a position; it was purely the result of your tip, more often the expression of esteem in which your father was held in the community.

There was also a type of café where you could buy a small meal, a pair of small frankfurters for Kcs 1 and a beer for Kcs 1, but our finances rarely supported such extravagances. Our real night out was to go to a wine bar where four to six of us shared a bottle of wine. We could get the cheapest bottle for about Kcs 18, which included the surcharge for the band. When we had dissolved a couple of lumps of sugar per glass, this liquid, Hungarian riesling, became quite drinkable.

The social events were dances. There were first of all dancing lessons, organised by the college, which were considered very important to teach you appropriate behaviour. Of course all the girls were accompanied by chaperons and it was imperative that they were addressed with due respect. They had to give permission for the dance. These functions usually ended at midnight. In addition there were dances organised by various sport clubs or cultural societies which often went on until 3 a.m. Again the girls were chaperoned and therefore 'out of reach' on the way home. There were however also dances in beer gardens where things were less formal and accompanying the girls home often afterwards was the main attraction.

The 'real' night out ended with a goulash soup at Kcs 1 and a half glass of beer at the station buffet. The station was two kilometres from the centre and it was open all night. We really felt that this was the high life when we walked two kilometres after the dance finished at 3 a.m., and two kilometres back after the goulash soup, thus coming home at 4.30 a.m., on Sunday morning.

I have never been very interested in ball games or team sports. I played tennis without really any special proficiency, perhaps mainly because I liked the tennis club dances.

Skating was very enjoyable from the age of eight onwards but I never reached any standard in figure skating nor in playing ice hockey. Ice hockey was however the most enjoyable sport to watch. It is so fast that one goal is attacked one moment and two or three seconds later the puck is in the goal on the other side. You really had to watch every second. As it was often very cold the shouting and jumping enthusiastically to support 'our' team was really a sport in itself and a very healthy activity.

As soon as I was old enough, probably about eleven or twelve, I was allowed to take up skiing, which became a sport I really loved. We were taken most Wednesdays and Saturday afternoons from school to the nearest ski slopes, about twenty minutes by local railway. When I became old enough to go out for the whole weekend our French master, who was a very good skier, took us on Saturday afternoon by coach or train to the Sudeten mountains. We climbed for about two hours on our skis covered with skins for climbing, arriving at the ski hut at 8 or 9 p.m. After a hot drink we went to sleep, putting on all extra pullovers as the heating was negligible. The accommodation was very primitive and washing in the morning was usually in melted snow. Then there was a cup of brown hot liquid called coffee and out we went onto the mountains. At about 1,400m above sea level it could be rather stormy and sometimes the fight with the elements was quite a battle, but you got your real reward on a sunny day when the snow glistened and you made your own tracks in the snow where no human being had yet been that morning. The area was wooded and making your way through the clearings amongst the snow covered trees gave you the feeling that you owned this mountain, particularly when you could move at speed (30/40 km per hr) and much faster during an open descent if there were no trees. In those days the ski huts would hold up to twenty or thirty people and there were no more than two huts on one mountain range. You could ski sometimes for three or four hours without meeting another party, a very different situation from today's ski resorts with ski lifts and big hotels. There were in my day no collisions with other skiers, as there were no ski lifts, you had to climb up by your own muscle power and if you could do that you usually also had the strength in your muscles to descend without tension, which would mean an immediate fall.

Swimming and hiking were my main sports in summer but these were not so directly connected with college so I shall come back to them later and first say more about the atmosphere of our life at college.

We were a two-stream intake called A and B. The streaming took place according to the knowledge of the Czech language. Although tuition took place in German, one third of the students in our form were ethnic Czechs. This was mainly because the parallel Czech school was usually over subscribed as about three quarters of the population were Czech, but also because some parents wished their children to have a German education as German is a world language and therefore career prospects were considered greater. The second third were Jews who generally were bilingual; and the last third were ethnic Germans who lived in the larger towns which generally had a largely Czech population.

The 'B' form consisted to a large extent of students who came from villages in the German speaking areas in the north of Moravia. They had to learn Czech as a foreign language so this consisted mainly of grammar.

In the 'A' stream the emphasis was on literature and general publication. Owing to the oppression by the German speaking Habsburg Emperors and governing classes, the Czech language and literature over a period of three hundred years prior to the establishment of the Czech state could not flourish in a natural way and we therefore read a great deal of nineteenth century Russian poetry in Czech translation. This I think had quite an influence on our thinking and attitudes.

I am sure that the consequences of this division were not foreseen by the authorities, but the result over the four years of this course was that these two streams developed a very distinct outlook on life and the nearer the Nazi period came the more this different outlook became noticeable. The 'A' stream was influenced more by Western, democratic and politically left ideas, while the 'B' stream tended more in the direction of the 'Sudeten German' and regimented, orderly ideas, which we felt were more influenced by the growing Nazi movement north of the border. This, however, was never spoken of openly and to a large extent it was an instinctive attitude, which although it coloured one's basic view of life did not lead to any outward clashes or difficulties. It may be that these two groups preferred different pubs or dances and read different newspapers.

I am describing this in much detail because it may help to understand the violent conflicts which we have seen in many areas since the Second World War and which are still going on.

For eighteen hundred years Czechs and Germans have lived in the same area. During the whole of the Middle Ages when Latin was the language of law, education and administration and therefore of the ruling class, the people in the villages could use their own languages and live together without major clashes. It was only when in the seventeenth century the vernacular became introduced into education and the running of the administration that language and 'nationality' became a problem.

Even then, the fact of living together in one community with so many common problems, inter-marriage and so on, did not allow this question to become a danger to the continuity of co-existence. It was only when the efficient and completely new propaganda machine of the Nazis started to use all modern means of communication and began to unleash the power of hatred in a completely new way that the national difference began to turn into a danger for co-existence and lives were in danger.

In the period I am describing, the early thirties, these forces were largely unconscious undercurrents and nobody could have believed that events which took place only less than a decade later could actually happen.

Thus my memories of this period of my life are extremely happy ones, with a great deal of comradeship and fun and with much cultural stimulation which reflected the position of the Czech lands right in the centre of Europe and with contacts in every direction. Theatre, films and concerts were all affordable and of excellent quality.

In November 1932 I contracted pneumonia. As I had periodically suffered from bronchitis the doctor thought it was one of the usual attacks and by the time it was properly diagnosed it had become really serious and for six weeks I was between life and death. Antibiotics did not exist, of course, and it was only after a long search that one of the doctors discovered that a professor in Berlin had successfully used some new drug with excellent results. It was later called M&B. If my parents would agree to this experiment this professor in Berlin would supply the drug provided detailed reports would be sent to him about treatment and my state of health.

Two nurses looked after me day and night. They were nuns of some order, whose habits I had seen often before, but I do not know which. The only present they would accept was a packet of coffee from time to time which they said helped them during their long night duties.

Although I did not know it at the time I learned a great deal from these two extraordinary and selfless women. I know today that because I was for weeks unconscious or in a delirious state my ordinary head hardly functioned, but there was an extraordinary direct relationship and I seemed very dependant on them for the help I received. They were two extremely different types: one was always cheerful and chatty, always willing to bend the rules a little so that life was that little bit more acceptable; the other one very serious, always fulfilling her duties absolutely, never saying an unnecessary word but always oozing a kind of goodness which evoked absolute confidence.

The chatty one told me she had once nursed the local Archbishop and still went to see him regularly. She told him of my case and he said he would pray for me. From time to time she would report that he had done so and would pray again. I felt I was not worthy of such high intervention and in fact the thought of not surviving had never occurred to me.

My best friend, with whom I recall playing from the earliest age I can remember and who had been very close to me all the time, used to visit daily and frequently was not allowed to see me, but he nevertheless came every day until I was well again. I did not know this at the time, of course; I was only told afterwards.

It has been a sorrow to me since my arrival in this country, that when I received a letter from him in August 1939, asking me to help him to come to Britain, I was absolutely penniless and the Home Office had just impounded my only one hundred pounds, to be returned to me when I left or became a British subject. There was nothing I could do and shortly afterwards war broke out and he ended in one of the extermination camps; one of the six million.

But back to my illness. After six weeks, possibly with the help of the M&B, I started to improve and four weeks later I could get out of bed and walk again. I became a great expert at taking my temperature and pulse as these details, morning, noon and night, had to be sent to that professor in Berlin.

By March I was able to attend college again. It was the year of my matriculation and the exams were in June. I was rather limited in the amount of physical activity I was allowed to do and this more or less forced me to study. It was a particularly beautiful spring. Very near to our house there was an entrance into the local park. I enjoyed going there early in the morning and studying two or three hours before breakfast.

I had a great deal of help from my college friends. Not all subjects could be studied from printed books and a great deal depended on notes taken during lectures. They were all willing to make their notes available and if necessary dictate them to me. The result of all this was that I passed my matric with distinction. It was the first and last time that I reached this top grade.

My health was now completely restored and the doctor said I could do anything within reason.

Chapter 10

Travelling

During the previous two years my father's business had run into a great deal of difficulty. It was the period following the great depression in the West. My father's business depended very much on exports to South America. Even if orders were received and goods delivered, payments were delayed by the various South American governments which made any normal cash flow calculations impossible. It looked very much as if this would be a long term difficulty.

A family council was therefore assembled, which consisted of my grandmother, my parents and various uncles. The extraordinary step was suggested that I should not join the family business founded by my great-grandfather; but should instead follow the trade of my mother's family and join an uncle in the manufacturing of woollen cloth. I was absolutely delighted by this decision as I had always felt that in making malt one does not 'do' anything; one only makes the barley grow and then stops it at the right temperature – the chemical change inside is done by God and not by man. Textiles was quite different; every process had to be done correctly and in the end the right fashion sense decided the success.

So when I was told of the outcome of the family conference I was absolutely delighted that fate had pushed me exactly in the direction I wished to go.

It was the end of June and I was to start work in September. So there were two months of freedom. There were fairly severe currency restrictions and you were allowed to take the equivalent of £10, in the buying power of 1933, out of the country.

So with two pals of my age and armed with the ten pounds we took a train to Bratislava, the capital of Slovakia, which is on the Danube and boarded a steamer bound for Bulgaria. The fare for the boat could be bought within Czechoslovakia and therefore left our £10 intact. These boats travelled extremely slowly and there was therefore plenty of time to see the countryside. We slept on deck, fed on tins of sardines and bread, which we brought along, and the luxury was Turkish coffee which was brewed the traditional way in the ashes of a fire made on deck. It was excellent and extremely cheap.

We stopped on the way in Budapest and Belgrade and ended up ten days later in Varna on the Black Sea.

One little detail I remember as extraordinary was a little island in the middle of

The family council and their children.

the Danube perhaps 200 or 300 metres long which was called Turkish Island, and which had been forgotten when the peace treaty at the end of World War I had been made and so this little area had remained Turkey in the middle of what I think was then Yugoslavia. We saw Turkish flags and then a fez, and we were told that it was all an accident. Perhaps this has made such an impression on me because it was the first time that the question arose, whether man is really in control of events.

In Varna we spent a week enjoying beautiful beaches and sea and one extraordinary event took place when one day we found that there was somebody from Olomouc, our home town, who had become a butcher in Varna. He had seen our names and addresses in the hotel register and as it had not happened for many years that anybody from Olomouc had come there he had left us this note. He presented us with a rather large quantity of *Moravské klobásy* (Moravian sausages) which provided us with food for several days.

Moravské klobásy are a famous speciality of the region and it is told that at some point at the beginning of the century Bohemia nearly lost its Home Rule which was being discussed in the Austrian Parliament, because all the Bohemian and Moravian deputies had discovered a pub that served outstandingly good *Moravské klobásy* and had therefore forgathered there for lunch. The constitutional catastrophe was only averted by one deputy who arrived in Vienna too late to go for his lunch and could warn his colleagues just in time.

Our journey took us from Varna to Istanbul, which gave me my first glimpse of the culture of Constantinople and the Greek Empire and also of the much younger Islamic and Turkish culture.

From there we took a Soviet freighter via Izmir (which then still had a horse drawn tram) to Athens. There we spent ten days feeding on the beauty and history and very little physical food except for grapes, the price for which in any other currency seemed to come out at less than 1.

One little incident at the Acropolis: an American woman was sitting there with a 'Baedeker'. When we approached she asked whether we could help her. She found it so tiresome always to read and then find out whether she could see what was described. If we could look whilst she read and say when we had seen it, she could tick it off so much more quickly!

In Athens we each of us received a postal order worth the equivalent of several pounds and the man at Thomas Cook knew of a way of travelling with a 70 per cent reduction of the fare for anybody visiting the Fascist Exhibition in Rome; so we were able to book an affordable return journey from Brindisi to Naples–Rome–Florence–Venice–Vienna and home to Olomouc.

From Athens via the Corinth canal to Corfu cost practically nothing as it was transporting prisoners to that island and discerning travellers would not wish to travel in that company. Corfu to Brindisi was the next journey, and then from Brindisi to Naples we took a night journey on an extremely crowded train with soldiers carrying full kit. It was so uncomfortable that there was no possibility of sleeping. A kind soldier taught me to count in Italian and also a number of other useful Italian words, knowledge which turned out very useful in later years.

Naples was extremely exciting, with Vesuvius, a living volcano rumbling under your feet, and the excavation at Herculanum and Pompei which gave such a vivid picture of Roman life.

As we had very little money but plenty of time we kept pestering the man at the steamship company running the boats to Capri that the student pass issued in Athens and written in Greek, which the man could not read, entitled us to a free trip to Capri. Driven to despair he finally agreed and we spent a marvellous day on the island.

Apart from the beauty of the island and the Blue Grotto, a little incident has remained in my mind. Shortly after the boat had left Naples, a lady tapped me on the shoulder and said: 'Is your father's name so and so?' (quoting the correct name of my father).

When I confirmed that she was correct she said: 'I concluded this from the resemblance,' saying that she knew my father well.

She then disappeared in the crowd without explaining who she was. It left me with a strange feeling that the world was a small place and that there was no escape so I would always 'be known'.

On our arrival in Rome a porter tried to carry our luggage. We managed to explain to him in a mixture of various languages that we would rather carry our own luggage but he could assist us by recommending a cheap hotel. At this his eyes lit up and he explained that his mother could accommodate us and he would take us there. This accommodation was indeed remarkable and has therefore stayed clearly in my mind. It was one room furnished with one large bed where two of us had to sleep and a third extremely narrow contraption which was the bed of the third person. The window would not open which in the town centre in August hardly made for comfort. It was however extremely cheap and we prepaid for the whole of our stay. We discovered later that the low price was due to the fact that Mussolini's Fascist government had just decided to bring ORDER into Italian life and all tourist accommodation had to be licensed and regularly inspected. This place was of course not licensed. Having concluded the deal very advantageously to us, the woman tried to improve her situation by selling us what she called *café latte*, which was a milky coloured base into which she carefully sprinkled three drops of dark liquid from a small bottle: 'coffee'. For some reason she always decided that we would abscond without paying. So whenever she saw us she would come and shout '*café latte*', and as soon as the drink had been delivered came the shout '*pagare!*' Two more words were thus added permanently to my Italian vocabulary.

There was a further difficulty about this drink. The dimensions of this woman were such that she could never decide which way it would be easier to negotiate the door, front or sideways. In this process the tray with the *café latte* always swayed dangerously. No disaster ever happened but it seemed clear to us that the day was not far away when it would become impossible for her to negotiate the opening.

One of the most important things we had to do was to visit the Fascist Exhibition and get a stamp in our passports confirming the visit so that we could travel at about a quarter of the normal cost on the railways. I am afraid I have no recollection of what we saw there. All I can recall is that we had to take a tram to get there and although the temperature was well in the mid 30°C the conductor would not let me travel without a jacket. So I had to get off and walk back to our 'digs', get a jacket and try again.

One morning we found ourselves on a crowded square where everybody was watching a balcony where a number of obviously high ranking Air Force officers were awaiting some important event. We were told that the commander of the Air Force, General Balbo, had just crossed the Atlantic with a number of planes and that this 'great hero' would speak any moment now. And indeed he did. The speech lasted a very long time. Italian is a language where the gestures are at least as important as the words and as we had been told what this occasion was about it was easy to follow. The crowd responded enthusiastically and soon shouted itself in to a frenzy.

In a way this was a very comic occasion; on the other hand it was clear that a lot had already been learned from Hitler who had come to power about half a year before this event, and that something of this orgy of hate that was to grip the whole of Europe a few years later could already be sensed. When the Italians attacked Abyssinia one year later I was less surprised than I would have been had I not seen Balbo on this occasion.

Another rather frightening occasion was a visit to the church of St Maria Maggiore. On the top of a long stairway there was exhibited, in a brilliantly lit showcase, a piece of the 'True Cross'. Whilst the pilgrims climbed this staircase on their knees saying prayers on each step, the 'unbelievers' were allowed to go up by a different way, inspect the relic from near by and look down on the pilgrims. As I looked down I suddenly had the impression, or perhaps a vision, that all these people were worshipping a piece of wood and a fear gripped me which then had no words at all but which I would today call a realisation of man's suggestibility. It occurred to me neither then nor later whether this impression was true in any objective sense but I was concerned with my suggestive vision of that possibility. This impression linked itself somehow with the frightening force I had felt on the same square when the crowd acclaimed Balbo.

1933 was an *anno santo*. You entered St. Peter's via some special doors and you could apply for an audience with the Pope. As the Vatican is also a secular state the application for such an audience had to be done via your embassy which resulted in a 'visa' stamped in your passport. This audience took place in the Vatican Palace. There was quite a long wait and various dignitaries walked past in very impressive robes and with an air of great solemnity and importance. Each time the feeling of expectation of the crowd of perhaps sixty to eighty people increased further. 'Extremely well stage managed,' a voice said in me. Finally the Pope appeared. In complete contrast to all the pomp that had gone before he was simply dressed in white and he moved slowly past the kneeling people giving them his ring to kiss. When he approached the three Jewish boys (half kneeling, as one must never kneel in front of another human being) he immediately grasped the situation, nodded and smiled and passed his hand rather quickly so that we did not have to kiss the ring. I was rather impressed as I felt that here was a human being. At some people he stopped and asked a question and with some Vatican citizens he had longer discussion about their problems.

Our 'visa' entitled us also to visit some parts of the Vatican museum not always open to visitors. We made the fullest use of this opportunity and spent two days there. There was of course a great deal we could not understand or take in.

From Rome we went to Florence but by now we were so full of impressions that any further sightseeing was mainly going through the motions.

When we arrived in Venice the father of one of the two friends who were with me had somehow traced us. He was there by car and was staying in the Italian Alps in a place called San Martino di Castrozza. He took us to his hotel where we had the first real four-course meal for weeks and slept in comfortable beds. The next day he took us to the little town of Treviso where the Vienna express stopped. We had just enough money left to buy a piece of bread and cheese which we ate sitting in the pretty square.

About midnight we caught the train. At the Austrian frontier in the early morning a lady in the next compartment heard us discussing with the vendor whether we could have one cup of coffee between us. She also came from Czechoslovakia and had recognised our accent. She invited us for a meal in the dining car, so we could conclude our journey in style. We had been away for nearly seven weeks at the cost of about £17 each, including the various postal orders which were sent to us on the way. When I arrived in my home town I did not have enough money for the tram, so I took a taxi and my mother had to pay.

Chapter 11

Textile Apprentice – Brno

Two weeks later I started work in Brno, the capital of Moravia, in a firm where an uncle of mine was a partner. I suppose one would describe his work as Designer/Manager.

He explained to me that my main privilege was that I was to have a desk in his office and would be shown everything, I would have to work in every department, on almost every machine and process, work shifts when needed, do overtime without extra pay and draw the lowest salary in the place. I would have the further privilege that when I did something wrong I would not be called '*Sie Pferd*' (literally you horse, with the polite form for you) but '*Du Ross*' (literally 'you steed'). I would have to become familiar with all the textile technical subjects and would be given private lessons by one of the lecturers at the Textile Technical College. The firm would pay for this and I would have one afternoon a week off for this purpose. At the end I would have to pass the equivalent of a 'City and Guilds' exam. My uncle also added that he expected that after my training period I would have to do my two years of compulsory military service, and after that he proposed to send me to Harr & Thompson in Vicar Lane, Bradford, who were one of the main wool suppliers, to finish off my education.

I was given a salary of the equivalent of five pounds per month net, the firm paying pension and sickness insurance. Both these payments were compulsory National Insurance, similar to the National Health Service introduced in Britain in 1948.

My first digs were a room in a flat on the first floor just opposite the tram terminal which produced a lot of clanging noises each time the tram was turned around to proceed in the opposite direction. As the trams ran all night this did not make for a relaxing existence, after spending the working day in the noise of a weaving shed or other machinery. I paid Kcs 220 per month (about £2) for this accommodation. This price included a cup of coffee in the morning and a weekly bath which was provided by bringing a tin bath into the room. It included light and a minimum amount of coal for a fire in a little iron stove in the winter. It seemed to be the normal price for such accommodation. When during the four years of my stay in Brno I moved to various other digs the prices remained fairly in proportion, increasing slightly for a real bath tub in a bathroom or a gas ring in the room so that I could make myself a coffee at any time and similar luxuries.

The team of foremen and designers in the firm of Eduard Ernst Essler, Brno-Obřany.

The mill was at the terminus of the No. 3 tram. I had to catch one tram into town, and another tram to the suburb of Obřany (about thirty minutes). My normal working hours were from 7.30 a.m. to 6 p.m. with a two hour lunch break from 12 to 2. When I worked shifts the hours were either 5 a.m. to 1 p.m. six days or 1 p.m. to 10 p.m. five days. In addition there was a third shift in busy times from 10 p.m. – 5 a.m., but that shift I never had to work.

I soon learnt to utilise this tram ride for reading. When the tram came to the loop at the terminal the wheels made a characteristic screech and I could read until this moment and be ready to get off when the tram stopped. In this way I read, for instance, the whole of the *Jewish War* by Josephus and various other longwinded writings by Thomas Mann who was then very much in fashion. After work in summer I loved to go to a rowing and swimming club which was another twenty minutes on the tram out of town in the opposite direction which tended to improve my literary knowledge a bit more. On Monday mornings, however, I had to read the newspaper and memorise the results of the football teams in which the men at the mill were interested. It would have seriously jeopardised my personal relationships had I not known the results and voiced my opinions. There was no harm in disagreeing but not knowing them was an unpardonable crime.

As I was taught over the next years the processes in each department I had also to calculate the wages there. Most wages were either paid piece rates or a combination of time rates with efficiency bonuses. Very few 'blue collar' workers were on pure time rates. The rates were laid down in agreement with the unions, and were identical for men and women. I never came across any other system. This also applied to office staff such as typists and telephone operators where general minimum wages for each job were laid down by law, particularly with regard to overtime and night work. The 'blue collar' workers' wages were public and open to inspection by the union and were posted up three days before pay-day so that the correct calculation could be checked. This did not apply to higher grade supervisory staff and managers.

These weekly wages calculations were always done on Saturday morning. At 12 noon the machinery stopped for cleaning until 1 p.m. when the mill closed for the weekend. It was always very important for me to have finished my adding up before 12 o'clock. At that moment the industrial noise stopped and one realised that we were in an agricultural area. There was the clucking of hens or a cockerel crowing or a cow in the distance and various other 'natural' noises and I found it quite impossible to add up any figures in this 'industrial silence'.

Every three or four weeks I took a train to visit my parents which was a journey of about 80 km and the return fare was about 13 crowns (just over two shillings at that time). Six years later the day return ticket from Huddersfield to Leeds was 1*s*.11*d*. for less than twenty miles: thus about three times the price.

Most of my main meals I had with my grandmother and I think that this family 'perk' had been taken into account when the salary was fixed. It would probably have been about £8 per month. I considered it as a matter of honour to stand on my own feet and it was quite possible for a young man to live in a reasonable way and enjoy life.

Food was very cheap and nearly always locally produced. Tins were very rare, and refrigeration was confined to the transport of special commodities. Most things eaten were therefore fresh or conserved by the old traditional methods. I only realised several years later in England, how much food preserved in different ways could be eaten and how the taste for fresh food can be lost. A good simple three-course meal was available in restaurants for 6 crowns (one shilling) and in country pubs for 5 crowns. For supper you could buy a reasonable number of hot sausages for one crown with a large slice of bread and a beer. This would come to 3 crowns (6*d*.) including tip.

There were also cafés usually open from early evening until midnight where you could get a coffee or beer at the usual restaurant prices and an additional surcharge of one or two crowns for the band and where you could dance or just sit and listen. This was in the days of big bands and crooners, and the hit tunes from Fred Astaire and Ginger Rogers films were the latest craze.

In a wine bar you could take a girl out and dance till 3 a.m., consuming a bottle of wine and a snack for just under one pound for the two of you. Such extravagances were of course limited to special occasions.

Industrial products were very much more expensive in relation to average wages, consequently all 'gadgets' were rare.

We got our first radio in the year before my matric and I remember that between 11 and 12 at night one could even very faintly make out Henry Hall from London, except on days when the 'atmospherics' prevented this.

We never had an electric fridge. What we called a fridge was a wooden box specially lined. From time to time a man came round selling you blocks of ice which were broken up and put into this box. I remember that a friend of my grandmother's was so rich that she had an electric fire for cool days when it was not cold enough to put the stove on. This was extraordinary. When I had left home and my parents decided they no longer needed both a cook and a maid, an electric 'Hoover' was acquired, as the one servant now had to do both the cleaning and the cooking.

Cars were very expensive and were considered to be mainly for the very rich. In the early thirties a small car would be between £300 and £400. I remember that just before the war a small Ford was just over £100 in Britain.

I do not know whether I have succeeded in indicating that the life my friends and I led in Moravia in the thirties included more simple pleasures and perhaps life was a bit nearer to nature and further from technical pursuits and gadgets.

Chapter 12

National Service

THE BIG SLUMP that started in the US and Western Europe in 1930 and 1931 was felt in our area about one or two years later. The worst unemployment was reached in 1933 and it was 1935 when the improvement became really visible in everyday life. There were a number of reasons why human suffering was less severe than in Britain or Germany. One important one was that the industrial centres were not as large as those in Britain, that the industrial revolution had been slower and was not accompanied by the same degree of migration of rural population to the industrial centres, so a smaller proportion of workers became 'industrial proletariat'. The mill where I worked, for instance, was about 4 or 5 km from the town centre and on the border of an agricultural area. Many workers came from the local neighbourhood, remaining on the small farms or at least had some family who continued to be farmers or smallholders. In the period of the deepest depression it was therefore possible to get some food from this family on the land, if there was no employment and National Insurance was not sufficient. This situation applied to the textile industry particularly in Moravia and also to the agricultural industries in that area. In the areas of the motor and heavy industry in Bohemia and in the coal industry the situation was more severe.

There was, however, a very well developed system of National Insurance, sickness benefit and pension scheme which had been established in the early 1920s. As distinct from the system established by Beveridge in Britain in 1945 it was based on state controlled insurance companies where the contributions remained available for the purpose for which they had been raised. Naturally this was not sufficient and particularly as far as unemployment benefit was concerned, the state had to provide considerable subsidies. In principle, however, these contributions remained separate from any tax income or other use so that they were left as the workers' property to which the contributors had a right and not a 'handout' decided by the government. The health service was excellent and provided everything: the general practitioner, specialists, medicine etc. I had my appendix removed which meant a stay in hospital for two weeks and all facilities were up to the standard of the best period of the NHS in Britain. I remember that the sickness benefit I received for the following three weeks of convalescence was greater than my salary as an apprentice. The justification for this was: when you are convalescing you not only have to provide for your food and lodging but you may also have to pay for some services which you can normally provide for yourself, or pay for transport when you could normally walk. As this was my right based on the contributions, the question of means testing could not possibly arise.

In the period of the worst slumps unemployment was kept lower than it normally would have been owing to some regulation that an employer could not dismiss more than a small percentage of his workers without the permission of the Ministry of Commerce. Before permission for a larger number of workers to be dismissed was given, the employer had to prove that the continued employment would lead to bankruptcy or a serious difficulty in continuing the operation. Loss of profit was certainly no reason for such permission to be given. This measure was based on the idea that an employer had a duty to provide work for his employees, at least until the ministry could find alternative employment for at least some of the workers. This measure seemed to work in that period of emergency because the patriarchal sense of responsibility on the part of the employer had not yet completely disappeared and also the loyalty of the workforce was considered a valuable asset which would pay when better times came.

I was of course far too young and inexperienced to know to what extent these laws were observed in the whole of the country, but in the four years in which I worked in that mill I do not remember that any worker was dismissed for other reasons than misconduct. There was short time working and laying off during particularly slack periods but no permanent redundancies.

When I started work in a mill in Britain I was very surprised by the attitude of secrecy as to the amount of wages a worker took home, particularly when I heard that husbands did not tell their wives how much they earned even when they sometimes worked in the same factory. It took me quite some time to believe that.

The most important sport was soccer, called football as rugby was unknown. I would certainly have lost face with everybody at the mill if I had not known the results of the local teams on a Monday morning. Spectator sports were played on Sunday.

In September 1937 the time had arrived to start my compulsory military service. I was passed fit A1 and was sent to the local cavalry regiment whose barracks were about fifteen minutes walk from our house. The regiment was called the 'Second Siberian Dragoons'. This was because it had been founded in Siberia in 1918. Czechs and Slovaks served of course in the Imperial Austro-Hungarian Army during the First World War. A large number of them, probably about 10,000, were captured by the Russians and given permission to form their own legion to fight the Austrians and Germans. When the Tsarist forces collapsed the Czechs tried to move on the Trans-Siberian Railway to Vladivostok, where the US had promised them ships to bring them back to Europe.

They set out on this route, but in the turmoil of the civil war the progress was very slow and finally the engines broke down and could not be repaired. It so happened that the Legion captured the gold stored in the capital of some Asian region, which gave them the financial means to survive, and in the general chaos they were forced to administer the area which at some period reached five times the size of the later Czechoslovak Republic. By 1922 things got organised sufficiently to use the railway again and they reached Vladivostok and finally came home. It is one of my early memories of childhood when I made red, white and blue paper flowers to decorate our balcony, to welcome them home. Nobody could have guessed that sixteen years later I would sit in the mess of the 1st company and listen to the stories which the Sergeant Major, who had been with this regiment during the whole time, loved to tell. They were of course extremely fascinating and got rather heroic after the first dozen beers.

On 1 October 1937 I had to report for my two years of compulsory military training at the 2nd Regiment of Dragoons, The Siberian. After a few days at the Regiment a silver stripe was sewn onto my epaulettes which meant that I had become a cadet and I was sent to the Officers' Training College at Pardubice in Bohemia.

This Officers' Training College already existed and was very important in the days when it trained the dragoons and *ulanen* of the Imperial Austro-Hungarian Forces, and the officer in charge of this college was still the same man who had once been in charge of training the cadets of the Emperor. Emperor or Republic, blue uniforms or khaki, meant very little to him, as long as the cadets were brought up with the right love of horses and a sense of honour and duty, and the conviction that they were the elite and privileged to serve (whatever there was to be served). Looking back at this today I wonder whether this was a last flicker of the age of chivalry of the Middle Ages and the knights who had served a principle which was only outwardly personified in the service of the lady. I do not suggest that the officers in question were aware of this. It struck me later at the end of the Second World War when I was interrogating German prisoners that there were never any cavalry officers who were suspected of war crimes. The only exception was an Estonian who probably had no connection with this tradition.

So in this spirit we were brought up to undergo the most rigorous discipline from 3 a.m. until 6 p.m. and be in bed by 9 p.m., having done all the necessary polishing and cleaning in our 'free time'. Any time left over was for our amusement!

This programme went on until Christmas when we were allowed home on

As Officer Cadet at the 2nd Siberian Dragoons, Officer Training College, Pardubice.

leave. Dressed in red trousers, and particularly well polished riding boots with spurs, I clearly felt very proud of myself.

Of this first leave to go home over the Christmas and New Year period, I particularly remember being invited to a New Year's dance at the local Air Force regiment. A very good looking girl had accepted my invitation and we were given a special welcome. I was of course a member of the senior service as the Czech forces had no navy. I think this was probably the moment of most chauvinistic pride that I ever experienced.

When we returned to barracks a severe frost had started. All water pipes had frozen up and no lavatories were working which meant the use of field latrines. Getting up at 3 a.m. to clean the horses and riding out on exercises long before dawn soon brought us back to earth again.

There were also the many hours of drill in the closed riding school where precision was the main requirement added to the purely physical demand. I remember one occasion after three hours of dressage training, when we were just walking round the riding school, I fell off the horse because my leg muscles simply refused to function. I had of course to mount immediately and continue.

But not all efforts were physical. After five hours of riding and barrack square drill on foot we were given a nice hot meal and without a break put into a cosy warm lecture room and instructed in various theoretical subjects. I remember particularly the lessons in 'order of battle' where you had not only to know exactly how many men and horses were in a regiment but also exactly which and how many weapons as well as how many rounds of ammunition were in the line, and how many would be brought in the supply columns. To fight sleep under these conditions was already a tremendous effort but to remember these boring numbers and details seemed a quite impossible proposition.

And yet when some years later in the British forces I was given a job which required me to know by heart the Order of Battle of the approximately 100 German divisions which faced our forces, it turned out that a great deal of the information that I had learnt with such agony was still remembered and enabled me to fulfil this task.

During the early spring of 1938, if I remember rightly, just before Germans invaded Austria, a French staff officer appeared and told us: 'Forget everything that you have learnt about tactics. In the next war everything will be quite different.' He then proceeded to describe to us the principles of mobile warfare, defence in depth etc., in other words exactly what later was called *Blitzkrieg*. From then on we were trained according to these principles. It has always remained a mystery to me that the French Forces in 1940 seemed to be unaware of these methods, when the Germans outflanked the Maginot Line in absolutely the textbook manner that the French staff had issued two years earlier and according to which we were trained.

In April 1938 our training course was completed and there was a Passing Out Parade followed by a ball. This event took place in exactly the same manner as it would have taken place in the days of the Emperor or Queen Victoria. Each cadet was allocated a girl whom he was to accompany to the ball. We all had to have our fingers manicured and clear polish put on our nails. The reason for this was that even on these occasions horses had to be cleaned and when you cleaned the horses' hooves dirt would stick to your fingers. Smooth lacquer on your fingernails prevented any dirt sticking. Armed with a bunch of flowers you then had to call on the girl's mother, formally introduce yourself and ask for permission to dance the Polonaise with her daughter; and officially hand over the invitation for mother and daughter. There were of course several inspections of your dress and your white chamois leather gloves. There had been several rehearsals so that every step would be according to protocol. The Minister of War was present for this grand occasion. In the end everything passed off well and we were sent back to our regiments.

I now had a second silver stripe on my epaulettes, which meant that I was a fully trained cadet, private. Everybody had to be promoted through the ranks to become an officer, a process that usually took nine months to a year. This system meant that the officer-to-be had lived very much closer to his men and for a longer time than was the case in the British forces before he became an officer and he had proved in practice that he could handle his men. The role of the sergeant major was rather different and was much more administrative than in the British forces.

The atmosphere at the regiment was rather different from the peace time atmosphere at the college. Here we were aware of the imminence of war and the training was not an exercise but a preparation for the war that we all expected.

And one day in early May the call came. We were given live ammunition, our sabres were sharpened and during the night we left barracks for the border area.

We were part of a 'Quick Division', which was the precursor of an Armoured Division. Armoured cars and tanks moved on the roads and cavalry through the woods. All supplies were motorised with the exception of the L of C (line of communication) transport.

Our company was the advance guard through a wooded area near the border and I was given a patrol on the flank. My three men were to ride at a distance in front of me so that I could just see them, and in case they got shot my task was to ride back and report that we had made contact with the enemy. At certain intervals we had to make contact with the main patrol on the road.

In this situation it was only natural for the four men to stick closer together

Being promoted 'in the field' after the first and unsuccessful attempt by the Germans to invade Czechoslovakia in May 1939.

than regulation required. So it was with us. We suddenly came to a little stream and my horse refused to cross. I just saw my comrades disappear in the distance. I jumped off and pulled the horse across. This had taken just long enough to be the right distance from my men. It was just time to make contact with the centre and there our patrol emerged at exactly the regulation distance. This was duly noted by the commanding officer and the next day I was promoted 'in the field' to lance corporal-cadet, for correct and courageous behaviour. The horse got an extra lump of sugar from me. In the afternoon of that day we halted in a village near the border.

As we later discovered, the Germans had realised that our intelligence knew of their invasion plan and that therefore the element of surprise had been lost. They decided not to proceed and gave out the story that they had no intention of attacking. After a few more days near the border we returned to barracks and there were another five months of peace.

The training continued and there was little time for contact with the outside world, so we were only vaguely aware of the political moves of the Western Powers. We still believed that the Franco-Czech-Russian pact supported by Britain was intact and any attack on Czechoslovakia would involve Germany in a two-front war in which the Czechoslovak resistance would play an important part. It was in this spirit that Czechoslovakia mobilised its forces in September.

My personal task was to collect horses from assembly points in Northern Moravia, for which task I was given a section of men. This operation took about three or four days during which we were completely out of touch with the world. The only thing we noticed was that we heard a few isolated shots which indicated that the Sudeten German population in that area were perhaps not as co-operative as they had been in May.

When we returned to barracks with all the horses our sergeant major welcomed me with the words: 'You may as well give me your pistol, it is all over.' To which I replied: 'What do you mean? We have not started yet.' It was then that I was told of the Munich Agreement. It was impossible to grasp immediately the folly of the Western allies of handing 24 modern divisions including several tank divisions to the enemy together with an arms production capacity in guns and tank which by far exceeded the British production capacity at that time. Only in the air was there a considerable superiority of the Germans and although we heard rumours of Soviet aircraft which had come to the eastern part of Czechoslovakia to help, we could not form an opinion either about the truth of this or of their actual capacity.

It was however immediately clear that the balance of power had decisively shifted and that no power could stop the Nazis occupying the whole of Central Europe whenever it fitted their plans. The old dictum of Bismarck's: 'Who holds Bohemia holds Central Europe', had once again become operative.

Having handed over the horses I retired to the stables of my section, told the Corporal to see to everything and asked him not to disturb me if possible and for the next two days I spent most of my time sitting on a box of oats and thinking and assessing the new situation.

At the end of this time I had clarified my ideas and sent a message to my father as, owing to the alert which was still in force, I could not leave barracks. My father came almost at once and I told him the only way for us was to prepare for possible emigration as the Germans would occupy the whole country not much later than in a year's time. (It turned out that I was far too optimistic; they occupied after six months.) My father could not accept the idea that German officers would break their word. They had been his allies during the First World War and he felt I was wrong. He promised, however, to set everything in motion that I had suggested.

In the meantime I went to my commanding officer and told him that I felt that as a Jew it was not right for me to train recruits who would eventually join Hitler's army. He immediately saw the point and sent me first on a chemical warfare defence course and finally I ended up as assistant to the brigade catering officer.

After about ten days I had my first day off and could go home to discuss the situation with my parents. I was still of the opinion that we had to try to leave the country with the utmost speed. My parents could not share my opinion and this led to the only serious disagreement that I ever remember having had with them. In the end they suggested they should help me leave but they would stay until I had established myself abroad. This help they gave me to the utmost of their ability. At the time I was very upset about my failure to persuade them to my view, and this failure indeed led to the fact that they became part of the six million victims of the Holocaust. Today I understand better why it was so difficult for them to accept the real situation and why they could not free themselves of the ideas and values with which they had grown up and had lived their lives up to that moment.

My father was of retiring age and had a short time before these events sold his factories to the largest and most respected agricultural co-operative. This deal included a lifelong pension, which under normal circumstances would have given him a very comfortable life for the rest of his days. As a person who had been an officer in the Imperial and Royal Army before and during the First World War he could not really accept the fact that these 'officers and gentlemen' would leave power so completely in the hands of Hitler and his Nazi gangs, although he had all the information of what was happening in Germany and now also in Austria.

My mother, as the daughter of a K&K Kommerzialrat (Imperial Commercial Councillor) shared my father's views. She spoke very little English or French and abhorred the idea of having to learn a new language at her age. She had been a pupil of Rudolf Steiner since the early 1920s and had both Czech and German speaking friends in that movement and I think she hoped that she would be able to keep in the background and not be noticed.

As we now know such hopes turned out to be completely wishful thinking.

CHAPTER 13

Contrasts

THERE NOW FOLLOWED a period of great contrasts in my life. The army service, which had been so strenuous, suddenly became very easy and enjoyable. It had been accepted that as a Jew I was not to be asked to train recruits for Hitler and I was given the task of seeing that all surplus horses were exercised. Owing to the mobilisation before 'Munich' a lot of horses from the Sudeten German areas were brought to the barracks. And when German troops following the Munich agreement occupied the areas, there was no possibility of returning them to 'enemy territory' and their dispersal was a slow process. In the meantime these horses had to be exercised. I was given sixteen men and each man had to lead one horse, so that thirty-two horses were taken out at the same time. As I was commander of this operation I had to lead in front riding one horse only. We started early in the morning, repeating this process five or six times in a day: one hour ride, followed by half an hour rubbing down and cleaning the horses. I had a marvellous time choosing the nicest rides through woods and fields and not even having to do the cleaning afterwards as my rank was now such that this was done for me, and I could spend some of the half-hours between rides listening to the amazing tales of life in Siberia which my sergeant major was always willing to tell and elaborate further so that no tale was ever repeated in the same way.

At the same time in the evenings I started applying for jobs in overseas countries in the hope of finding employment somewhere and thus perhaps being able to emigrate legally when the time came that Germany would occupy the now defenceless remainder of the country. Nobody I met doubted that this would happen; the only question was when.

So my life was spent between these delightful autumn days on horseback and the desperate efforts in the evening to try and ensure survival by finding a job before it was too late.

After some weeks this job of exercising horses came to an end as they were either allocated a permanent place in the squadrons or returned to farmers if they had come from the border area which had remained Czechoslovakia.

I was now sent on a training course to become Brigade Gas Defence Officer. This entailed a lot of instruction in chemical weapons and the defence against them. The use of gas was however considered unlikely. The possibility of an attack by aircraft had not yet been thought of as likely, and the difficulties of preventing contamination of our positions owing to unexpected changes of wind etc. was considered too great to be a practical possibility. There was also the fact that mobile warfare with attacks deep into enemy territory and defence in depth over 30 or 40 miles mitigated against the use of chemical warfare. As gas was never used during the years of World War Two it appears that the conclusions of our staff were correct. We therefore concentrated on laying smokescreens, and a lot of instructions on meteorology and weather forecasting. Our methods at the time were of course extremely primitive and the little knowledge I acquired just enabled me to appreciate the colossal advances that were made during the war and in later years, which amongst other things made safe flying a possibility.

When I had completed this course I was posted as assistant to the Brigade Catering Officer, which turned out to be a much more interesting job. I joined this team just before Christmas when the big problem was to calculate how many live pigs would be required to supply 3,486 times 250 grams of cooked meat for each soldier. My commanding officer calculated so accurately that the meat of only one pig was left over on the day. He was rightly very proud.

The army had a recipe book where each ingredient was given to an accuracy of a tenth of a gram and it was my task to multiply this with the figure of reported strength on the day, which was usually a figure around three and a half thousand. I had then to round up to the nearest sack or drum or whatever containers the commodity was stored in, then to calculate how many wagons and horses would be required to fetch this from the depot and indent for the right number of wagons and horses. This had then to be distributed over five kitchens; miraculously, this mostly ended up as edible meals which in many cases were even tasty. In later married life I had quite some difficulty in realising that the unit for purchasing potatoes was not a sack.

On 13 March 1939 I was given two days leave and I went to Brno to the mill where I had worked before I was called up and discussed with my uncle what I would do if my military service ended before I had the possibility of emigrating. It was decided I would work under the weaving foreman and re-condition some old looms, which meant taking them to pieces, replacing worn parts and re-assembling them. This would improve my technical knowledge. There would be no resistance to that occupation.

Satisfied with this proposal I returned to Olomouc on the afternoon of the 14th and as I had not to be in barracks until midnight I stayed at home in the afternoon and invited a friend for dinner. His family had had a wool merchant's business in what had become the occupied Sudeten area and they were busy trying to bring out as much as they could, so that they could continue to live. It was known that sooner or later the Germans would sequestrate the business so it was a race against time.

In the early evening I had a phone call from the regiment telling me 'off the record' and in secret that the Germans would begin their occupation in the early morning of the 15th. I should stay at home and ring mid morning to see what I should do. Naturally my father, my friend and I were very excited and discussed all the likely turns of events. My mother had gone to a concert and arrived later. We told her excitedly what was going to happen. To my surprise she listened to what was to take place, made no comment, and started to tell us in great detail calmly about the concert which had been a remarkable event. At that moment I understood that her many years with the teaching of Rudolf Steiner had given her the ability to detach herself from the ordinary turmoil of life. This ability stayed with her and the last descriptions I was given later about her life in the concentration camp at Terezín was that she worked there as a nurse and that the peace and calm that she managed to maintain was a great support for my father who suffered very much in those conditions.

But back to the 'Ides of March'. After a very good meal we all went to bed and on the morning of the 15th I rang the barracks and arranged to visit in civilian clothes and go straight to the major's office.

At the gate there was our sentry as well as a German one. The Czech sentry recognised me and although he knew I was only a cadet officer for whom normally arms were not presented, he gave me a very smart present arms salute, and the German sentry, thinking I was some important officer, immediately followed suit.

When I came to the major's office he greeted me warmly and told me that our ways would now part and that I would have to leave the country where my ancestors had lived for many generations; that he could do no more for me than give me an immediate release from the forces under some regulation which could be 'bent' to suit my case. The formalities took about half an hour during which time my status changed from a defender of my home country to a civilian who was now at the mercy of the Occupying Powers. And later that morning it was brought home to me what this meant. Now that I was no longer a member of the armed forces I could apply for a passport. So armed with my release papers and all the necessary documents I went to the passport office.

To my surprise I found my entry barred by an SS officer (SS = Sturm Staffel – the elite paramilitary organisation of the Nazi Party). As the man turned round I saw that it was an old friend of mine who was about two years older than me and we had both been members of a Boy Scout type of organisation. We had often gone on day's outings together and as he had not only been older but also taller and stronger he had often looked after me and carried my rucksack when I had been tired.

He recognised me, of course, but continued to stop me from entering the

The Germans march in.

office. I could not believe that he was serious and I said to him, 'Don't be silly, Rudi, I only want to go and fill in an application form.' On hearing himself called by his Christian name his attitude softened somewhat and he proceeded to explain to me that he was now under the order of the Führer, and that only people who had a clearance from the German authorities could enter.

So there was nothing to be done but to return home and find out from friends and acquaintances whether there was another way to obtain a passport. And indeed, as all Jews and known political opponents of the Nazis were in the same boat, a system of spreading important information developed at amazing speed and within a few days I had discovered the following: in an area where there was an German ethnic majority or a large ethnic German minority, as in most Moravian towns, the Germans had taken complete control of all Town Halls, which were the authorities that issued passports and other documents like copies of birth or death certificates.

In areas where there were no ethnic German minorities, as for instance in Prague, the German authorities had not yet taken over the local administration, partly because they hoped in this way to obtain more co-operation from the ethnic Czech population.

In order to receive a passport you had to prove that you had been resident in that particular locality for at least a month. And the Czech police authorities were very willing to issue passports at great speed if these legal requirements were met and they did not particularly check whether the dates of registration of residence were somewhat ante-dated. Obviously one expressed one's gratitude to such a police officer. On hearing this I of course immediately took a train to Prague and took a room there and became a resident. A friend of mine who had been in the forces with me took the same action. His family, who had rather wisely withdrawn a fair amount of cash before Jewish bank accounts were frozen, supplied us both with rather lavish pocket money with the result that in this period of severe stress, tension and danger I led a life of luxury and entertainment such as I had never known before. These two contradictory situations made life particularly alive and intense. A corresponding situation would recur in my life in a number of very different circumstances again and again.

During this time I experienced several instances of a typical sense of humour which undoubtedly helped the Czechs to keep their sanity under the difficult situation of oppression, injustice, hunger and cruelty which they experienced for forty years either under Nazi occupation or during the Communist regimes. We were sitting for instance in a pub where there were some German soldiers singing some songs. The Czechs applauded wildly when they had finished and the Germans beckoned to the locals that they should also sing. The Czechs then proceeded to sing anti-German songs, in Czech of course, and at the same time laughed and waved to the Germans. The Germans, having no idea that they were being insulted, also laughed and cheered which of course increased all our amusement.

In a more refined form there was an occasion at the races when German officers talked and joked with some Czechs. It was a speciality of Czech intellectuals to make some harmless jokes in German which, however, if translated into Czech were insults. Again the Germans had no idea why these apparently dull jokes caused such hilarity.

As soon as I had received my passport I returned home to continue my efforts to obtain a permit to go to another country.

An aunt of mine who at that time lived in Cuba was making efforts to obtain a visa and an entry permit but at that moment nothing had arrived yet, so I put my name down for a transport to Israel and started learning Hebrew. These illegal transports were organised by Jewish underground organisations. They were not only illegal from the German point of view but were also particularly dangerous because the British refused to allow these illegal immigrants to land, and many were turned back so that they ended up in German concentration camps; some ships were sunk and people drowned, some were interned in other places like Cyprus and Mauritius, but some managed to get through. When I later received the permit from my aunt to go to Cuba, I gave up my place on this transport to a friend. I later learned this transport got through to Palestine and my friend lived in Israel for many years but he died before I could visit that country so I never saw him again.

During the weeks which I spent in Prague, the Nazis had increased their control of the towns in Moravia. In Olomouc many of the prominent Jews and of course all prominent left wing personalities had been arrested. The 'political' detainees were mostly sent to the concentration camp in Buchenwald. Although this was not an 'extermination camp' the large majority died there, but one doctor survived and when I returned to Olomouc on leave in 1946 I met him and heard tales of horrors that he had suffered. When you hear these things from somebody you have known from childhood and it is not a statistic but the story is personal the impact is quite unforgettable. The way this man, whom I had known as a very polite gentlemen, grabbed the cigarette I offered him with the speed of a wild animal grabbing food, is one of the examples of human degradation which I will never forget.

During the six weeks after the occupation most Jewish businessmen were arrested, taken to the Gestapo headquarters and interrogated for periods of one to four days. I did not hear of any specific atrocities in that period and only a few people apart from the ones previously mentioned were actually sent to concentration camps. But the feeling of the German police or the paramilitary organisations (the SS and SA) being able to enter your house without any explanation or warrant to take you to the police or Gestapo caused a great amount of fear and tension which led to a number of suicides. No appeal or legal intervention was possible, and the sudden change from a free democracy based on equal rights for every citizen to a state where paramilitary and Nazi party organisation were above any law, with the ethnic Germans the next group, no longer under the complete authority of the Czech state organisation and with political opponents and Jews having no rights whatsoever, was a shock which nobody had really been prepared for, even though information about this situation was known from Germany, Austria, and the Sudeten area.

It was very interesting that very often the high and mighty and rich citizens collapsed under the strain whilst a lot of the ordinary and people and those lower on the 'social scale' now showed inner strength, which reflected a much more real set of values.

There was a man called Pinchas Scheck, who had arrived some twenty years earlier from Galizia. Galizian Jews were considered 'inferior' by the native Moravian Jews whose ancestors had lived in the area for many centuries and were often also well-to-do compared to the 'immigrants from the East'. Although Galizia had been an Austrian province, living conditions were very much more difficult and many of these Galizians were in fact refugees from the Polish and Russian pogroms of the earlier part of the nineteenth century. Mr Scheck opened a small furrier's business in one of the side streets in the town centre. He carried on quietly and attracted little attention. One soon got accustomed to the fact that his shop was always closed on the Sabbath and all Jewish holidays. This was unusual in a very assimilated community.

Pinchas Scheck was also arrested during this period but even a thorough investigation by the Gestapo could not find any misdemeanours or irregularity. The chief officer of the prison presented him with a paper to be signed so that he could be released. It happened to be a Friday night. Mr Scheck very quietly explained that he could not write on the Sabbath and asked to be given this paper on Sunday. The Gestapo chief in turn explained that Sunday was his holiday and he could therefore not release him then. Mr Schech's answer was that he would wait until after the Gestapo Chief's Holy Day and sign on Monday. The officer's answer was that he expected a posting any moment and if his successor was not so favourably inclined, he might send him to a concentration camp instead of releasing him. Pinchas, quite unmoved, answered, 'If it is God's will I go to a concentration camp, so be it. I cannot sign today.' He was released on Monday.

When my mother heard this story, she pointed out to me that here was really a MAN and she stressed very much that while she did not believe in the importance of outer religious performance, when a truly felt principle and action is taken according to those principles it will earn respect even from one's enemies. The force with which my mother said this made a very great impression on me, which has remained alive until today.

From then on again and again I came across people who were considered important in the framework of the old country but who often lost their dignity in the situation of the new country and turned out to be unprincipled and not trustworthy. On the other hand those who had seemed less important were not affected morally in their outwardly very humble and difficult situations and often ended up as respected members of the new society and frequently were able to establish a stable and happy family life.

A short while after the occupation there was the time of the Passover Festival and we intended to go to a service for the first time since these events. When I looked out of the window I saw flames rising from the synagogue which was not far away from our flat and could clearly be seen. It was of course clear that this was not an accident but a deliberate act of the Nazis to mark this important Jewish festival.

As we later established, the SS had not only put fire to the building but also actively prevented the fire brigade from taking any action to extinguish the flames. They were however unable to prevent the Cantor (*Chatan*), an elderly, physically weak man, to enter the burning building and together with two helpers to rescue the Torah-Scrolls. They carried them to a small house in the corner of the grounds which had been the residence of the rabbi, who had fled at the first sign of trouble. This small building served as the synagogue during the following months and was still in use when I left the country. During the war the Germans destroyed even that so that when I returned in 1946 it was a completely empty site.

CHAPTER 14

Permission to Leave

IN EARLY APRIL my permit to enter Cuba arrived, for which my aunt had spent all the spare money available to her at the time.

I was now faced with the task of finding a way to leave the country and secure a passage on a ship. This was quite a difficult matter. No exit permit was given unless you had booked a passage, no passage could be booked unless you had first paid a passage there and back, in case the country you were going to found some reason not to let you in. And no money could be obtained from the bank as all Jewish accounts were temporarily frozen. It seemed a hopeless situation. From that time on a number of events started to happen which, when I look at them after more than half a century has passed, look quite miraculous and although at the time I considered myself very lucky, I had no time to ponder how extraordinary they were.

The day after the receipt of my visa for Cuba I was walking along the main square of our town when I met a girl whom I had not seen since I left Olomouc in 1933 but who had been in the same crowd when we were students, I asked her how she was and what she was doing and she told me that she was engaged to a boy from New York but as she could get no entry permit to the States, she was trying to go to Cuba, where her fiancé would meet her. They would get married there and she could then travel with him to New York. She had just heard of a German ship that was sailing to Cuba and which accepted payment in German marks, which would be released by the local bank so that this difficult hurdle of money could be overcome.

I of course immediately contacted the HAPAG, one of the important shipping companies in Hamburg, who confirmed that this ship would indeed be sailing and they accepted my provisional booking.

I had now just over four weeks left to obtain an exit permit which was a series of bureaucratic processes designed to take normally about twelve weeks.

But at this moment the next improbable event took place. My father was stopped in the street by my former professor of German and Economics and one time form master. He told my father that he expected that I would wish to emigrate. He had now become the head of the local Nazi teachers' organisation and was therefore in a position to recommend an acceptance of an application for an exit permit, if I wished to make such an application. He gave his present address to my father and suggested that I should go and see him.

The only reason I can imagine why he was making this offer to help me was that during my years at the college particularly during the study of Economics, he always held the opposite view to me. His were very right-wing, i.e. pro-Nazi, and mine were left-wing and anti-nationalistic. This led to a number of discussions in the classroom when I would openly oppose his ideas and hold on to my point of view. I think he probably had admired the fact that I was not willing to make any compromise in my views, even if I should cause him displeasure.

The next day, armed with the Spanish permit and the confirmation of my booking to Havana, I went to see him. We talked for at least one hour, discussing my views on Zionism, which the Nazi doctrine did not directly oppose, and the likelihood of me trying to join the British or American forces in case of war. As the only country I would be able to enter was Cuba and Cuba was considered a relatively friendly country and in any case hardly a danger to the German Reich, he felt he could recommend an acceptance of my exit visa. He then disappeared into the next room and returned with a small brown sealed envelope addressed to the Gestapo HQ, and told me to take it to the address given on the envelope. I could not know of course whether this really contained a recommendation or if it was a request to send me to the appropriate concentration camp.

The next morning I set out to the indicated address and as I had this special letter which from the type of envelope indicated to the Gestapo officer that its content dealt with a Party matter, I was ushered past the waiting crowd, some of whom I understood had had to queue there for many days, and came straight to the office door.

The door was opened by a young man who immediately recognised me because many years before he had helped to fix my skates at the ice skating club. For this service he regularly got a tip of the equivalent of 2d. instead of the usual 1d. He now repaid me by immediately securing my interview with the appropriate officer.

After a lengthy interview and, by Gestapo standards, very mild shouting he provided a letter which I had to take to the German police.

This was in the familiar distinctive Gestapo envelope. The German police HQ was on a large square and there was a queue of people right around the square where the applicants waited for their turn, which I was told could be several weeks. The Czech police had to keep these queues in order. When I approached the policeman at the end of the queue I held the letter in my hand and said in Czech, 'From the Gestapo,' meaning that I had this letter from the Gestapo. He however mistook my meaning and thought that I was from the Gestapo. To my surprise he led me past all the waiting people right to the front door of the office. Just as I arrived there the door opened and one of the less successful applicants came flying out past me and landed on the ground. The arm of a German police officer appeared, grabbed me and pulled me into the office, and then a push and I found myself standing before the officer in charge. All this happened so quickly that I had no time to realise what was happening. I was still holding the letter. The police chief took it out of my hand and after the usual questions and shouting he inquired about the relevant dates and on learning that the ship sailed on 13 May he gave me a permit to be in Germany until 12 May. I later found out that this was a frequent device so that on the last day I would be in Germany without permission and therefore entirely in the hands of the authorities.

I returned home triumphantly, having got through these formalities in such a short time. It was now even possible to spend about two weeks in Brno at the mill and take a loom to pieces and reassemble it and bring the world of textiles back to my mind, although it seemed far too much to hope that I would be able to use my textile knowledge in Cuba.

Via the usual rumour, 'bush telegraph', I had also heard that it was possible to send personal luggage abroad which exceeded the weight the German authorities allowed emigrants to take with them. So a large trunk was packed and sent to some forwarding agent in Cherbourg. Once aboard one could then give instructions for a final destination. We contacted some friends abroad who would at the right time give instructions for onward dispatch.

The Germans allowed emigrants only 10 Reichsmarks to be taken out of the country. This sum would then probably buy you a simple night's lodgings and one meal. A few days before my planned departure we discovered that it would be possible to obtain permission to transfer one hundred pounds abroad through an arrangement with a British Aid Organisation, the 'Stopford Fund'. Although we had known of the existence of this organisation it became clear only now that this possibility existed also for emigration to Cuba. So my parents and I immediately departed to Prague to deal with all the necessary formalities. It soon transpired that in order to get permission to transfer the £100, the Nazi organisation required the equivalent of £300, as an 'Emigration Fee' which was their name for this bribe. Whilst the £100 could be drawn from the otherwise blocked bank account of my father's, the equivalent of £300 had to be paid in cash in Czech crowns, i.e. it had to be 'black money'. At that time this was a very large amount and as my parents had always been very honest it had never occurred to them to put some money aside when this had still been possible. I had been in the Forces for nearly two years and the Czech army pay did not even cover the occasional snack or drink during a morning break. A frantic search started therefore to find some friends who would be able to lend this amount. Whilst a number of them were willing to help nobody had this amount of money. It took until one day before my departure to have borrowed the necessary sum and the deal was done. It meant however that I left my parents with these debts, a

My parents and myself just before departure.

situation which they accepted without any complaints, but which was nevertheless very painful for me.

The 9 May, the day of my departure, arrived. Whilst we had of course discussed various plans how we would meet again, we all knew that this was rather unlikely.

As it was time to say goodbye my mother gave me some last advice: 'When the time comes, when you wish to get married, don't think of money or position, just picture what I would have said if you had brought her home. If you are sure that I would approve, then marry.' I heeded this advice. As the train drew out of the station and I waved, I just saw my mother fall back into my father's arms.

In such very emotional moments I have always found that I have taken a very ordinary action with very great intensity and that all the minute moves remain very sharply in my memory. It now became terribly important to have a good Czech cup of coffee before the train reached the German frontier when the dining car would be changed to a German Mitropa car, where they served what the Czechs called the Saxon 'flower coffee', because it was so weak that you could see the flower designs in the bottom of the cup. I went to the dining car and ordered my last Czech coffee. I can still see the cup in front of me whilst the train began to enter the mountainous areas of the sandstone formations which are extremely picturesque and form the border area between Bohemia and Saxony.

I took the train to Berlin where my uncle with whom I had stayed as a child was still living. He had managed to arrange for all his family to leave the country and to supply them with some money for the early stages of emigration.

He met me off the train in Berlin and took me to his house, which he had mysteriously still managed to keep, although there were no longer any servants except for the gardener/chauffeur, who was still the same man who had been there in my childhood. I believe his wife acted as the housekeeper.

Once again I was in a situation of absolute contrast. A poor refugee with 10 marks in my pocket, I stayed in a house in the same street where Field Marshal Göring had his villa, in the exclusive suburb of Grunewald. From there to the centre of the town leads a very wide road called the Avus which was also a racetrack for cars, and when I had been there as a little boy it was a special treat to be taken along this road at what seemed the tremendous speed of 60 kph. On this occasion my uncle took me again along these roads to the centre of the city. The Avus was still the same except that now some massive concrete monuments with lots of swastikas had been erected to glorify the Third Reich. Being driven like a VIP around all the sites of central Berlin, which in a way was the centre of the enemy who had just engulfed my country and who threatened at any moment to enlarge this Reich still further, was again one of those situations where everything was being photographed in my mind. I was very pleased when this journey came to an end.

I was given a typewriter to take to my aunt in Cuba and various little items for her which could be fitted into my suitcase. My uncle then gave me sufficient money to make my stay in Hamburg a bit easier and also some money to buy HAPAG travellers cheques which one could use on board. He took me to the train to Hamburg and we said goodbye. This was the last time I saw him. He had so selflessly supported not only his immediate family but also a number of more distant relatives and friends, that he was still in Berlin when war broke out and it became impossible to escape. He became one of the six million victims of the Holocaust.

On arrival in Hamburg I took my luggage to the shipping company who told me about all the formalities that had still to be done and was told that as a Jew I had to stay at a certain small hotel that the authorities had specially allocated for that purpose.

One of the formalities I had to do was to go to the police to register my departure. There the police requested that I produce a certificate from my hometown certifying that I had never been in prison and that I did not owe any taxes. As this was one day before my departure this could only be done by telegram which would cost 5 marks. So I paid half the money I was officially allowed to have and was told to come back the following morning to collect this document.

Certificate of good conduct (Führungszeugnis).

CERTIFICADO DE SALUD
GESUNDHEITS-ZEUGNIS

Certifico que he examinado al señor (a la señora, a la stra.)
Ich bescheinige hierdurch, daß ich Herrn (Frau, Frl.)

Anton Haas

y que no está atocado(a) de lepra, tracoma, enajenación mental, epilepsis en su forma de
untersucht habe und daß diese(r) nicht an Lepra, Trachom, Geisteskrankheit, Epilepsie,

gran mal, tuberculosis, parálisis, ni séa ciego(a), sordomudo(a), ní alcohólico(a) o toxicómano(a)
Tuberkulose, Paralyse leidet, weder blind, taubstumm, noch Alkoholiker oder Rauschgiftsüchtiger ist,

ni de cualquier otra enfermedad que pueda comprometer la salubridad pública o convertirse
noch an irgendeiner anderen Krankheit leidet, welche die öffentliche Gesundheit gefährden oder zu

en una carga pública.
einer öffentlichen Last werden könnte.

Hamburg el den 12.5.1939

HAMBURG-AMERIKA LINIE, HAMBURG

R 3169 (August 37 Peru)

CERTIFICADO DE VACUNA
IMPFZEUGNIS

Certifico que, en esta fecha, he vacunado contra la viruela
Ich bescheinige hierdurch, daß ich heute

al señor (a la senora, srta.)   *Anton Haas*
Herrn, (Frau, Frl.)

gegen Pocken geimpft habe.

Hamburg el den 12.5.193 9.

HAMBURG-AMERIKA LINIE, HAMBURG

März 1935

Health and vaccination certificates.

When I called the next day I was told that no communication from my hometown had been received and therefore this certificate of good conduct could not be issued and I could not leave the country. After a lot of pleading on my part and shouting on the part of the policeman he finally agreed that on payment of a further fee he would issue that certificate. I suppose by the standards of the time this was extremely decent behaviour by a German towards a Jew. Had I not had the extra money which my uncle had given me I would now have been completely penniless.

It was now eleven o'clock in the morning and we had been told that we could not go on board until four o'clock in the afternoon. The girl from my hometown whom I have mentioned earlier and I discussed the best way to spend the time. My permit had expired the previous night and if any policeman, Gestapo, SS man or soldier, stopped me I would be immediately arrested. It was therefore not advisable to wander about in the streets. I knew of a very expensive restaurant where I had been with my parents some years before and I concluded that such a place would be frequented by the Nazi hierarchy and would therefore be the least likely place where we would be asked for papers. So we went to the Alster Eck, which, as the name says, is at the edge of the lakes in the central part of Hamburg. We ordered a meal with many courses so that a great deal of time could be taken up with it. In spite of the extra money we had we realised that the bill exceeded our cash. I took out a HAPAG cheque which was really only valid on board ship, presented it as if it were the most natural way of payment and added a good tip in cash. Fortunately this worked and fortified with good food and wine we now took a taxi to the docks to board the ship. At this moment I felt hardly like a poor refugee fleeing from his country and yet another part of me was well aware that the situation was rather grim and my prospects for the future were anything but easy.

A last reminder of the situation was when we were walking to the boarding area when two SS men suddenly grabbed two would-be passengers, knocked them to the ground, kicked them and then took them away. Everybody continued to walk as if they had not seen anything, hoping to reach the ship without any such fate befalling them. Those were my last moments on German soil.

On board ship we were treated exactly as normal passengers on a cruise which was a great surprise and relief.

So I sailed on Friday 13 May 1939 on the MS *St Louis*, a cruise liner of the HAPAG (Hamburg–America line) expecting to land in Havana about the end of the month.

We found ourselves in a very paradoxical situation. The passengers consisted of nearly one thousand Jews, the vast majority German or Austrian nationals with about thirty former Czechoslovakian nationals which the Germans now

Sailing on 13 May 1939.

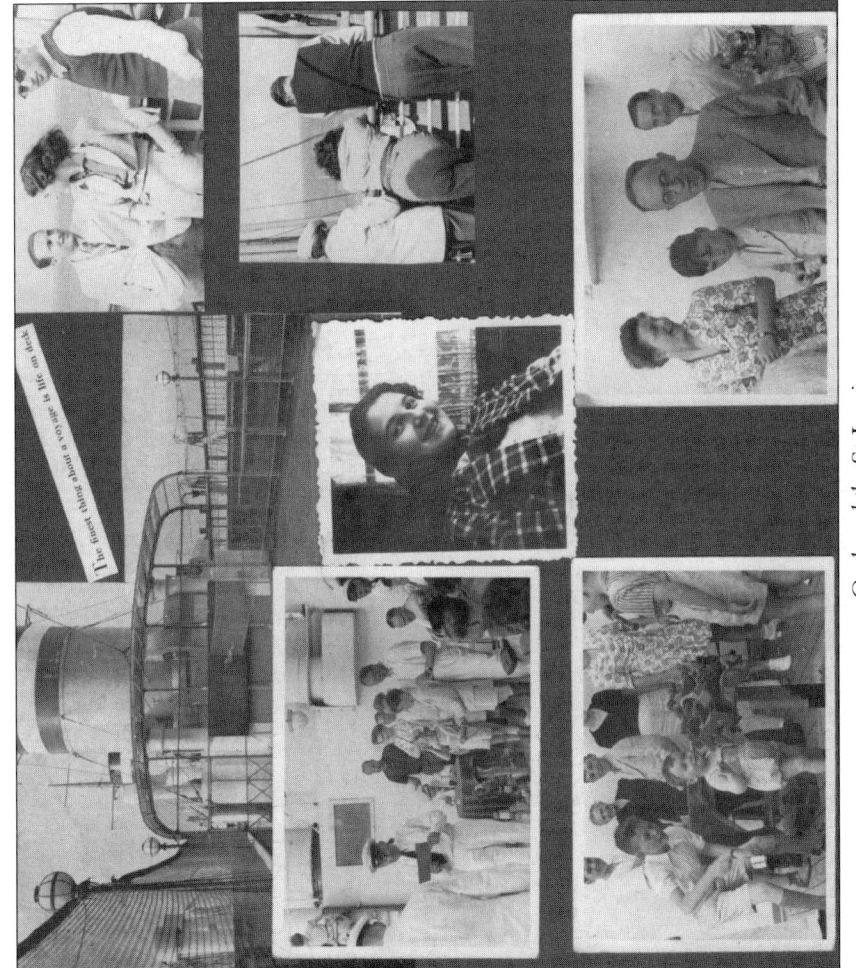

On board the St Louis.

considered citizens of the protectorate of Bohemia and Moravia. Many of the German Jews had been suddenly released from concentration camps. The only qualification for the release seemed to be that they or their families had been able to pay for the passage and that they had some friends or family abroad who had been able to pay about £100 in a 'hard' currency in Cuba, which was the fee the Cuban government demanded.

We had no idea why the Nazi government had suddenly decided to make such a 'humanitarian' gesture. And it was only many years later, when I read a book and saw a film called *The Journey of the Damned*, that I learned the details of the Nazi plot that lay behind this scheme.

For the moment I gave no thought as to how this situation had come about. It was a marvellous feeling to have left German soil although the Nazi flag on the mast was a constant reminder that we were not yet free.

On board we were treated like normal passengers on a cruise, with only small differences from the normal luxury liner. Although there were a first and a second class everybody was allowed on all parts of the ship and the food was identical for everybody.

The contrast of this existence on board is difficult to describe. We had just escaped the terror and humiliation of the Nazi regime and in three weeks we expected to be penniless in a strange country, with a most uncertain future. In the meantime we were on an ocean cruise, putting on our dinner jackets every night, dancing and enjoying ourselves. In this atmosphere friendships were quickly formed and life was very intense. My memories of those weeks are those of a very enjoyable and relaxed holiday.

Just occasionally there was a reminder that this ship was still 'German soil'. One evening the engine stopped – 'Man overboard'. A fifteen minute search for the man took place, then the journey continued. The rumour was confirmed after the war. A member of the crew was considered too friendly to the Jewish passengers and therefore disloyal to the Führer. So the 'party supervisor' Führungs-Offizier caused him accidentally to slip and fall overboard.

CHAPTER 15

Final Destination England

ON ARRIVAL IN HAVANA the process of checking documentation for disembarkation started and we were told we would disembark *mañana* (literally 'tomorrow'. But *mañana* means not only tomorrow but also 'at some time in the future' or 'perhaps', or even 'never', as we discovered.)

Each day the relatives and friends arrived in little boats around the ship and we could shout messages, always with the hope that we could land *mañana*. Gradually rumours trickled through that the Minister who had issued the entry visas had absconded with all the money and his successor had declared the visas illegal. It was only discovered after the war that all this was pre-arranged with the Germans.

The feeling on board grew more and more tense and fears grew more and more particularly among those people who had been in concentration camps and realised more vividly what could await them if we were not allowed to land.

My aunt also came every day and we all hoped that *mañana* we would be allowed to land.

Somebody cut his veins and jumped ship. He was rescued by the port authorities and taken to hospital, thus entering Cuba. Naturally this event caused other people to try something similar. The young and fit stood guard day and night to prevent suicides. Again my strongest memory is of an amazing contrast – the apparently hopeless situation and yet I remember the joy of a beautiful subtropical sunrise.

Eventually, Cuban gunboats escorted us out of the harbour. All the time the American 'Joint' Jewish Aid Committee negotiated with the United States, British, French, Dutch and Belgian governments to find a solution.

We sailed towards the coast of Florida until we were stopped by United States coastguards. The captain stopped the engines and for a day we watched huge coloured octopuses and sharks around the ship. Then we were officially told that we were sailing towards New York. I looked at the sky and decided the direction was more towards Europe and with my last marks sent a telegram home: 'RETURNING VIA SOUTHAMPTON – SECURE LANDING.' My parents understood and telephoned some friends in London. A guarantee to cover any costs for me was given by these friends and this in the end saved my life.

Naturally the mood on board began to change. Rumour followed rumour and

Mañana. The little boats with our relatives waving to us, 'We hope tomorrow.'

fears grew as it became clear that we were in fact sailing north-east. The ship had rations for the journey out as well as for the journey back but we had spent well over two weeks waiting in Habana and sailing up the US coast. The food was therefore now getting a bit more basic. The crew on the whole behaved in an exemplary fashion. Some people who had been able to leave tips on the outward journey had now run out of money and felt embarrassed not to be able to do this now. Some waiters noticed this and started leaving the expected tips under the plates in such a way that the tip was visible and that it looked as if things were as they had been before.

The solution, which was arranged by the 'Joint Jewish Aid Committee' was as follows: 250 passengers would be allowed to land in each of Britain, France, Belgium and the Netherlands. If one could get a guarantee in one of the countries, this would reduce the amount the 'Joint' had to find and in this way I became part of the British contingent. The 250 passengers each sent to France, Belgium and the Netherlands went into camps, where they still were at the time of the German occupation, so that only the British contingent survived.

The *St Louis* sailed back to Antwerp and the British contingent was transhipped onto a German troop ship, the *Rhakotis*. We had another two days wondering whether the war would start before we reached Southampton. However, on the morning after 21 June, six weeks after our departure from Hamburg, I saw the Union Jack going up on the mast and only then felt we were safe.

Again came this amazing contrast – in the morning I was still in the hands of the Germans; at teatime I found myself in a suburban house in Shortlands, Kent, listening to a lady whose big excitement of the day was that she had bought a blue hat for £1 in a sale at Selfridges. This hat was to go with a coat, also blue, but the two blue shades clashed terribly. Perhaps because of my elated state at being finally free, this impression was so strong that even now, more than half a century later, I can still see these clashing colours clearly in front of me and feel the 'horror' of this situation.

The same afternoon I was given the address of a firm of textile manufacturers in Huddersfield, which was owned by a Czech who was a friend of my family. I immediately wrote an application, received a positive reply by return of post, and having been given the address of some charity that helped refugees was able to receive the money for my fare to Huddersfield and pocket money for one day which enabled me to take up this offer, as on landing in England I possessed only two shillings which I had acquired illegally before leaving home.

I had my interview at 9 a.m. and as I had no money for a night's lodgings I took a night train which meant changing trains at 4 a.m. at Stalybridge. Waiting for this train in a typical North of England drizzle on a cold June morning, watching the water dripping down the smoke blackened rocks, was a very strong and not exactly elating impression but the feeling that I was miraculously in England with a possibility of work in my own trade, instead of in Cuba with no prospects, was marvellous.

My first impressions of Huddersfield can be described as somewhat mixed. The neo-classical front of the railway station was very impressive but the fact that there was no station restaurant or café which was open all night as in every continental town was less so. It was 5 a.m. and I was told that the only possibility of getting any breakfast was in a covered market which was fortunately near the station. There I found a café which brought my first acquaintance with the English mug of tea of the strength that I later encountered again under the name of 'sergeant major's tea'.

My interview went rather well and the firm arranged for me that I got an immediate Labour Permit so I could stay and start at once. The conditions of this permit were that it would be reviewed every six months and I was not allowed to earn more than two pounds per week, which after deduction of the 'stamp' for the 'Friendly Society' (health insurance), left me with a weekly income of 38*s*.6*d*. I considered myself of course extremely lucky at having escaped the concentration camp and also to find myself in Britain rather than in Cuba, but I found the attitude of the British government both very degrading and unjust. I had been forced to emigrate in the first place owing to the direct intervention of the Chamberlain government which made it impossible for me to defend myself in my country by imposing the Munich agreement. Secondly, as a Jew I felt that the British government, by accepting the Balfour declaration and the mandate in Palestine, had the responsibility for arranging a way for me to live and work. Thirdly, they had accepted a guarantee from a British citizen that I would not be a burden to the British taxpayer, a guarantee which was in addition backed by the Joint American Jewish Aid Committee. When my only possession, namely my £100 for which my father had paid £300 to the Nazis, was impounded by the British government to be returned to me when I left the country or became a British citizen, I really lost my faith in justice meted out by government. I felt very much that I was now a second class human being without the rights of a human being, which had been so strong in the constitution of the country I had grown up in.

In absolute contrast to this impression of mine of the government attitude was the attitude and behaviour of the people I met.

One of the first things I had to do was to register with the police, an occasion which has remained very clearly in my memory. On entering the office I was asked to sit down. Such a thing was inconceivable in Nazi Germany where you had to be at attention and were shouted at, but also different from the attitude of the Czech police where the official was considered to be the representative of the ruling power and the attitude that the 'civil servant' was the servant of the public did not exist. This of course I only learned later so that the fact I was asked to sit down was so strong an impression and so important for me that I can still bring it back visually and physically. In order to fill in the necessary forms the police sergeant had to ask a fairly large number of questions. What seemed so extraordinary to me was that he accepted my word on all occasions without any cross-examination or trick questions. In other words he treated me as an honest person.

My employer had found me some digs where I paid thirty shillings for full board. The trolley fare was 2½d. each way, i.e. 5d. a day x 6 made 2s.6d. a week which left me with 6s. a week for other expenses.

In the same boarding house lived a Mr Brown who was a salesman for bath salts. As soon as he heard from my landlady about my financial situation he invited me to a show at the Palace of Varieties where a ticket cost one shilling, a sum which I considered well beyond my means. The following weekend he invited me to come to his auntie's in Southport, which was my first experience of the North of England 'high tea', and also my first car journey across the Pennines and the moors, which after the rich agricultural country of central Moravia seemed extremely depressing. This was so warmly compensated for by the warmth of Mr Brown's kindness. The feeling of this contrast remained with me throughout the following thirty years which I spent in Yorkshire.

My first job at the mill was to weigh and check all the cases of yarn which arrived. The first time I was in town with the lad who was doing this job with me he invited me to a pub where he bought me a pint of beer and refused to allow me to pay for a round.

My lunch consisted of some sandwiches, a little bag of tea and another little bag of sugar. This was eaten in the 'canteen'. The canteen was a small room adjacent to the boiler room and consisted of two tables and benches and one tap where boiling water allowed you to 'mash' your tea. These visits to the canteen and the boiler room led to my acquaintance with the boiler man who very soon invited me to Sunday tea at his house. This occasion was quite a revelation for me. As I knew exactly the same trade in Czechoslovakia at about the same period of time. I think it was really possible to judge the difference of standard of living in the two countries. Whilst the boiler man in Brno would have lived in a flat consisting of a livingroom-kitchen and a bedroom, and possibly an additional bedroom for the children, his counterpart in Huddersfield lived in the usual three bedroom house, with kitchen, dining room and sitting room downstairs with a small garden. In Brno the meal would have been served on a scrubbed wooden table with the minimum of cutlery; in Huddersfield there was a white tablecloth with 'silver cutlery', laid in the same way as in any middle class family. The food value of the meal would have probably been equivalent but very different in its composition. It was my first experience of a typical northern English Sunday high tea and included certain things which in central Europe would have been great luxuries, such as tinned pineapple as one of the courses. The great variety of cakes and buns served from the three-tier stand, which became very familiar to me, was a great novelty then. The warmth of this welcome and the tact with which any reference to the fact that I could not now afford anything but the absolute necessities of life was avoided, is something I have never forgotten.

This memory may be particularly strong because it contrasted so very much with the only upper-middle class contacts I had in those days. A cousin of mine was married to Tom Hopkinson, later knighted, editor of the important weekly the *Picture Post* who, on hearing of my arrival in the country, sent me two torn shirts of his, together with a very politely worded note that he would rather not see me at his house in Cheyne Row, Chelsea.

Chapter 16

Yorkshire

After the first few weeks the number of deliveries of yarn reduced somewhat and I was given the additional job of bringing yarn to the warpers. They were all members of a very strong union which tested their knowledge, ability and experience and recommended a wage to the employer. As far as I remember this grading was always accepted by the manufacturers. The result of this system was that the warpers were always craftsmen in the old sense of the word. Most of them came from villages further up the Pennines in the Holme Valley where really broad Yorkshire with a number of Celtic words was still spoken. Although my English was quite reasonable, this broad dialect was of course an entirely new language to me, and this led to a great deal of amusement at my bewilderment but taught me not only some of the dialect but also a great deal about the local sense of humour.

I soon discovered that the Moravian and the Yorkshire weaver had a great deal in common! Much slower and broader speech than the people in the capital about two hundred miles away in both cases. Very reliable and nearer to the values of the land in the countryside. The same kind of good-hearted humour without any malice. Both had the quality of calling a spade a spade. By the nature of the industry woollen mills had always to be in areas with moist air and plenty of soft water. This meant that they were usually in hilly areas with a lot of rainfall and because of these geographical conditions the units were mostly smaller than, say, in the cotton industry. This in turn brought about a closer contact and greater team spirit.

I later discovered that this applied to most European woollen industries such as Verviers in Belgium, the German industry near the Schwarzwald and the North Italian industry.

It thus came about that in the course of a few weeks I felt very much at home in the workplace, and I was now able to look at some of the differences. The most outstanding one appeared to me the higher technical knowledge of the ordinary worker. When a loom stopped in the mill in Brno the usual thing was for the weaver to come to the foreman with the remark: 'My loom does not run.' The foreman had then to eliminate the various possible faults until he hit on the right one. I was very surprised when in the same situation I heard the weaver say: 'My weft-fork is catching.' The foreman could therefore go straight to the right place and rectify the fault. I ascribed this difference not so much to any technical college training as to the longer tradition of the British industry, which had started with the invention of the power loom, which in turn had been based on the cottage industry of handloom weaving about four hundred years ago. In Moravia the industry had only started around the 1870s and this was only indirectly connected with the Saxon and Polish industries.

The other side of the coin was that workers in Britain were very much more conservative and resisted any change, whilst in Czechoslovakia they simply accepted the latest methods as there was no very old tradition.

In my experience this difference applied particularly to calculations of cloth construction and wages calculations. I had learnt in college to calculate the weight of a cloth by taking the number of ends and picks per cm^2 and simply converting into m^2 by a transposition of the decimal point. The 'count' of the yarn was calculated by so many times 1000m per kg. The British design office worked on weighing grains (of which there were 7000 to a pound if I remember rightly), then converting this into ounces per square yard. A large number of calculations were required which needed a number of 'ready reckoners' and possibly a slide-rule to accomplish the result. When I first got to the design office in Huddersfield and was shown this system, my first act was to go to town and purchase a metric set of weights which saved me many hours of calculations.

Perhaps this is best illustrated by the example that in Brno I was able to calculate the wages of about 100 employees in one morning, followed by a further two or three hours of the various calculations of deductions and bonuses which in those days were done with a hand operated multiplication machine. During a period in 1949, fifteen years later, when I worked in Scotland, a very capable girl required 40 hours to calculate 60 wages. It would seem that the calculation in Scotland would cost about ten times as much. It may be that this is an extreme example and it is of course now history as with the introduction of metric weights and measures in the textile industry and with decimal currency these differences will have ceased to exist, and today the computer has taken the calculation time practically out of existence.

Whilst this difference between the system of imperial weights and measures compared to the metric system was obvious to me from my arrival in this country it took many years of living here before I began to see that the attitude went very much deeper than the matter of efficient calculation. The imperial system relates to the measurements of the human body and is a natural way to divide into fractions, whilst the metric system relates to the circumference of the earth and thus to the measurement of the physical universe expressed in decimal system. After living in this country well over half a century I have no idea why this makes such a difference to attitude and what the consequences really are but I mention this at this point in my story, because it struck me as one of the differences between the British and US world and the Continent of Europe. Interestingly enough it seems to me that modern Australia is on the side of the Continent in this matter.

I had no difficulty in adjusting to the people in Yorkshire and felt at home in a very few weeks. What was much more difficult was the adjustment to different outer circumstances, and mostly in connection with what one's head would think were very unimportant matters. The most emotional moment I remember in the whole process of becoming a poor refugee, moving from one country to another, was when I received my first shirt from the laundry. It was neither properly ironed nor properly folded, and the charge was about five times as much as I had been charged in Brno. It was quite a struggle to suppress my tears. Even at that moment my head was quite aware how trivial this was and yet it seemed to me to describe my present position better than anything else.

Another difficult moment was when my trunk which I had sent to Cherbourg from Czechoslovakia and which I was able to redirect to this country, arrived here and I was asked for £12 for carriage and customs clearance, six times my weekly income. I really felt like a beggar when I went to my boss for a loan for this amount. He was very magnanimous and made me a present of this cost, which enabled me to have all my winter clothing and my typewriter, which I considered a great treasure at that moment.

About ten weeks after my arrival in England the Nazis invaded Poland and I listened on the radio to Chamberlain's broadcast declaring that a state of war now existed between Britain and Germany. It was a very strange feeling. Previously I had a clear task in front of me for this expected occasion. Now that it had really happened, there was nothing for me to do. This was the first occasion when I had found out how to set about it. I presented myself to the recruiting office, explaining my previous military training and said that as a member of an allied nation, I expected to be able to be of some use in a corresponding unit. The recruiting sergeant took all my details, measured and weighed me and announced that I was one inch too short for the British cavalry, whether on horse or in a vehicle did not matter. I was not very impressed with this attitude at the time when Britain was so desperately short of trained personnel but there was nothing to be done, but to say: 'Call me when you want me.'

The outbreak of the war meant that the restrictions on my working permit and earnings limit were lifted and when the winding foreman, who was a member of the territorial army, had to join his unit I became winding foreman. The technical side was easy as the winding frames were very similar to the ones in Czechoslovakia. What was new for me was the wage calculations using a 'ready reckoner'.

Very soon after this I was given a new task. When the firm had moved from Brno to Huddersfield, they started weaving the same cloths in the same settings (i.e. the same number of threads per inch) as they had done in Czechoslovakia. They had purchased the same yarn and some of it had simply been delivered to England. When the first pieces came off the loom it had become obvious that there were far more breakages of threads than there had been 'at home'. After some experimenting they realised that the reason was the climate. Owing to the humidity in the air the yarn became much bulkier and this increased bulk caused more rubbing and thus more breakages of the threads during weaving. It took several experiments to establish the right settings. As there were about 100 looms which had started production simultaneously and as there were usually four or five pieces on one warp this meant several hundred pieces with a very much increased mending time before the difficulty could be overcome. The mending staff of the mill was therefore inadequate and the only way of overcoming this was to send pieces to 'outmenders' to mend some pieces in their homes. These were usually women who had previously learned this highly skilled trade in the mills, but who now for various reasons could not go out to work. I was equipped with a van and two strong lads to carry the pieces and started driving all over the district to take these pieces to about forty different addresses, leaving usually two pieces at a time, collecting them the following week and leaving the pay for the work that had been done. This turned out to be an extremely interesting job for me. In the first place, I acquired a knowledge of the district in a way one would normally only have been able to have after a very much longer time. Visiting all these houses I saw how people lived and even learned a great deal of the variation in living standards in the district. Huddersfield is situated at the confluence of two rivers, the Holme and the Colne. Both valleys had had textile industries for a very long time, but owing to various circumstances very different types of production had developed in each. The Holme valley had the first worsted cloth production of high class and speciality fabrics such as imitation fur fabric pile and loop fabrics. The Colne valley produced the cheaper woollen fabrics which had to be made in real bulk and had therefore much bigger units for bulk production. The central area of the town had an important engineering industry which employed mainly men, whilst the women travelled to the textile mills in the valleys.

Owing to the recession in the inter war period these divisions were no longer quite as definite at the time when I arrived there but it was still marked enough to notice a clearly different standard of living and different education in the different areas, and certainly a different attitude to craftsmanship. What all districts had in common was an amazing honesty, reliability and trust.

The houses were always left unlocked. I just walked in and left the pieces at a previously arranged spot and collected the ones that had been worked on. The women had little books where they entered the time spent, giving the details when this had exceeded standards. They marked places with chalk where more important repairs had been necessary. This was then checked at the mill by the person in charge of the department and the piece rate calculated. On my next trip I would then bring the money, and if nobody was there leave the money in a jar or vase on the mantelpiece. During the three or four months when I was doing this job I do not remember a single case of any dispute, either about the accuracy of the calculations or the fact that the money had been left. In some cases when the woman was out at work the husband would 'work nights' and was therefore asleep upstairs when we called. Sometimes he would wake up and enquire who was there. We told him and in no case do I remember anybody coming down to check.

When somebody was in when we called we were often offered a cup of tea, which then led to conversations which taught me more about the way of thinking of the people in my new surroundings.

Some old traditions survived. One of them was the Monday wash day. In some villages in the Colne valley it was impossible to deliver anything on a Monday. It was an area of back to back houses with neither front nor back gardens, so the only way to hang out the washing was across the road. No car could pass after about 8 a.m. until the washing was dry and taken in. I cannot remember what happened in heavy rain, but the frequent drizzle certainly did not stop this procedure.

The weather played of course a great part in my early impressions of England and the West Riding of Yorkshire in particular. As I had arrived from the Caribbean where it had been subtropical, I felt very cold on arrival. I landed on midsummer's day and the early temperatures I encountered in Huddersfield were around 10 to 14 degrees Celsius at mid-day. I enquired when the summer started but all the replies I got seemed to me rather vague, such as: we do not have high temperatures here but then it is not very cold in winter, the difference in temperatures in summer and winter is not very great, and so on. Then one weekend summer broke out and there was almost cloudless sky and warm sunshine. I had been told about an open air swimming pool in Holmfirth, which could be easily reached by a bus ride and a twenty minute walk up the hill. So I dressed in what I considered appropriate for the occasion, namely a white linen suit and a straw hat, with white and yellow suede shoes, and set off on the bus. Together with an expatriot colleague from the mill we started walking up the hill and soon I heard some strange noises behind us, as if we had joined a crowd going to a football match. I turned round and saw that all the urchins of Holmfirth had gathered to view this strange apparition in white tropical suit and hat on the way to the swimming pool. A foreigner was a novelty in Holmfirth in those days, and one dressed in such unusual dress was a real sensation. All went off peacefully as we changed into swimming suits just like everybody else and I suspected that when we swam a whole length in these ice cold waters we were considered even with some admiration. There was no temptation to wear my tropical clothing again, as this had been 'the summer' and we never saw bright sunshine again.

The predictions of the winter turned out to be just as inaccurate as the hints about the warm weather had been earlier in the year. One incident stands out particularly in my mind. I was driving the van with the pieces for mending up a long hill on the main Huddersfield to Bradford road towards a roundabout called Odsal Top. With me in the van was an old employee of the firm, who had only arrived just before the outbreak of war. His English at the time was practically non-existent. He came from Moravian peasant stock and had not yet lost the ability of seeing through the outer trappings to the reality of the situation, an ability which country folks often have. It was probably late October and as we started to climb the long hill a sudden snowstorm started and before we reached the top the four-lane road had become one sheet of ice which brought all traffic to a halt with lorries sliding in all directions. We stopped and got out of the van. Because of the heavy traffic in that area there was a continuous line of vehicles in very unusual positions as far as the eye could see. My friend looked up and down this picture of chaos, gravely assessing the total situation. He suddenly nodded and uttered a statement consisting of three words which characterised the whole position of this country: '*Pánbiček jim pomůže*', which roughly means: The Good Lord will help them.' Having solved this situation, we got into the van and waited. His judgement proved absolutely correct, as within the next minute 'the good Lord' sent bright sunshine, and after a short while the ice had melted and the column of lorries and cars could continue their journey. I was reminded of these wise words whenever there was a situation for which this country was ill prepared, and where, against all logic, the disaster which every person not born in these islands expected without any shadow of doubt, never happened. When I got married about a decade later I told this story to my wife and these three words were amongst the first words of Czech that she learnt and she has always quoted them whenever I was worried about the future and tried to convince her 'with all my logic' that the disaster was just around the corner.

Very soon after the outbreak of the war I decided that the digs I was in were too expensive for me and also that the expense of 5*d*. per day trolley-bus fare could be avoided by changing to some digs just by the mill. So I moved to Mrs Bailey, a policemen's widow, who seemed to be favoured and respected by many local people. It was here that I first experienced good, traditional English cooking.

There was first of all the marvellous English breakfasts and on Sunday the real Yorkshire pudding as a separate course before the main course of roast beef. I was also introduced to puddings with custard. One had, of course, got used to the seven day rotation where each day had its definite and almost unchangeable menu.

I had also to learn the use of a hot water bottle which was absolutely necessary in order to survive the change from central heating to the absolutely unheated bedroom. The extremely small size of the bedroom made it also advisable to keep the window at least a bit open. On a November night this meant that one could watch the fog rolling in and settle on top of the blankets.

Even before Christmas snow appeared and I was very pleased that I had brought both my riding boots and another pair about the same height so I could walk about in the deep snow, which was about 40 cm at the time. There were of course no snow ploughs and traffic came largely to a standstill. Soon the weather changed, the snow melted and normal life was resumed. I knew now how to take the statements which I heard since my arrival: 'Oh, we never have very cold winters and never a lot of snow.' It was a statement of hope, not fact.

I have tried to describe the main impression of the new way of life that I experienced on my unplanned and unexpected arrival in this country. The overriding feeling, however, was that I had come to a country where honesty and the observance of both moral law and legal requirement were generally upheld, and where a contract whether written or verbal was considered binding and a given word was usually kept. This gave me a feeling of stability, safety and justice and the impression that the rights of the individual were being upheld. All this had been absent in the Nazi dominated area and the contrast was very strong.

What I found absolutely puzzling was the attitude of the people I met to what I had been brought up to think of as the British Empire. It was now called the Commonwealth. Again and again I heard the statement: 'We are only a small country,' whilst to me Britain was still the head of the biggest group of countries in the world, even if perhaps not, at this moment, the biggest military power. I found very few people who seemed aware of the fact that miraculously Christianity was a minority religion among citizens of the British Commonwealth and still fewer who held any opinion with regard to the problems that this was going present in the future. Everybody I met seemed to think that things were as they were because it was right for them to be so and the general feeling of confidence that this gave was so infectious that I assumed that there must be many things I did not understand, and would perhaps learn in the future.

In the meantime I could occupy myself with living and getting to know as much as possible about the country I was now living in. I started to read first of all love stories and thrillers, which I thought would teach me most about the language that was generally spoken around me. After a time I started to read the plays of Bernard Shaw which I thought would improve my language.

Apart from my contacts with other refugees my relationships were mostly with working class people at the mill. I learned the difference between 'a mild' and 'a bitter' and got the taste for fish and chips for supper. Occasional visits to see 'Huddersfield Town' play was the most important moment of the week.

'Middle class' contacts were mostly confined to a drink at the Queens Hotel which sometimes led to the remark by my acquaintance: 'You must come and see us sometime,' always carefully avoiding a real invitation.

Chapter 17

Early Days of the War

THE COUNTRY WAS NOW entering the 'phoney' war, when nothing in particular happened and the war seemed more like a cricket match than a *Blitzkrieg*, with a bit of fighting 'before lunch' and some artillery bombardment 'before tea'. My personal life seemed equally phoney to me as all my efforts in my career seemed temporary as I expected to join the forces sooner or later.

Then came May 1940 and the *Blitzkrieg* started in earnest. By accident a friend of mine who had been in the Czech Forces with me had joined the firm where I worked. I had been in charge of section 1 of the first company of our regiment and he had been in charge of section 2. The last big exercise in which we had taken part in the early autumn of 1938, just before the mobilisation which ended in the disaster of 'Munich', was a scheme where our units had to cover the erection of a pontoon bridge which would allow light tanks to cross and 'leap-frog' our position, penetrate swiftly to a depth of 30km behind 'enemy lines' and fan out to disrupt the supply lines and thus prevent a prompt counter-attack by the 'enemy'. This enabled the heavy tanks to cross the river and cover the advance of our infantry, which could then establish a firm bridgehead as a base for the leap-frogging of a large armoured force which could then advance about another 30 to 50km behind enemy lines. All this had to be done within hours instead of days, as had previously been normal tactics. The Czech Minister of Defence and Czech general staff watched this exercise and we were given to understand that it was very important.

When the first report of the German crossing of the Leopold Canal in Belgium appeared in the papers it was exactly like reading our own exercise two years earlier and we could work out exactly what would happen next. When on the third day, exactly according to our exercise, large German armoured columns were advancing both south and west, we knew that the whole northern part of the Maginot Line had been outflanked and that nothing could stop the German forces reaching the Channel coast. What we did not know at the time was how demoralised the French forces were and that no counter-attack of any weight against the now exposed southern flank of the German forces would be made.

As I discovered at the end of the war in interrogation of high ranking German staff officers they did not know this either, and were therefore convinced that such an attack would come and so secured this flank first. This short delay in reaching the Channel coast gave the breathing space which enabled the withdrawal and Channel crossing of the British and some Allied forces to take place.

This was the time of Churchill's famous speech, which I heard in a pub. The electrifying effect on the people around me gave an impression which was probably as strong as the content of the speech itself. For the first time since the crossing of the Leopold Canal, my black mood lifted and I saw the possibility that under Churchill's leadership some miracle might occur that would change the situation.

In the meantime the only war effort given to me was to do some 'fire watching' on the roof of the block of flats where I lived which also contained a garage with petrol pumps; and wait.

Later that year I was offered a designer's job in a mill at Wibsey in Bradford, which was of course quite a promotion and meant that I was back in the actual job I had been trained for. Owing to the circumstances of the war there was rather little creative designing to be done. The 'Utility Scheme' for cloth had been introduced, which meant that the structure of the cloth was given by regulation as the quantity of wool or yarn was rationed. It meant in practice that all that was possible was to vary the different stripings in men's cloth and to a limited extent the basic colours. I had been given this job because the managing director, the designer and other executives had joined the forces and only a manager who was beyond military age was left. I therefore had to do a number of things which were not strictly a designer's job and which made it rather more interesting to me as I became more familiar with the running of a mill in this country. One of the interesting details was the fact that the mill had done a lot of exporting to China, where customers selected the cloth according to a picture which was put in each piece of cloth. They were generally pictures of ladies in Victorian clothing. With the outbreak of the war this trade had stopped but some stock of the pictures was still in the warehouse.

I now moved to Bradford and found myself in a boarding house where three officers in the Army Pay Corps, which had its headquarters in that town, also lodged. This turned out to be extremely interesting for me as they came from rather different backgrounds and political views and their discussion and disagreements were very stimulating and instructive. All three held the rank of captain and did fairly similar jobs. One of them, a Labour politician before the war, had been sent to Vienna to study the huge municipal building programme in that town, had generally travelled in Europe and had taken part in the Spanish Civil War on the Republican side. He had been Mayor of one of the very left-wing boroughs in East London. He was also an amateur actor and was as active as wartime duties would allow at the Civic Theatre in Bradford. The second one was an accountant from Manchester with rather extreme Conservative views and a member of all corresponding Conservative clubs etc. I had the feeling that had it not been for the war he would have never spoken privately to a person who did not share his views, let alone to a foreigner like me. But given the circumstances of the war he accepted the situation rather well, and apart from the odd remark about his 'Bolshy colleague' became even quite friendly. The third one was a lady who owned a leather glove factory, who belonged to the type of Liberal minded Conservative middle class who knew how to say the right thing and remain calm, collected and controlled in every situation in life, except when domestic animals such as cats or dogs were concerned.

The long evenings in the blackout, with very little inducement to go out and take part in the entertainment that wartime Bradford had to offer, meant very interesting conversations developed and if anybody had designed a course to teach me about the views, manners, taboos, interests and generally all attitudes to life in wartime Britain, no better curriculum could have been found.

It now became possible for me to join the Home Guard which in the early stages meant barrack square type drill in Manningham Park and later I was selected for telephone duties at the local HQ which was considered a 'classified job' for which as an alien, even if a friendly one, I had to swear an oath of allegiance. Watching the pompous face of the Home Guard major during this ceremony, it suddenly seemed to me a rather paradoxical situation, but I was nevertheless very pleased to have been selected. The announcement of the German invasion, which was the main *raison d'être* of this switchboard, never came, so we had to make do with less important messages.

When my language qualifications were realised I was sent on a course to be trained as an interrogator for prisoners of war. Together with other German speakers we spent two weeks on Doncaster racecourse, pretending to be either German prisoners or interrogating officers. We were accommodated at the best hotel in Doncaster, and it was a very enjoyable time even if a lot of study was also required.

This hotel, the Danum, was to be some years later the place where my wedding reception took place. It is a pattern in my life that I find myself returning to certain places for entirely different reasons which become important in my life.

After my return from this course I was given a commission and apart from being an interrogation officer, I also became second in command of the security of Bradford. The only Army unit stationed in Bradford was the Pay Corps, who did not have their own intelligence or security unit, so the Home Guard was entrusted with these duties. This led to the following somewhat unusual situation. In my capacity as Security Officer I had sometimes to inspect the lorries of the Pay Corps and report on their alertness and security arrangements.

Mr and Mrs Churchill and Sarah Churchill at the time when I was 2nd in Command of security in Bradford.

Although I held the King's Commission and was a lieutenant, I was also an alien and a civilian, who according to the Aliens Order had to obey a curfew and be at my registered address each night at midnight. I therefore had to go to the Aliens Officer of the Police and ask for a permit to be out of doors each night, when I was on duty. The Police sergeant of course very soon saw the absurdity of this situation and gave me a permanent pass. It was this following of commonsense rather than the strict letter of the law which made life in Britain so much more delightful than any other country I had ever been to.

I was soon sent on a further course, this time run by the Intelligence Corps rather than the Home Guard. I was billeted in St John's College, Cambridge. Most lectures took place in beautiful rooms in the area, which had possibly been some club in peacetime. We ate in the college dining hall together with the masters and students, which gave a most interesting glimpse of English university life.

During this course my knowledge of Army organisation, which I had acquired so painfully during many hours in the Czech Officers Training College, came in very useful and soon I felt I had mastered the structure of the German Army.

Whilst I was on this course some events took place which lifted the curtain of happenings for me for a moment and some historic event could be seen as it unfolded, bringing significant consequences. This was the battle of Bir Hakim. Whilst the course was in progress the report of this battle came in, and from these reports the senior officer guiding this course showed us the progress and the effectiveness, strengths and weaknesses of weapons on each side, the approximate losses on both sides and the likely strategic outcome.

The Afrika Korps had hoped to reach the border of Egypt in one swift advance before a major British counterattack could be mounted. This they hoped would open the way to the Suez Canal and onward.

When they reached the area of Bir Hakim they encountered a much larger tank force than their intelligence had reported. In fact there appears to have been about 200 tanks. As the battle developed it became clear that the German guns had a larger range and bigger penetration than those of the British. The British anti-tank guns particularly were of a smaller calibre and did not penetrate the German armour satisfactorily. Although I could not remember the actual figures it seemed to be that the penetration of the Czech anti-tank guns used by the Czech forces in 1938 was stronger than the British in 1941. My instructor neither confirmed nor denied this when I asked on this point. The result of this battle appears to have been that about 180 British tanks were disabled, but although the German losses were much smaller it meant nevertheless that the Afrika Korps had to stop and regroup and as their supply lines became more and more difficult owing to Allied air superiority, the possibility of reaching the Suez Canal never occurred again.

It was explained to us that Churchill had shipped all available tanks on the long route via the Cape and the Suez Canal, as soon as he had seen that the Germans had not invaded as the consequence of reaching the Channel coast. The German High Command could not imagine such a gamble and were therefore taken by surprise at the amount of armour facing the Afrika Korps. Nothing that I have seen or read since then has altered my view that it was this courageous decision probably in 1940 that prevented an Allied defeat in the Middle East.

But back to more pedestrian happenings in the Home Guard: in the early days there seemed to be practically no weapons available. Either we had rifles and no ammunition, or ammunition for the wrong rifles. We were largely occupied in drill which it seemed to me had been designed during the First World War. Later however useful weapons particularly anti-tank weapons and anti-personnel grenades appeared. The Home Guard also did a lot of ancillary duties, which relieved the regular forces. But there were also the episodes which later formed the story for the 'Dad's Army' programmes. One occasion particularly stands out in my mind. Three German-speaking Home Guard officers were selected, of whom I was one, to attack a Home Guard Battalion HQ at the other end of town. We were dressed in completely correct German Army uniforms, armed with German light machine-guns and set out in a car across Bradford at about 3 p.m. on a Sunday afternoon. Just as we were traversing the main square, Foster Square,

As an officer in the Home Guard.

in front of the cathedral, the car misbehaved and the engine stopped at some traffic lights. There was nothing to be done, but for two of us to get out and push whilst the third one stayed inside and tried to start the engine. As it was slightly uphill my colleague shouted to a passing soldier, 'Give us a push, lad.' He immediately came to help and there were two 'German enemy soldiers' and one British one pushing the car across the square. Finally the car re-started. We jumped in, thanked the soldier and drove off. Neither he nor any of the passers-by had noticed anything unusual. We 'captured our objectives'.

The result of this exercise was that some of us were sent round munitions and aircraft factories around the area with pictures of German uniforms and weapons, to increase the awareness of what the enemy would look like if he came.

Not all my time was spent in uniform and I continued my job at the Mill. Because rationing became stricter there was less and less designing to do and it became rather boring. When I was offered a different job in Huddersfield I therefore took it. This turned out to be rather interesting and stimulating. It was a woollen mill making mainly ladies' cloth and coatings. By this time the Wool Control, the authority dealing with the allocation of raw materials to the manufacturers, had discovered that there were certain waste products which were only available in such small quantities that it was impossible to categorise and allocate them. It was therefore decided to make a new category called 'free materials' which could be used outside the general rationing scheme.

Perhaps it will help if I say something about 'waste' in the woollen industry. Traditionally everything that in the slightest resembles a fibre can be re-used. At the top end are the by-products of the worsted industry: The waste from carding and combing the wool, called noils, are the raw material for making fine woollen coatings particularly velours and 'face cloth', such as billiard cloths. Then come the spinning wastes, which have to be 'pulled up' before use and therefore yield somewhat shorter fibres; lower down the scale are 'shoddies' which are produced from pulling up cloth from already woven fabrics. Top of this group are new tailor's cuttings and pulled up unused knitted fabrics, called misleadingly for the layman 'cashmeres'. The pulled up woven rags are called 'mungo' which now yield very short fibres. The term 'mungo' is derived from the words 'must go': i.e. it must somehow be made possible to spin even these very short fibres. The waste from mungo which is now impossible to spin is used for stuffing cheap upholstery and the waste from that makes good manure. So nothing is ever wasted in the traditional woollen industry.

At the outbreak of war every type of wool that was traded was defined and categorised, given a number and its use controlled by quantity and price. The same was done with all waste products just described. Each manufacturer was allocated a certain amount of raw materials from which he had to produce a given yardage of 'utility cloth' in a variety of weights and qualities which the 'makers up' had to make into a more or less defined number of garments of given qualities and standard so that each person was able to purchase with his clothing coupons an amount of clothing which would supply his real needs. In each process a small fluctuation for accidental waste was allowed. This allowance enabled the efficient manufacturer to build up a small surplus which could then be sold outside the control of the Utility Scheme, which allowed the production of a small amount of goods which were 'different' and usually inordinately expensive.

This scheme worked extremely well and as far as I could tell was very much more effective than any scheme in any other country.

In spite of this very efficient classification there were always some materials, particularly wastes, which were made in very small quantities and defied any classification, as I have said. To utilise these required very short runs and constantly inventing new fabrics and not always knowing at the beginning how it would work out and one had to be ready to make adjustments in the course of production. This was not only a very stimulating occupation but also brought me into contact with many people in the trade who turned out to be very useful connections after the war.

In early 1943 the Allied Forces Act came into operation which gave Allied nationals the opportunity to join the British forces on equal terms with British nationals. I volunteered, and after some slight difficulty, because I was in a reserved occupation, I was called up and received my papers to report to the Primary Training Centre Gravesend which was part of the main centre at Maidstone, Kent.

CHAPTER 18

British Forces

THE ALLIED FORCES ACT was passed in 1943 to enable Allied nationals to join the British Forces with equal status to British citizens. As various communities of continental Europe were overrun by the Germans, refugees from those countries established governments in exile which were allowed to form their own fighting units. These 'governments in exile' were not necessarily representative of the political spectrum that had previously existed in their countries, and some of their citizens therefore felt that they could not give their allegiance to them. In addition separate 'governments' were formed by such Allied nationals who had reached Soviet countries and it was therefore by no means certain which faction would eventually govern the now German-occupied countries after the end of hostilities. The Allied Forces Act allowed such nationals, who for these reasons did not wish to join their own forces, to take part in the war effort.

I had made this decision as soon as this Act was planned early in the war, and therefore received my calling up papers as soon as it had become law, and was in the first batch that was formed. It was a somewhat unusual unit. I was instructed to join in my Home Guard uniform and thus arrived as second lieutenant. I was smartly saluted by the sergeant to whom I had to report and I told him that I was one of the new recruits and that I also held the rank of sergeant cadet in the Czech forces. The bulk of the unit were similarly unusual recruits. There was for instance a former Norwegian naval officer, two Yugoslavs who had served for several years in the French Foreign Legion, an ex intelligence agent from the Belgian Congo, and people who had served in other Allied forces. The number was made up by some Allied refugees who had no previous Army service.

There are certain procedures which are the same in any army and where the new recruit gets into difficulty. One of these procedures is the issuing of kit. On the first parade where the kit is checked the recruit has some items missing, gets shouted at by the sergeant and is asked to pay for the items he has lost. The experienced soldier always knows how to 'acquire' some extra items 'just in case'. So our unit surprised the sergeant by the fact that not only were no items missing, but there were also sufficient items to replace the ones lost by the recruits who had not been in other armies before.

Not everybody spoke English. The Army authorities, with quite remarkable foresight, had found a sergeant who not only spoke French but also knew correct words of command in French so that in the early part of the training orders could be given bilingually.

On the first evening the Yugoslavs asked for permission to go out. The sergeant said that no recruit could go out until he had learned to salute and no instructions had yet been given, 'But we know how to salute,' came the reply, 'and we also know how to get over the wall, if we get no permit, and then you might get into trouble!' In panic the sergeant fetched the colonel, who with Salomonic wisdom decided to examine us there and then and those who passed this saluting test were given permission to go out.

Another unusual moment in the early training which I remember was when the corporal gave a demonstration of how to get down behind the Bren gun into the firing position. One of the ex Foreign Legion chaps piped up: 'If you do this in the Sahara you are dead before you fire the first shot! Get up, I will show you.' This was said with such authority that the corporal automatically got up and we were given a demonstration which was much quicker and would certainly be more effective.

Gradually everything settled down and by the time the six weeks of the PTC (Primary Training Centre) came to an end we had become more or less indistinguishable from any other unit at this stage.

When it came to the question of which units we should be allocated to, I naturally gave my qualifications that I had received in the Czech Cavalry which in this context meant light armoured units for reconnaissance and my Interrogation and Intelligence experience in the Home Guard. If neither of these qualifications were available I volunteered for paratroops, which we were told at the time were wanted for North Africa. It appeared that my case did not fit with any of the existing rules and a special officer from the War Office came to interview me. After a long interview a captain informed me very politely that although I was eminently qualified for service in the Intelligence Corps, for service in that unit it was laid down in Regulations that the applicant must have British born grandparents and as I could not produce even one British grandmother he could not see how he could bend the rules. When I pointed out that according to the Allied Forces Act, Allied nationals had to be treated in the same way as British subjects and my ancestors had all been born in the area which was Czechoslovakia, he admitted that he had a problem which would have to be resolved by a higher authority. As there was no possible precedent for this situation, the decision would take several weeks and would I mind very much if he sent me, temporarily of course, to a Pioneer Corps depot, to await the answer. Although I minded very much, armies are not institutions where a private can contradict a captain, and as I was promised it would only be temporary, I could do nothing but agree.

I was sent to a Pioneer Corps depot in Buxton, Derbyshire, which was a unit for 'under-developed people'. On arrival I had to hand my rifle into the quartermaster's store as it was considered that weapons would be more dangerous to the members of this unit than to any enemy. I was given a large wooden baton instead and became camp policeman. My duties were mainly to guard the camp at night, I think mainly to watch that nobody left the premises. In the morning I had to go round the town on a bicycle and wake the soldiers who were billeted in houses in the town, shouting the usual 'wakey, wakey', 'rise and shine', 'show a leg' and other not quite so polite terms. Having completed this round I could then, together with the other 'night policeman', have breakfast and go to bed. In the afternoons we were allowed into town where the only possible amusements were the WVS canteen and the occasional picture. In intervals between police duties I sometimes went on route marches up and down the Peak District, a very pleasant countryside, which I enjoyed as much preferable to sitting in the little hut at the entrance to the camp.

The 'several weeks' promised by the War Office lengthened into 'a month or two' but finally the approaching 'D' day brought the decision that I had to report to the Interrogation Centre at Kempton Park racecourse. This order was of course not given in open language like this, so that all I knew was an address where I had to report to the following morning at a given time.

I was given the necessary papers but could not get my rifle because this was locked in a special part of the quartermaster's store and he was off duty. So I was instructed to travel without my rifle and told that it would reach me at my new unit. Indeed after several weeks at Kempton Park I saw my name on the list of people who had received a postal parcel. Hoping that this would be a cake sent to me by some friends, I immediately dashed to the place where it was to be collected and to my surprise I was handed my rifle very carefully wrapped in canvas and brown paper, thoroughly greased that it should not go rusty. I was of course disappointed that it was not the expected cake and it struck me as somewhat odd that a soldier should be sent his weapon, in the middle of the war, by ordinary post.

In prisoner of war camps personnel who enter prisoner of war compounds are never armed as there would be a danger of them being overpowered, so all I had to do with my rifle was to hand it into the quartermaster's store. The sergeant considered that it would be a good idea if I left it in the marvellous wrapping and grease as that would relieve him of the effort of cleaning it. The rifle stayed there wrapped in the store in this way until I was posted abroad.

As is usual with intelligence postings I was told one day to collect my kit and be ready in thirty minutes when a jeep would take me and another colleague to an address in central London where we were told to report to Mr so and so 'on the other side' who would give further instructions. There was of course no time to unpack my rifle so it was carried in its perfect wrapping together with my kit bag by an orderly on to the boat. The same procedure was repeated in a corresponding way each time I was moved in Belgium, the Netherlands, France and Germany and only on my de-mob over three years later had I to carry it myself, when it was handed in, in Hull. It elicited the remark by the quartermaster that he would not have to clean that one.

My commanding officer had soon discovered that owing to my previous training in the Czech forces and in the Home Guard I had a good knowledge of German Army Order of Battle and organisation and that my German was good enough to deal with a barrack square full of prisoners by giving them correct commands according to German army drill without giving them the feeling that they were commanded by a 'foreigner'.

The procedure in those early days after 'D' Day was as follows: prisoners who appeared of particular importance were interrogated at once in France. All others were embarked on the landing crafts on which the Allied troops had just been taken to France and across to a British port. There a train was waiting that took them straight to Kempton Park railway station, where they were counted and marched immediately onto the 'Barrack Square', which was an area just behind the grandstand of the racecourse.

Just before the departure of each train we had been given as much information as was available about the section those prisoners had been taken from. From previous information we had some idea which German Divisions were in the area, and by learning all the numbers of regiments and special battalions by heart, it was possible to call them out and make them fall in in the same sequence that they had been in on the front line only some hours earlier. This gave the impression that we knew a great deal about them and any questions during the preliminary interrogations that followed were very frequently given freely and in a relaxed manner, particularly as they were simultaneously told about the hot shower and the meal that would follow. The aroma of this meal was usually wafting across the interrogation huts at the time.

The arrivals of these trains were of course very unpredictable and they had to be dealt with at once whether day or night. This meant rotas of different teams. We usually had continuous periods of readiness for about ten days and then 24 or 36 hours off duty.

The result of this was a very strange psychological experience. For ten days we lived as if we were in Normandy, talking to prisoners who had been there some hours before, having constant detailed maps in front of us, sometimes knowing in fair detail what was going on in a certain section, and seeing it very much as the Germans reported it.

After this period came the day off when we took a train or bus to London. There was an official news blackout of about two days and people were often discussing events which we had known about two or three days before, and they were guessing future events of which we already knew the outcome. It seemed quite unreal, particularly when we were given free tickets to West End shows. At 4 p.m. you might have been mentally in the front line and at 7.30 you saw a West End comedy, and the next day you were mentally 'back in Normandy'.

This life brought a tremendous intensity and constantly brought the question: which reality is the real one, or how can all this co-exist? There was of course also the third reality of ordinary Army life, with the sergeant major checking on the making of beds, the meal times and all the ordinary routine.

Apart from meal times the intelligence staff was always kept separate, so that our life in the mess was very much more interesting than in an ordinary unit. All were of course linguists and between us we probably covered every European language and some others as well. A large percentage were university graduates, many of them with unusual life stories and experiences, although we never asked and some did not wish to give their previous history.

For instance, for some time the man in the bed next to me was a Gruzin (Georgian), who seemed to be of peasant stock although he never confirmed this. He would tell very interesting stories, particularly about customs and traditions which were so entirely different from ours. When a photograph of Churchill, Stalin and Roosevelt at one of the conferences appeared in the newspaper he interpreted from the position of the hands of Stalin what he meant to keep, and what not. It turned out to be correct in the years that followed.

As the war proceeded, our duties became more general in the sense that apart from the immediate tactical information our interrogations had to deal with various other problems, such as the effectiveness of the technique of the Nazi indoctrination and what was later called brain-washing. I had already, in my Home Guard training in 1941, been given examples of the effectiveness of this technique when we were told of a German airman shot down over Britain. He had been convinced by the propaganda that London had been destroyed by German air attack. The Interrogating Officer took him by car into the West End and drove him along Piccadilly. He asked him: 'Now do you believe that London has not been destroyed?' 'No,' answered the airman, 'I do not know how you do this trick, but London is destroyed, as I have been told.' The German was allowed to get out of the car, and touch the walls to convince himself that the buildings were real and that the people he saw were ordinary people. They got back into the car and he was asked again. 'I am completely puzzled, how you do this, but I am still sure London has been destroyed,' was the answer.

We found similar cases of such brain-washing, particularly amongst U-boat crews or people who, by the nature of their jobs, worked in more isolated conditions.

It was expected, and nearly all interrogations confirmed this, that young Waffen-SS officers gave answers which were absolutely the party propaganda line, and they seemed to be entirely incapable of thinking in any other way. They produced these answers even when talking to each other and when they could not be aware that they were being overheard.

At one time prisoners were interrogated in a long hall where there were about a dozen tables in a line. Most of the Interrogation Officers in this room happened to be Jewish. A young German soldier made a statement about how terrible Jews were and proceeded to describe in detail what they looked like. 'Can you see one here?' asked the Interrogating Officer. The German looked around and said, 'No I can't.' 'Have you ever seen one?' was the next question. 'No,' said the soldier. 'Would you recognise one if you saw one?' 'Most definitely,' was the answer. The German was about twenty-five and not particularly politically involved, but the hatred for these 'subhuman Jews' whom he had never seen was very obvious.

We had to fill in a questionnaire with prisoners which was so designed that people who had been indoctrinated in the Nazi party line gave standard 'Nazi' answers. Those who had retained a certain ability to think for themselves gave answers that varied even if they did not express any thought of a different political opinion.

Amongst young SS units the stereotype was nearly 100 per cent. More surprising was the fact that amongst older soldiers (aged 35 to 45), politically not especially involved, 80 to 85 per cent of the answers still followed the party line. This was towards the end of 1944.

The only group where we found a lower percentage of 'party' answers were professional officers. There it was probably in the region of 45 to 55 per cent. As this group was above average in intelligence their answers might not have reflected real beliefs. They supported however 100 per cent the question of military aggression for the greater German Reich, and if they had reservations about any invasion or aggression by the Reich these were purely on strategic grounds.

Whilst these were the results of these enquiries at this particular time, in connection with a limited number questioned, I had never in the following fifty years found any evidence that these findings were basically incorrect.

When after the initial heavy battles in Normandy the war became more fluid the number of prisoners increased and included a large number of non-German nationals. It was necessary to find out why and how these soldiers had come to be in German uniform. Had they volunteered? Were they forced to join? Were they traitors to their own countries? What was their real nationality? Had they lied to the Germans, or were they now lying to us? Each nationality behaved differently and a great deal of knowledge of the local situation and its history was required to decide even how the problem should be approached. In my experience the Dutch were the simplest. On the whole they were courageous enough to say that they were (a) Dutch nationals even if now in German uniform and (b) that they had been members of a Nazi organisation; these cases could immediately be handed to the Dutch authorities.

CHAPTER 19

Problems of Nationality

INTERROGATION OF THE Poles was not a simple matter. To approach the problem one had to look at the history of the country. During the first millennium of the Christian era most of the area which at the outbreak of the Second World War constituted the eastern part of Germany i.e. Prussia, Silesia, parts of Saxony and Pomerania, were inhabited by Slav peoples. During the tenth and eleventh centuries the Germanic people started to push the Slavs eastward. This movement became particularly strong at the time of the Crusades when the Order of German Knights added a religious aspect. To the east of the Poles were the Ukrainians, White Russians and finally the Russians themselves who found themselves under constant pressure from the west. Various Mongol invaders came from the east with the result that all these peoples were pushed west which in turn caused the Germans to feel under pressure and under the slogan *'Drang nach Osten'*, expansion to the east, constantly kept the Slav people under threat of invasion. The religious division in the area constantly reinforced discord and strife. Eastern Germany was largely Lutheran Protestant but the Poles were ardent Roman Catholics always ready to fight on the side of Church and Pope. East of them came the Ukrainians who belonged to the Uniat Church which is a form of orthodox Christianity recognising the Pope, and east of that Russian Orthodox Christianity.

In the nineteenth century Poland was completely divided with Imperial Germany occupying the northern part, the Austro-Hungarian monarchy governing mainly Galizia and some parts of the Polish Ukraine, and Tsarist Russia occupying the eastern parts.

When Tsarist Russia collapsed the Poles, with the help of British and French Expeditionary Forces, occupied large parts of the Ukraine, took Galizia from the Austrians and established a Poland which was rather larger than the area inhabited by 'ethnic Poles'. This process of constantly moving borders had gone on for many centuries, with the victor always oppressing the defeated group and trying to make them speak the language of the victorious power. At the outbreak of World War 2 the Germans once more annexed the eastern parts of inter-war Poland and declared all those who could speak some German to be *'Volksdeutsche'* i.e. ethnic Germans, gave them full German citizen rights and called them up into the German forces. There were of course those of purely Polish descent who at the beginning of the war tried to be on the winning side and to be 'Germans' and those who, although they spoke German, felt themselves as Poles and tried to escape from the clutches of the Nazis.

Of course the people who had lived in the area for many centuries had freely intermarried. There was understandably a great deal of confusion and not surprisingly many changed their minds as the war progressed.

Perhaps I have now described some of the complexity of the task British Intelligence was faced with when it had to be decided whether a person arriving in German uniform was in fact a German and an ordinary prisoner of war under the Geneva Convention, or a Pole who was an Allied national who should be handed over to the jurisdiction of the Polish forces in Britain. This was further complicated by the fact that there were two separate Allied Polish armies and governments in exile. One was in Britain, which was in a way the successor to the Polish government that had attacked the Soviet Union in 1921 and included some rather 'right wing' elements. The other government and army which had been formed in the Soviet Union was reputed to have a rather 'left wing' orientation. It happened a number of times during the war that a person who had been considered a German by the Nazis was called up into the German forces, was captured by the Allies, joined the Polish forces either east or west, was captured by the Germans in the next campaign, rejoined the German forces and arrived in Britain to face our interrogation team. We called these people 'shuttle service' boys. We had to decide whether they were patriots or traitors or just victims of circumstances. It will have become clear that these decisions were extremely difficult, and even though no decision was ever taken by one person alone, so much had to be left to a subjective opinion that we could rarely be certain that the right choice had been made.

It may serve as a good example of the intricacies and difficulties of these decisions which by necessity changed the lives of many people and their families if I describe in detail a particular case where I had to take part in making the decisions. A prisoner, about twenty years old appeared, giving his place of birth in a village near the town of Těšín in Czech, Cieszyn in Polish, and Teschen in German. This town was in Silesia near the Czech, Polish and German borders and was, with its immediate surroundings, part of Austria until 1918, then part of Czechoslovakia until 1938, when the Poles annexed it after Munich. After the outbreak of the war it became part of Germany. The boy's mother had been to German language schools in the time when it was Austria, the father had been to Polish schools, but the boy had been to Czech schools; and all of course held Czechoslovak nationality. Then they became automatically Poles in 1938, and German citizens in 1940. The Czech government had never recognised either the annexation by the Poles or the Germans and the Poles had not recognised the annexation by Germany. Because of the German mother tongue of his mother the boy had the right to declare himself as a *Volksdeutscher* which made him a German in international law. He was therefore *legally* a citizen of all three countries: Czechoslovakia, Poland and Germany. It was decided that he should be free to decide for himself and he was first given an interview with the officer of the Czech forces. This interview was confidential and he emerged from the room saying that he was Czech. The same procedure was repeated with the Polish officer and he returned with the statement that he was a Pole. I had then to interrogate him with the aim to establish whether he wanted to be German. After a short interview he agreed that he could be considered a German. By that time it had been possible to put him at ease and he could give a sincere answer to the question: 'What do you *wish* to be?' 'I do not know.' I then tried to find out his real mother tongue. 'With my mother I often spoke German, with my father sometimes Polish; when friends were present who are mostly Czech then we spoke Czech'. Impasse again. Then I asked, 'But when only you three are together, what language do you speak?' 'Shlonsk,' came the answer and the lad blushed a bit. Shlonsk was the local dialect which was a mixture of Moravian/Slovak/Polish dialect containing a lot of German words, and it was considered very 'low breeding' to speak this local dialect. As I had been born less than 150km from Těšín and that area had been part of the catchment area of my college, I had met a number of lads from those parts and could therefore assess the position and also verify the boy's statement. Owing to the co-operation of both the Polish and the Czech officers present we could come to the decision that the lad would be classified as an Allied National and not be drafted into either the Czech or the Polish forces, and in this way be repatriated to his native village whichever power would be in control of that area at the end of hostilities. It will be easily appreciated what a combination of favourable factors was necessary for such an outcome and how millions of people displaced by that war could never rejoin their families or native areas and had to spend the rest of their lives in exile and unhappiness merely by unfavourable circumstances.

A very different problem to the Polish and Czech question arose with the Ukrainians. The anti-Russian attitude seems to have been very much more widespread than amongst the Czechs and Poles and as soon as the area had been overrun by the Germans they were very quickly influenced by Nazi propaganda. A Ukrainian general called Vlassow was able to gather a considerable force which fought with enthusiasm for the Nazis against the Allies. There can be no doubt that all these were Soviet citizens and by taking up arms against their own country, they were traitors and when captured by Allied forces had to be handed over to the jurisdiction of their own country. They received very harsh treatment by Stalin and his government, but one must not forget that the Soviet Union at the time of the battles on the beaches of Normandy was still facing about three times the number of German forces than were ever employed on the Western Front of Europe in 1944/5. They had faced this onslaught from 1941 onwards and stood alone from the time of Dunkirk until the opening of the second front. Any leniency towards such a 'Quisling' army as the Vlassov forces could have led to defeat of the Soviet Union and the possibility of final victory of Nazi Germany over both East and West. Today when the Ukrainians have attained freedom and the injustices done to them by the regime of Stalin are becoming widely known, it is nevertheless important to remember that many of them fought with Hitler from their own will, even if influenced by propaganda.

What I personally saw of Ukrainian prisoners in British hands did not fill me with much admiration. They did not show much courage about their personal convictions and hid their membership of the Vlassov forces until faced with facts of the true situation. I did of course only see a small number of the total force captured, and can therefore only give my subjective impressions.

On one occasion a lot of prisoners arrived on the Barrack Square and every effort to make them obey my German orders ended in confusion. Getting more and more exasperated I forgot myself and started swearing at them in Slovak, which is reputed to be the second best language for this purpose, after Hungarian, in Europe. To my amazement after the second swearword a tremendous movement started on the square. I continued my orders in Slovak and in no time this formless mass had become orderly units following commands. It turned out that these were 'Hungarian' troops. Hungary had joined the Germans with extremely little enthusiasm and most of the soldiers in front of us were from 'Upper Hungary', a part of Slovakia which the Hungarians had occupied at some time during the war. These Slovaks showed even less eagerness for fighting and when the first opportunity arose, they got themselves captured. They were extremely co-operative but had of course little strategic or tactical information to impart, though they could supply a lot of general information which was probably more reliable than the Germans were willing to give.

I only met one Russian in German uniform. My only function in this matter was to hand him over to a Russian speaking interrogator. I cannot remember how it came about, but we had to wait so we had a lengthy conversation. He spoke Russian with odd words in French or German and I answered in Czech with odd words in other languages. He had come from a family of lower nobility who were professional Tsarist officers and his father simply continued in this occupation after the Revolution. He himself was brought up by an aunt who had a flat in Leningrad (now again St Petersburg), who had managed to keep her antique furniture. He described an eighteenth century chest which sounded very similar to one we had in our flat in Czechoslovakia, a coincidence which I found extraordinary. Because of his family connections he had also become a professional officer and at the outbreak of war was a lieutenant. He was captured by the Germans, but he was either unable or unwilling to tell me how he had become a private in Hitler's army. At this point the Russian interrogator appeared and I do not know what happened to him.

A very different type of investigation had to take place with the prisoners who were citizens of the eastern and south eastern republics of the Soviet Union. They were largely peasants and most of them illiterate. If they arrived in Britain together with their original interpreter which the Soviets had provided when they were recruited, then it was easy to establish where they had come from, and the chances of returning them after the war to their home region was pretty good, but if their original interpreter was not with them it was at best possible to establish the *oblast* they had come from. An *oblast* was a rather large administrative area, perhaps similar to a county. To find their home village or town was a task rather beyond the ability of the Soviet administration even if a rather higher priority had been given to this task than there actually was.

A typical report of the wartime activity of these people was as follows: 'Where do you come from?' 'From a village 8 km south-east of *the* town?' 'Which town?' A blank look and some sign of puzzlement usually followed and a repetition of the statement: '*The* town.' They had gone there to do their purchases at times, and sometimes it was necessary to go there for business with the authorities. They did not know the name of this town, and were unaware that any other towns existed. One day as they were working in the fields the local policeman or municipal functionary came with two people in uniform. They proposed that they should come with them and carry food and other materials for the horses and they themselves would be well fed and the farm would be looked after and even paid. This seemed a good and fair deal. They agreed and went off with these people. For a long time all went well and was as it had been promised to them. Then suddenly there was a lot of noise, shooting, explosions and chaos. 'In the end the men who had been looking after us disappeared and some others came dressed in different uniforms and said we could work for them instead. They gave us new clothes and so everything continued.'

Many of these people had the tradition of putting their new clothes over the old ones. It was therefore very important that intelligence staff saw them *before* they had their first shower and before they had gone through the de-lousing process. In this way much of the wartime history could be verified. One man said, 'Then we worked for them and all was really as before. But then again a lot of noise and explosions and lots of things from the air much more terrible than the first time. Then some very wicked men came dressed like you,' pointing at our khaki uniforms 'and took our horses and cart away, put us on a ship and here we are. What will become of us now without our horses?'

There were of course a number of educated members of the Eastern Soviet Republics, Kazaki, Uzbeki, Turkmeni and others, who had joined the German forces voluntarily because they were either anti-Russian or, more rarely, anti-Communist. Many of them had been persuaded by the German propaganda that if they helped to hold the Russian forces for a certain time the British, French and Americans would make peace with the Germans and they would then together destroy the Soviet Union.

Many of these Eastern people showed a great deal of cunning, which defeated many of the Western interrogation techniques. Some for instance would answer every question with 'Yes' for a period of time and then for a similar period every question was answered by 'No', pretending not to understand. On the whole they showed far less physical fear than Europeans.

An interesting fact was that their movements changed the further east you went. European movements were very much more 'dog-like' whilst the agility and speed of movement of the Easterners was much more 'cat-like'. At one time a group of about thirty prisoners – if I remember rightly, they were Kalmucks – arrived in the camp. Whenever they received their food there were three or four standing there claiming that they had received no food. It was at first suspected that the guards had somehow not given them the right number of rations. It was then arranged that Intelligence staff counted the number of plates which were put several yards in front of each prisoner who were standing in line, each one in front of his plate. On a given command they had to collect their plates and return to their places. When they stood in line again, three of them were without plates. The missing empty plates were later found in the barbed wire but none of us had actually observed how these three had transferred their food on the neighbour's plate and thrown the empty plate into the barbed wire, so swift were their movements. They were also intelligent enough never to try this again once they saw that we knew their method.

One of the most interesting groups of people from a general human point of view were the Gruzini (Georgians). I never found out what they call themselves in their own language. The number of educated people was very much higher than in any other group. This seems to have been connected with the fact that a large part of the intelligentsia seems to have been anti-Russian and had therefore voluntarily joined the German forces. They felt that they had been taken advantage of and rather looked down on the Russians whom they considered slow and unintelligent. A number of the Soviet leaders were of course Georgians, including Stalin and Beria and many more in less important positions. The University of Tbilisi certainly produced some very capable undergraduates and graduates. I met some students who could write, apart from their own writing, in Russian and in our alphabet and speak Russian, French, English and in some cases German. The speed with which they seemed to grasp things appeared extraordinary. I wondered sometimes whether they had developed a mental agility corresponding to the physical agility of the peoples of Eastern Asia, at the same time being sufficiently 'Western' to be able to understand Western thought and values.

CHAPTER 20

Joint American/British Unit

AT A SLIGHTLY LATER STAGE of the war I was transferred to a joint American/British unit which dealt with the interrogation of high ranking officers or other special prisoners. It was located in a beautiful stately home inside large wooded grounds and thus very pleasant. It was only at very rare intervals that we were allowed out into the world past all the security barriers, but pleasant surroundings were a fair compensation for our own imprisonment.

I was not doing any interrogations there myself but was in charge of the Map Room. This entailed reading daily all the communiqués of all the armies under General Eisenhower's command and sticking a pin into a map showing the position of each division on the front line. I then had to read the interrogation reports, which gave changes of the positions of German divisions. Each morning the interrogation officers would come to study the map and I had to point out the specific movements that had taken place and where perhaps our information on the German order of battle appeared deficient. This daily briefing I had to give created the illusion for me that only two people could really know what was going on: Eisenhower and myself!

A very thrilling moment came when the American Forces crossed the Rhine quite against any prepared plan and owing to one of those strange accidents which play such a big part in the course of wars.

By a series of mishaps on the part of the Germans they failed to blow up a bridge across the Rhine and when General Paton's tanks of his 3rd Army reached the bridge, to everybody's amazement they just drove across and Paton, being a capable general, soon got his troops organised and established a deep bridgehead east of the Rhine. His message to the Allied Headquarters simply said: 'Have outrun all maps, send maps.' By these particular circumstances the war was probably shortened by several months.

Another very exciting moment was at the time when the British Forces were preparing for the advance in the Netherlands (later called the battle of the Reichswald Forest), whilst the Germans were preparing for an attack in the south. Each day we watched the pins representing our divisions concentrating more and more around the Reichwald area whilst the pins representing the German forces collected in the south. It was obvious that somewhere in Germany there was a map demonstrating the corresponding pins, and showing that this colossal gamble was going on. Who would be ready first? Whoever was to move first would have a tremendous advantage and the other side would have to take defensive measures and lose the initiative. Over two hundred front line divisions, about one hundred on each side. Five or six million men and all the planes and their crews, all dependent on who could complete the preparations first. All these lives at risk. And we were just sitting and watching the pins on the map and repeating to ourselves: 'This is not a cup final!' In the end we were first.

Being in an American/British mixed unit was an interesting experience. What particularly struck me was the working relationship of different ranks whilst on duty. In the British specialist units the rank completely ceased to matter whilst on duty within our own offices. The Americans kept to much more formality such as a second lieutenant saluting and calling a first lieutenant 'Sir' in a very formal manner. When off duty these formalities ceased, whilst we treated each other more formally off duty. There were occasions when certain extra food had to be paid for in an American mess whilst in the British mess it was either free or not available.

Having pointed out some differences I must say that it was very easy working together and very interesting because of the many different aspects that were dealt with in one unit. I remember for instance an Air Force woman from Texas. We both liked peanut butter at teatime, and if I could have understood more of her broad Texan accent it would have been still more interesting. She was an expert at interpreting aerial photography of bomb damage and, I was told, quite outstanding at her job.

As our troops advanced further into Germany the task of this special unit changed and I was posted back to my original unit.

Information from the underground in occupied countries and from agents in Germany was now much easier to obtain. The Germans were now calling up the last possible reserves called '*Volksturm*', a kind of Home Guard but organised into fighting units for use on the front line. We had very accurate information when and how each battalion was recruited and what deficiencies there were in the armament. When some members of such a unit were captured, I could ask them as an opening question: 'What happened to your heavy machine gun?' because I knew that this particular weapon had not been supplied and the unit had had to go into action without it. After this they obviously assumed that we knew everything and supplied every bit of information that was asked for, thus filling all the gaps in our knowledge.

At that time the Germans launched their last major offensive operations and their hope was that if this was successful they could perhaps negotiate a separate peace with the Western Allies. This could then bring peace with the Soviet Union. I propose to describe all the information that I gained not only at the time but also after the end of hostilities when we had to gather information for the historic assessment of the campaign. What I can describe is therefore largely the picture from German sources and not an overall objective assessment.

By then the Allies had liberated practically the whole of France with the exception of certain fortified ports which the Allies had bypassed but which nevertheless restricted the use of ports for supply purposes. The whole of Belgium and the Netherlands was also in Allied hands. The bridgehead over the Rhine had been established and all these vast forces were mainly supplied through the port of Antwerp.

The Germans had just enough supplies of fuel for one major tank battle with at least some air support. By massing all the available tank divisions and concentrating the attack into southern Belgium they hoped to break through the Ardennes which they rightly believed were lightly held mainly by one American Division (101st) who had shortly before arrived from the States. Then it might be possible to reach Antwerp, interrupt the whole of the L of C (Line of Communication) of the Allies, and prevent the re-establishment of supplies, by the new secret weapon, the V2 missiles.

As it happened the American Division together with other units managed to delay the German advance, suffering tremendous losses. This however gave General Montgomery the possibility of moving a strong tank force into the area.

In the words of a German major general, one of the commanders of the German tank forces: 'When we saw the Allied tanks racing at full speed with their headlights full on, we knew that they would cut us off and the campaign would be lost.' If this is true, and I have never heard anything to the contrary, then one of the decisive decisions in this battle was Montgomery's decision to disregard any risk of air attack by the Luftwaffe and get the tanks in position before the Germans. If this report is indeed true it shows how important psychological factors remain in warfare, when by switching on the headlights the Allies not only gained an important tactical advantage but also demoralised the enemy.

It seems to me from other information that the fuel supply indeed started to fail and therefore the supply situation was made very much worse by the Allied bombing of railway and other communications, a development very difficult to assess. Because these raids also caused many civilian casualties they became rather controversial after the war. It is a controversy difficult to assess as nobody has really been able to collect the necessary correct information.

CHAPTER 21

Interrogation

During the early part of 1945 we came across the first formal concentration camp guards who had been posted later to fighting units and became prisoners of war. I remember in particular one report on a camp in northern Germany. The inmates were a mixture of 'political prisoners', i.e. people opposed to the Nazi regime; and what the Nazis called 'special criminals' which often meant homosexuals, some gypsies, people who had committed 'race offences' i.e. 'Aryans' who had been suspected of sexual relations with Jews or any friendly acts towards Jews or gypsies, and any other 'crimes' which were not defined in the ordinary criminal codes. They were used as slave labour and were escorted to work in nearby factories and systematically starved to death according to a programme worked out quite scientifically, so that the State could obtain the maximum number of working hours at the minimum of food expenditure. The speciality in this camp was that prisoners were tattooed with artistic patterns and when their time came to be killed their skins were tanned and made into lampshades which were intended for sale. The guards who reported this were on the whole people between 35 and 45 years old, of relatively little education and politically not involved. They considered the action of the commandant and the team who committed these actions as wrong but were by that time so dehumanised that the enormity of the crimes they reported was not realised by them. This was a process of shutting off of any moral human reactions which we came across again and again on the part of people who were found to witness or even commit such crimes and atrocities. After carrying out these interrogations, I myself and some of my colleagues were physically sick.

About one week before the end of the war we came across the first prisoners who had been guards at transports when the Germans started to move inmates of extermination camps and other concentration camps from the east to the west. The purpose of this manoeuvre seems to have been twofold. The SS command seems to have believed that if the Russians captured these camps, they would kill the guards without any trials, or with trials in very summary form. They therefore largely withdrew the SS guards and possibly dispersed them over ordinary Waffen SS units which were ordinary fighting units originally formed largely from the Hitler Youth organisation.

The guards were replaced by units that had previously guarded airfields or ammunition dumps or performed similar duties. On the whole they were men between 40 and 50 who had been in the forces for several years and for a long period of time been accustomed to obey orders and not to think for themselves.

They were told to 'stack' the prisoners into open goods wagons in the way timber (pit props) is often stacked. The journeys took three or four days and there was no food or sanitation. On arrival at their destination the guards were told to lower the sides of the wagon. A large number of them fell down. Some managed to stand up. The standing ones were told to fall in and were counted. The lying ones were counted on the ground. The number of both groups were reported and then the standing ones were marched off. 'And the lying ones, were they dead?' I asked. The guard in question looked at me in great surprise and for several seconds seemed to try and recall the situation. 'I suppose so,' came the final answer. It had never occurred to him. He had never thought of the 'standing' and 'lying' ones as human beings at all. How could a human being let another human being just die on the floor like that? After my question it occurred to him for the first time that life and death were involved. How could a human being act like this? The only way could be if these guards were no longer human in the ordinary sense, but beings where all human impulses had either temporarily or permanently been put out of action. Again and again we were to come across this terrible phenomenon. It seemed to be made still worse that one could not even call them 'beasts', bestial or wicked. They were simply 'somethings' that could still walk and talk but somehow were no longer human, without knowing it themselves.

One of my first assignments at the end of the war was to look after the welfare of the former commandant of the concentration camp at Bergen Belsen, Dr Kramer. This took place in a fortress in eastern Belgium, where a number of non-military persons were held. Kramer was a tall and exceptionally strong man, over 6 feet, reportedly a doctor of medicine, which enabled him to think up the various medical experiments and cruelties which took place. My job consisted mainly of talking to him every morning, seeing that he was properly looked after with a toothbrush and similar toilet articles. It was also his only possibility to talk to somebody in his own language. At the time when I first saw him he had been imprisoned there for several days and had just had time to think, to become aware of the situation and realise some of the deeds he had done. Increasingly every morning, he complained of the 'brainstorms', which kept him from sleeping. He cried like a child when these moments of clarity came. I realised during these moments and the conversations that took place at that time that when a certain limit is transgressed some higher power or energy manifests itself and a man ceases to be a man in the way we normally understand this word and some form of suffering and punishment is lawfully meted out to such a person which is far more terrible to bear than the punishment given by his fellow men. I saw very clearly that this man had already been judged and condemned before he even stood before a human court. In a way that I could not explain at all at the time, it gave me the feeling that there was a higher justice and it was even possible to feel some compassion for this unfortunate wretch without having any different view about the unbelievably terrible crimes which he and his helpers had committed.

One of the people held in this fortress was Heinrich Himmler's brother. His views, opinions and social background gave a very interesting insight into the family of one of the leaders of the Nazi movement. The brother, whose Christian name I do not remember, was a school teacher. I believe he taught in a secondary school and the strongest emotion he expressed was that owing to the fame of his brother he could not go undisturbed in the pursuance of his profession and found himself under public scrutiny which he always tried to avoid. He seemed to indicate they had both come from an ordinary middle class family and received the almost standard grammar school education. Heinrich, according to his brother, had always been an arrogant and over-ambitious fellow and did not listen to his brother's warnings that he should not meddle in politics. 'And now it has been proven that I was right.' This conversation took place very shortly after Himmler's surrender in the north of Germany. My conversations with Heinrich's brother went on for a number of days and it became more extraordinary that the two brothers were so different in outlook and that one could have remained an ordinary schoolteacher with ordinary middle class views whilst the other became one of the leaders of the criminal clique pursuing their goal ruthlessly without any inhibitions brought about by the moral laws according to which human life had been judged for thousands of years.

One afternoon another Interrogation Sergeant and I were told to wait in the Major's office. To our surprise the safe had been left open and very visibly there was a booklet lying there marked 'secret' in very big letters and entitled 'Proposed policy of the demobilisation of the German Forces after the end of hostilities'. Quite obviously attracted by this title we took it and started to study it.

It dealt in great detail with how during a screening process prisoners should be categorised according to previous political orientation and various other criteria including their immediate usefulness in building up a new democratic Germany. Officers above a certain rank and officials above a certain grade should be held and examined in greater detail. Just as we had finished reading this, the Major returned to the office, took the booklet and locked it in the safe without saying a word.

The next day the two of us were posted to Flanders to an area where there were about six large prisoner of war camps and we were told to organise their screening so that about 2,000 prisoners could be moved each week and 2,000 new ones would arrive. This might have to be stepped up to perhaps 2,000 a day. The only other instruction was to report to the Commandant of the camps with our suggestions on how we were going to do this.

Fortunately, my friend had an almost photographic memory and thus we were able to reconstruct the leaflet by working late into the night and were able to put a reasonably coherent plan before the Colonel in the morning. The Colonel had great misgivings from the start that some sergeants were going to tell him what to do. When he heard that all senior officers should be held for further investigation he really blew up, saying that officers were gentlemen, he would do no such a thing as we suggested. We could of course not tell him that this was not the Crimean War or another campaign of the last century, and all we could do was salute as smartly as we could and retire. We managed to get through to our Commanding Officer in London and explained to him the general difficulty. He immediately went to Brussels to the Headquarters L of C and arranged that more or less the same wording as we had put to the camp Commandant would be published in 'orders' the next day. When the Colonel now received what we had suggested as 'orders from above' he accepted the situation and from then on the demobilisation of the German forces proceeded according to this plan.

The next morning we had a telephone call from our sister units in northern Germany and Norway. They had already been told that we had a system according to which the German forces were being screened for demobilisation; would we tell them how it was being done. We shall never know whether the major in the Belgian fortress had left the safe open on purpose or whether it was pure accident, but in any case in this somewhat informal way the demobilisation of the German forces and the preparation for a new democratic Germany proceeded fairly accurately according to the method the War Office had foreseen early in the course of the war.

It was only when we had started the screening process that we realised the tremendous responsibility that it entailed and the impossibility of doing justice to the task which we had been given. In practice we soon realised that the large number of prisoners that had to be 'processed' allowed us about two to five minutes to make a decision on who should be demobilised, who should be held for a short period, and who should be sent to a country where he should remain for a long period, which usually meant sending people to camps in Britain or Canada where they would stay until the situation in Germany had stabilised. It also meant deciding who was an East German and should be sent into the Russian Zone or who should go into the Western Zone, and deciding who was a *'Volksdeutscher'*, i.e. a person born in an area outside pre-1939 Germany who had volunteered to be German. These people were now sent to post war Germany, whether they had been born in Poland, Czechoslovakia, the Ukraine or Romania, or were 'Volga Germans' from Russia.

In short we felt we had to play God in five minutes. The only possibility in cases of grave doubt was to put them back for further interrogation, and because of shortages of accommodation this possibility was rather limited.

One of the more amusing decisions was how to define who was a German and who an Austrian. At the end of the war Austria had been declared an 'Allied' country. Conditions in Austria were therefore much better than in Germany. Many Germans who had at some time during the war years been stationed in Austria, therefore claimed to be Austrians. This problem was solved by relying on the Austrian love of food, and the fact that Austrians love going out for meals and each pub or restaurant has its special dishes for which it is famous among the locals. Even the people who couldn't afford meals knew where they would have gone, had they been able to afford it. This enabled them to boast to their acquaintances and pretend that they had been there.

For some reason this knowledge was not easily imparted to strangers. Once we had discovered these facts, our method was as follows. If a prisoner claimed to be a native of an Austrian town or village, we ascertained from a known citizen of that town what speciality they ate in which place. In some instances they even knew what one would eat at a certain place on a certain day of the week. Armed with this information, we then only had to interrogate the prisoner as to what he used to eat in which place. If he knew, he was an Austrian, if not he was classified as German. Once we had established this method, any lengthy investigation could be dispensed with. I do not remember a single case where this decision was disputed.

A very different problem was the decision about people from the Eastern republics of the Soviet Union. Would the Soviets treat them as traitors and shoot or imprison them? Would they be technically able to find out where they came from, and be able to repatriate them to their native village? It was of course impossible for all these thousands to be settled in the West. At some point the Soviet authorities said that they would talk to them and give them the choice whether they wanted to go home. They thought that most of them would wish to do so. Thus one day a fairly high ranking Soviet officer in a beautiful uniform with a lot of gold braid appeared in the camp. About 2,000 men were assembled on the square. It was the same place where the prisoners had been assembled when they first arrived and had been given an address telling them about the shower and the meal they were going to receive.

The Soviet officer made a very moving speech in Russian about how Mother Russia would welcome them back and either bring them back to their home, or find work for them. He appealed to them to volunteer to come home. When he had finished there was first a complete silence, and then a shout from 2,000 mouths: '*Jawohl!*' They had experienced before that after a speech from the rostrum and shouting 'Jawohl!' they had been given a good meal. They had neither recognised that the person addressing them was in Soviet uniform, nor that he had addressed them in Russian and not German.

The Soviet Officer descended from the rostrum more quickly than he had ascended. The men were nevertheless 'voluntarily' returned to the Soviet Union. There was in practice no other possibility.

At one period, very shortly after the end of hostilities, about one hundred textile workers had accidentally accumulated in our group of camps. There was at the time an extreme shortage of cloth in Germany and most of the factories had been destroyed or could not quickly be brought into operation for other reasons. Having been in this trade I knew that a lot of machinery in Britain was idle because of shortage of labour. I therefore worked out how these prisoners could be employed producing cloth for Germany, alleviating the extreme shortage. I suggested a system where the money the prisoners would have earned could go into a fund for charitable purposes, so that nobody would have either an unfair advantage or be penalised. I must mention that I received a reply from the War Office amazingly quickly, explaining that this was against the letter of the Geneva Convention, and nothing could or would be done. In the end bureaucracy reigned supreme, as owing to some clerical error these largely anti-Nazi prisoners were not sent to Germany to await employment in their trade but ended up in Canada in a camp for Nazis to be held there until things in Germany had stabilised. Thus with all the best intentions on the part of everybody involved, the opposite of the original aim had taken place.

As time went on, we saw more examples of where this giant administrative machinery seemed to have taken on a life of its own and things happened contrary to the good intentions of all concerned. This was obviously depressing for any efforts to build a sensible future. It gave everybody a feeling of helplessness and there was no explanation for these happenings.

Gradually our tasks changed to the interrogation of officers in order to establish the history and course of the various campaigns during the war. This was very much more interesting work. Whilst we were able to crosscheck various German reports, we could of course not establish a balanced view, as we had no information from our own side. For me the most fascinating aspect that came up again and again was the fact that much of the success or failure of most campaigns depended on accidental circumstances beyond the control of the immediate participants.

The various reports on the situation after 'Dunkirk' was one of the most interesting examples. Most officers, including General Staff Officers, agreed that the German High Command had been correct not to pursue the French forces to the south after they had been defeated on the Maginot Line, when the Germans had carried out an almost textbook exercise of mobile warfare in depth by outflanking the strongly fortified lines. We had been taught the theory of this in 1938 in the Czech Officers Training College by a French Staff Officer. I was therefore not in the least surprised when the German officers knew that according to the 'textbook' of this form of warfare the French should have withdrawn as quickly as possible which would extend the German lines of communications to the utmost possible and then counterattack with highly mobile light armoured forces and break through the now extended German positions and cut off their supply lines. A number of German officers also confirmed what we had already been told two years earlier in Czechoslovakia, that it was the French Staff Colleges who had developed the theory of what became later known as the *Blitzkrieg* and that the Germans were really following the French lead. Not a single person I spoke to could understand why apparently the French Command seemed to be the only ones who did not know what their own military textbooks said.

The Germans therefore spent the next three weeks securing this exposed flank. Nobody I spoke to suspected that the absence of the awaited counterattack was due to the degree of the demoralisation of the French forces. It was only after that time that the full extent of the breakdown of French morale became clear and that the Germans could really contemplate the invasion of Britain.

The following amazing story was told about the German preparation for this invasion. When the German Forces had reached the Channel coast, the German High Command (OKW-Oberkommando Wehrmacht) sent a message to the Command of the Navy to prepare 'the invasion fleet' to move to the Channel ports. To this came the surprising answer: 'Which invasion fleet?' It then emerged that the basic instruction to build such a fleet, given by the OKW long before the war, had never reached the Navy, and no such fleet had been built. The only tentative suggestions about how such an absurd situation could have happened, was that the original order might not have come from the OKW but from the party organisation, the *Reichssichereitshauptamt* (the Nazi Party Security High Command). At the time of this order the Navy was still entirely commanded by professional naval officers, who might not have accepted orders from the Party. Needless to say, there was never a confirmation of this report.

When this situation was realised emergency measures were taken to improvise landing craft, by cutting off the bows of ordinary ships and constructing landing doors. Since I have no naval or shipbuilding knowledge whatsoever I cannot judge the technical meaning of these measures. According to these reports the

Emergency Invasion Fleet was ready in late summer 1940, and was moved to the Channel ports.

An exercise was ordered and several landing craft, fully manned, took part. When they were in mid Channel an unexpected wind sprung up and these improvised craft proved less seaworthy than expected and sank. Several hundred men were drowned. There were rumours in Britain at that time that a considerable number of German bodies had been washed up on the beaches of the Channel ports.

One must take into account that what I have just written was information obtained from relatively junior or middle ranking Army officers only, as on the whole the German Naval and Air Force officers were interrogated by Navy and Air Force interrogators respectively. Nevertheless the picture that emerged gave us an impression of the general situation and an inkling of the relationship and tension between the German Services, as well as the divergence of emphasis between the professional Forces Chiefs, the Führer and the staff he had surrounded himself with. These were not always held in very high esteem by the traditional, professional officers.

When I read Churchill's description of the operation 'Sea Lion', which was published four years later based largely on the official records of both sides, I was surprised that the basic 'feel' that I had received in 1945 had not to be radically altered. Many of the reported rumours were of course never confirmed as facts. There still remains the amazing statement reported by Churchill in his *Second World War*, volume ii, page 268 that: 'The German Army Command had from the first regarded the invasion of England with considerable qualms. They had made no plans or preparations for it; and there had been no training.' The Navy had made its own plans and it would seem that Admiral Raeder had never discussed it with the Army Command. It will probably puzzle future generations, just as it puzzled me in 1945/6, how this most aggressive country in the world at that time, with its admired ability of scientific planning and ruthless cold logic, could have engaged in total war without ever making a plan how to fight it after the successful conclusion of Stage One, especially when one compares this with the meticulous and detailed planning of the destruction of the Jews and Gypsies, when all details for this negative task were thought of and bureaucratically recorded.

A very interesting picture of the Battle of Britain was given to us by a Luftwaffe officer, who in the final stages of the war was the Air Force Liaison Officer in Hitler's Bunker during the last phases of the war. Our interrogation was really about the happenings in the Bunker, which I will describe in detail later.

During this interrogation it emerged that this officer had been in charge of a major portion of the German Bomber Command and was very proud of his role in the operations during August and September 1940 and he liked to talk about it. In order to get him to talk freely about the happenings we wanted to know about, namely the last days in Hitler's Bunker and Hitler's death, we spent quite some time talking about things which he liked to talk about, and when a friendly and relaxed relationship had been formed, we could then introduce the subjects we wished to discuss. Another interrogation officer and I met daily over a number of days in a hut in the PoW camp, where we sat around a table, had numerous cups of tea and offered lots of cigarettes. No notes were taken, and although we made a report of his account of the Battle of Britain I do not think that it was of the slightest importance as the Air Force interrogation officers who had seen him earlier on Air Force matters would have obtained all the technical information. It was however a very interesting experience for us.

He had been in charge of a group of airfields in France charged in particular with the bombing of the fighter bases in southern England, with the aim of destroying the ability of the Royal Air Force to resist the German air attacks. Whilst the reports that he received showed quite considerable destruction of British fighters and damage of airfields, the losses of Luftwaffe planes exceeded this. At one point he calculated that at this rate he could only continue for thirteen days at the present intensity. He contacted Göring who immediately came to France. Göring was of the opinion that the whole war could be won by these Luftwaffe attacks and resisted any change of tactics. Finally, after another two days, he accepted a change and the massive daylight raids ceased. What he had not known at the time was that the ability of the RAF to resist an attack on that scale was several days shorter than the German ability to maintain this attack. It would appear that the faulty intelligence at that particular moment plus the emotional make-up of the leaders, played an important part in the course of this campaign, and perhaps the whole fate of the war.

In 1942 a British/Canadian force made a surprise attack near Dieppe in order to establish a bridgehead in France. I do not know whether it was intended that if this attack was successful, it would become the beginning of the 'Second Front' or whether it was intended to be only exploratory. It turned out to be less successful than expected and according to the Commander of one of the German Armoured Divisions involved, the reason was the following. He was taking part, together with another Armoured Division and a corresponding support force, in a major exercise. They were stationed somewhere in the south-west of France and were moving north. The scheme was that the Allies had landed north of Calais and this force was to prevent the formation of the bridgehead. They had already been travelling quite some time when a dispatch rider appeared and reported an Allied landing near Dieppe. 'You idiot,' the Commander answered, 'you mean Calais, it is Calais where they are landing in this scheme.' 'No sir,' replied the dispatch rider, 'They have *really* landed at Dieppe.' The officer immediately went to the telephone, confirmed the truth of this report, ordered the sharp ammunition which was carried in the rear of the column to be brought forward and went full steam ahead. The Germans arrived two hours earlier than our Intelligence had considered possible. Because of this accidental happening the Canadian losses in particular were terrible.

After the fall of Paris in 1944 the Allied Forces under Field Marshal Montgomery moved north, and it was hoped that by an airborne attack it would be possible to capture the important bridge at Nijmegen in the south of the Netherlands before the tanks reached that area. This would enable the Allied armies to move straight across and ahead and it was hoped that this would shorten the war possibly by six months. The paratroopers met however very strong resistance and had larger losses than expected. Although there was some heroic fighting the attack was only a limited success. One contributory factor was as follows.

Two days before this attack a Cyclist Battalion had been posted near the northern end of the bridge. At that time the Germans were already having difficulty in finding sufficient fuel for mobile units, and a large number of the young and fit men had already died, been wounded, or put out of action by frostbite on the Russian Front. It became therefore necessary to recruit older men in the 40 to 45 age group, and put them on bicycles. This saved precious motor fuel and was faster than horses and in addition bicycles did not eat the precious feed. This is how the men of this battalion described their part of the battle of the bridge to me:

'After we had arrived, we were told to dig trenches. It was cold and misty and we sat in those wet trenches. It was very miserable. Suddenly in the early morning these aeroplanes appeared, and out came these parachutes. They were slowly floating down just in front of us. We had never fired a shot in anger. But there they were, just in front, so we shot at them. We hit quite a few.' Not exactly like the film that in later years was made about these landings!

CHAPTER 22

Yugoslavia

THE INTERROGATION which was for me personally one of the most interesting ones was the one of the Chief of Staff (Intelligence) of the Army Group South/East, which was responsible for the area of Yugoslavia, Greece and the rest of the Balkans.

To put this into a better perspective it might be useful if I described what I already knew about the area which then formed the republic of the Slovenes, Croats, and Serbs, called Yugoslavia (which means the country of the South Slavs). It seems impossible to follow the happenings without some knowledge of the history of the area. The Slav peoples who inhabit this area at present appear to have settled there in the first centuries of the Christian era, at first under Roman and then under Byzantine influence. The Serbs adopted Byzantine i.e. Orthodox Christianity, the Croats and Slovenes became Roman Catholics. In the thirteenth century the Turks started to conquer the Balkans. In the fourteenth century they defeated the Serbs at Kosovo, which is even today an important shrine of the Serbian religion. During the following century the Turks occupied the whole of the Balkans and came to the gates of Vienna in 1529. Had the Austrians not been able to stop the advance the whole of Central Europe would have come under Turkish domination. From that time on the Turks were gradually forced to retreat until only the relatively small area around Istanbul remained Turkish. This process lasted from 1529 until 1921 when the present borders were established. The northern parts, i.e. Slovenia and Croatia, gradually came under Austrian and Austro-Hungarian influence with the consequence that on the one hand Austro-Hungary became the oppressors. Liberation from this occupation came with the formation of the South Slav Republic. On the other hand this area came under the influence of the Roman Catholic Church which was so very strong under the Habsburg dynasty. This Slovene and Croat area could also benefit from the higher standards of living and education in the Austro-Hungarian Empire. Serbia and the other southern parts stayed much longer under Turkish rule and part of the population, such as some Bosnians and Albanians, accepted the Islamic Faith. The whole way of life was more under Eastern influence which could clearly be experienced in their music and other cultural activities.

As the Serbs were the largest ethnic group and over this long period had to struggle against the Turkish overlordship, they felt they were entitled to be rulers in the new state (1918) and by 1934 the country had become a dictatorship under the Serbian royal family. None of the grievances were forgotten, including the defeat of Kosovo, a region which today has an Albanian/Islamic majority with one of the most holy Serbian/Orthodox shrines, and is one of the areas of tension which remains unresolved. I had visited Belgrade in 1933 and as it is not too difficult to understand a bit of Serbian and Croat when one speaks Czech, I had acquired some knowledge and feel of these various tensions and views. An uncle of mine had served in Sarajevo during the First World War as an Austro-Hungarian Officer and from him I had heard a lot about life in Bosnia. As Czechoslovakia in the early 1930s had surplus qualified technicians a number of acquaintances had gone to Croatia where new industries were being developed and I therefore heard about the general situation there and how in fact it was much easier to establish industries there than in Serbia because the education system in Croatia was much nearer to the Czech system and training of workers therefore much easier. Knowledge of German was also more common in both these areas but not in Serbia. I had also heard a great deal about the different nationalities that make up that country and the frontiers which frequently altered during the course of history so that different people moved in and out of the area during the centuries. At the outbreak of World War Two the kingdom of Yugoslavia had about 15 million inhabitants, including about 7.5 million Serbs, 3.5 million Croats, 1.5 million Slovenes, 0.5 million Hungarians, 0.5 million Rumanian, 0.5 million Albanians and 0.5 million Germans. 82 per cent of the population worked in agriculture and forestry and only about 9 per cent in industry. Only 4 per cent lived in large towns, the rest in villages and small towns.

When it came to evaluate the report by the Wehrmacht Colonel about other events during the period of 1941 to 1945 my position of being once again 'in between' enabled me to understand some of these happenings with the different 'persons' that make me up. The Serbian and Russian position I could grasp and feel with the Czech in me. The distinctive Croat reactions were felt by the knowledge of the way of thinking of the old Austro-Hungarian monarchy and even the Bosnian feelings as a religious minority could partly be followed by my Jewish reactions. The German aims and actions, and also their fears, were very clear to me. Having experienced the whole war through British eyes I could appreciate the difficulties and understood the very involved and contradictory influences which acted on everybody in this area.

The military events in this theatre of war are of course well documented today and have been described in great detail. I will therefore describe only my own impressions and evaluations of these events.

Colonel H. was a professional German staff officer and like most of these professionals not a Nazi in the strict party sense. He supported, however, like all

German officers I have met, the expansion of Germany, particularly to the east and south-east. He detested Hitler's 'non professional' conduct of the war and his 'military adventures' even if they appeared to be successful. He was rather pro-British and would even put up with the 'cultural upstart' Americans if it all led to a defeat of the Russian and Asiatic 'Bolsheviks'. As the war was over and we were no longer 'the enemy' his reports were models of objective reporting in the best tradition of European Intelligence, distinguishing as accurately as possible between facts, hearsay, observation and opinion.

The picture that emerged was for me as follows. His opinion of Italians as soldiers was not the highest and he felt that when the Germans had to take over in that theatre of war the Germans had to pull chestnuts out of the fire for them and he spent as little time as possible on their exploits or the lack of them, and as I was also not very interested in this aspect this was very acceptable to me.

He confirmed that the Royal Yugoslav Army was very lukewarm about the war and was on the whole quite pleased to surrender after the King had fled to Britain and had formed his government in exile. There remained contact by the underground forces of that Army with the British Headquarters in Egypt, but it was easy for German Intelligence to penetrate the communications and they were therefore well informed about all the planned actions, and knew the codes. The possibility of effective resistance to the Germans was therefore rather limited. The population, particularly the Serbs, were aware of this basic situation and the influence of this force therefore waned more and more. It took until late in 1942 before the British High Command accepted the consequences of this situation and supported other resistance groups more strongly.

The Germans very cleverly exploited the anti-Serb feelings of the Croats in creating a Croat National Movement who worked with the Germans against any Allied resistance. They also managed to get the support of a 'Quisling' Serb movement. There was a Serb pro-Allied underground movement as well as a Croat one, both supported by the Allies. In addition there was the Communist supported movement headed by Tito covering all national groups in Yugoslavia. Tito, a Croat whose family name was Brož, had been a sergeant in the Imperial Austro Hungarian Army who on capture by the Russians had joined the Yugoslav Legion which was formed for the creation of a Yugoslav state. He went to Moscow after World War I to be trained both politically and militarily and after the defeat of the Royal Yugoslav Army started the organisation of a resistance movement which was the only one of all the various movements which was 'clean': that is, their integrity was never compromised by the Germans. All the other groups suffered from traitors which led to terrible hatred amongst the various groups and to large numbers of atrocities. The Allied resistance groups were supplied by air by the Allied forces. Owing to the defections in all these groups the codes of all groups were known to everyone including the Germans and their groups. When the details of any impending air drop was given over the 'secret' radio wavelengths and in 'secret codes', all four or five different resistance forces raced to the drop area and savage battles developed between them for the possession of these arms. This lead to further hatred and atrocities, as Serb fought Croat and pro-Nazi fought pro-Ally, but also each other. All this I could easily verify because one of my colleagues in my unit had been dropped, at one period, in Yugoslavia with a wireless set to receive the messages of impending weapon drops.

The Tito units were at first only supplied by the Soviet Union and direct contact with the British only came into operation later in the war. Little by little the Tito forces gained the confidence of all the various groups of the population. It was Tito's great achievement that he could show clearly that he was above the national, racial and political divisions and that he was working for the good of the whole of the country. This clarity of purpose aimed at uniting the country and, if not forgetting the possibility of revenge, at least made it appear less important than the building of a country. The interrogations made in 1944/5 enabled me to see the possibility of understanding Tito's aim of uniting the country and using economic pragmatism to perform 'the miracle' of forming a 'Communist' state, which could resist and become independent of the Soviet Union and at the same time keep close relations with the 'capitalists' of Western Europe.

Without these interrogations I would have found it much more difficult to follow the subsequent developments in that country. As long as the superior understanding of Tito directed the happenings in that country economic conditions started to improve, but these developments in turn contained some of the elements of the later downfall. The economic situation in Slovenia and Croatia improved very much faster than in Serbia. By the mid 60s the standard of living in Slovenia was nearly twice as high as in Serbia and the GDP in Croatia was not very much lower. The Serbs saw that in a Federal Republic where they formed the majority of the population they had a very much lower standard of living with no prospect of a major change in the situation. The reasons went back to the early part of the century as well as the entire war period. When no successor to Tito could be found who could keep the forces for unity in the country flowing, an opposite movement started and nationalism in all parts became stronger with the richer regions aiming to become independent and not have to share their wealth with the poorer majority. And the majority of Serbs, finding it impossible to unite the country by persuasion, turned more and more to try to achieve this by force. As always in such circumstances other problems raised their heads which later on were those between Yugoslavia and Greek Macedonia involving a member of the European Union. There was also the

'Albanian problem' in the Kosovo region and the fact that the Bosnian problem had now changed from a 'Turkish' problem into an 'Islamic problem'. The major European powers showed themselves entirely unable to understand the situation at a time when the 'moral power' of the EU could have still made a difference and been accepted, if it had shown a promise of improvement to each of the groupings involved. When the situation had deteriorated to a military situation, it helped to think of the very clear explanations of Oberst H. who had described to me that even the large Forces of the Nazi Army South/East, of something like 30 divisions, could not really conquer and pacify the Yugoslav region. Nothing had really fundamentally changed. The hatred and desire for revenge that had made the situation so bitter in the 1940s had been re-awakened and the European powers had not understood and not taken the necessary action when there was still time.

An interrogation which gave a very different kind of information came to light when we discovered that an Army major had been dealing in an official capacity with money transfers from and to Switzerland during most of the war. I believe he was a lawyer in civilian life who knew a great deal about international law. According to his statements the German authorities controlled firms in Switzerland, some possibly ultimately owned by organisations like Krupp, I G Farben and Opel. There were other firms in Switzerland who in turn were ultimately owned by Dupont, the ICI, General Motors etc. It was his job to see to it that the dividend which accrued during the war years from the profits of the mutual shareholdings should reach the shareholders across the 'enemy lines'. He gave quite a few details and stated that his efforts were on the whole successful and as far as he was aware none of the multinationals involved suffered any serious losses from the fact that their holdings were the other side of the enemy lines. We completed our reports and handed them over of course without any possibility of verifying any of these statements. As the German firms in question were by then under Allied control and often Allied management it is unlikely that the truth of these reports would ever be published, and it must therefore remain entirely my own personal opinion, that it seems unlikely that the German Army major in question would have invented everything, particularly as it could not have brought him any personal advantage, that I could see.

During 1946 various German officers managed to be released from the Soviet prisoner of war camps and cross over into the British zone. One fairly high ranking officer arrived with both his German *Soldbuch* (paybook) and a Soviet identity document written in Russian. The name on the Soviet slip bore no resemblance to the spelling on the German documents but was a phonetic transcription of the way the Russian clerk interpreted the name. The officer suspected that his name was on a Soviet wanted list, possibly for war crimes, which was why he had crossed over to the British zone as soon as possible. When we asked him how it had come about that he had been released when his name was on a wanted list, particularly as in view of his rank he should not have been released at all, he replied that he had removed his badges of rank, and as there was nobody in the camp who could read Latin writing nobody could understand what it said in his paybook. We questioned him in greater detail about the conditions in the PoW camps and his reports we could verify later from other reports: As the number of Soviet soldiers guarding the camp was very low, any administration and record keeping was extremely difficult. There was even difficulty in keeping records of the number of prisoners in the camp and in view of the numerous movements in that period they had quite some difficulty in anticipating the right number of rations required. As the authorities issuing the rations had the same administrative difficulties prisoners sometimes went hungry, neither from any bad intention nor because of a basic lack of food but mainly from this lack of organisational ability to establish the correct numbers. When we had verified this situation from other interrogations, we could believe that the possibility of identifying the name, rank and previous record of prisoners was rather limited.

During all these interrogations I never came across a single case of cruelty or crime that was inflicted on prisoners from any central plan or by a higher authority. No prisoners were ever starved by intention, although inefficiency and corruption must have accounted for a fair number of cases.

This contrasted very much with the treatment of PoWs on the Eastern Front and in concentration camps by the German forces and the Nazi Party, where all ill treatment seems to have been planned with amazing efficiency from the centre.

Prisoners who had lived in Siberia and for various reasons had been recruited into the German forces told us about the Soviet scheme to make the population literate in backward areas. The region was divided into definite areas of a certain number of square kilometres, which would justify the building of a primary school for a definite number of children. If there were more children than this number, this was just unfortunate; they could not benefit from this drive for literacy. The school itself had a given number of teachers and an absolutely fixed curriculum. The right books for this curriculum were provided. A number of such primary school areas qualified for a secondary school with an equally standardised programme. At that stage universities or other tertiary education were planned but according to the people we spoke to, none had yet been put into practice. How far these rigid plans were really adhered to we did not find out, but it left us with a realisation of what tremendous effort the Soviets had to make to develop the country to the standard of a Western European country and we ended up with an even greater admiration for the achievement of the Soviet war effort which in spite of these difficulties had managed to keep 300 German

Divisions (about 3 million front line soldiers and 21 million men in the supply columns) at bay from 1941 till 1944 and finally gain the upper hand at Stalingrad.

Under these circumstances it is not surprising that the Soviet forces could not supply their prisoners with any more than the basic necessities and that there was plenty of room for organisational mishaps and corruption which brought hardship. These rumours of 'Soviet atrocities' and the rumours of the luxuries that were available in American camps made all Germans very keen to be captured by the Western Allies rather than the Soviets. The German Military Command was still hoping that by surrendering to the West it would be possible to avoid 'unconditional surrender', particularly as certain rumours of the negotiations which the organisers of the 'Hitler *Putsch*' of July 1944 had had with American Intelligence in Switzerland filtered through, and filled the officers with hope that a war against the Soviets together with the Western Allies might become a possibility. They therefore encouraged these rumours and withdrew as quickly as possible on the Eastern Front during the last two months of the war.

According to some German officers the retreat of some German Armoured Divisions in Saxony was covered by American fighters so that they could surrender to American forces rather than the Soviets. This rumour, as far as I know, reached Soviet Intelligence. Together with other such rumours and a few actual anti-Soviet acts this seems to have created the background for the 'Cold War' long before any reports of such a possibility appeared in the press. As the Soviet fears of an attack by the Western powers after what the Soviets considered unprovoked attacks in 1920/21, and the breach of the treaty of Alliance between the Soviet Union, France and the 'Little Entente' which was supported by Britain, was very well known by all Intelligence and Diplomatic Services, it will always remain a mystery to me why no measures were taken by the West to allay the fears of the Soviets that the Allies might make a separate peace with Germany; or if such measures were taken, why they were not published.

One of the intriguing questions at the end of the war was the fate of Hitler and his immediate entourage. The unravelling of this question was like a detective story, which gave me very interesting moments apart from the basic question itself. One was an interview with a major general who was in charge of the communications between the Führer's Bunker and Himmler's HQ in Northern Germany. On 30 April 1945, he tried to make contact and suddenly the Führer himself was on the line. He described the conversation verbatim and at the moment of the mention of the words 'the Führer', his eyes lit up and this state lasted whilst he was repeating the words. Then his face took on again its normal appearance. It was then that I realised the hypnotic power that Hitler must have had on those surrounding him.

A very interesting report was the description of Major Freytag-Von-

Loringhofen who was one of the last persons to leave the Bunker and who brought Hitler's testament to the West. All these details are described in *The Last Days of Hitler*, by H.R. Trevor-Roper (Macmillan & Co 1947).

Freytag-Von-Loringhofen described in detail how he took off on the 'Avus', the race track leading from Central to West Berlin. I had been taken on this road a number of times as a boy and also on my way to Cuba on 11 May 1939. To hear the exact details of this officer's take-off almost exactly six years later, which I could so clearly picture in my mind's eye, was a moment which is still with me, in great clarity.

I have already mentioned the Luftwaffe officer who was the representative of the Air Force in Hitler's Bunker, when I described the German decision about daylight attacks on Britain. He was a Bavarian who could reproduce the accent of Hitler as he came from just over the border in Austria. He was the only person I have met who was not influenced by the hypnotic power of Hitler and who had preserved his sense of humour. He had a very good memory and was able to give a great deal of the conversations that took place and reproduce certain parts of Hitler's actions and speech verbatim, complete with gestures and table thumping which was quite hilarious. In a way it was quite pathetic that the man who planned to conquer the world and who made millions of people tremble should end his life in a cellar quite detached from real life and any real power, still continuing his speeches as if he controlled the destiny of the greatest power of his age, finally ending his life with his closest followers according to some imaginary Teutonic *Götterdämmerung* (Twilight of the Gods).

These interrogations took place in one of the huts within a prisoner of war compound for high ranking officers. In order to get a relaxed atmosphere only two interrogation officers were present and some tea was brought as well as numerous cigarettes offered. No notes were taken during these discussions and we sat around a table in a quite informal way. As I have said before, this Luftwaffe officer had kept his sense of humour and hearing all the bombastic speeches and orders with many gestures and other details as they took place one week before the unconditional surrender of the Third Reich was at once hilarious, tragic, unbelievable, a tremendous relief that these terrible war years had now ended, and yet just a report to be written and handed in. Once again this was a moment of tremendous contrast that seemed to reappear in my life at certain times.

CHAPTER 23

A Historical Perspective

LATER INTERROGATIONS were to a large extent concerned with war crimes committed by the Nazi organisation and the Holocaust, and the preparation of material for the war crimes trials.

Before going into these details it may perhaps be of interest if I described our way of life during that particular period. In the early period we lived with the troops guarding the PoW camps although we usually had some separate accommodation and only joined the units for meals, in my case, in the sergeants' mess. At first we lived as two interrogators in one tent. There were two kinds of German speaking personnel in PoW camps: interrogators who were Intelligence Corps personnel who only stayed in the camp for the duration of the jobs assigned to them; and interpreters who were part of the permanent staff of the camp in order to mediate between the camp Commandant and his staff and the prisoners. They knew which prisoners had abilities that would be helpful and they helped us to make our life more comfortable. A carpenter who was given some bits of wood made some camp beds for us which if hardly luxurious allowed us not to sleep on the ground which in the wet climate of Flanders was a great treat. Some hot water was organised for washing and shaving. When the system was fully developed a guard appeared with three prisoners. The head batman 'knocked' at the tent and reported that it was morning, took our boots and gave them to No. 2 to clean, and No. 3 brought the hot water. At a later stage I was billeted in a partly bombed house near another of the camps and again a team of three PoWs came to look after us and saluted smartly when we drove off to the mess for breakfast. When they saw me carry a lot of records and books which I needed for interrogation one young man made me a box with a handle to carry it like an attaché case. It was covered with black cloth. I used to carry a book in it which was a list of all suspected war criminals, and in no time it was known all over the camp that it contained that book and all PoWs showed great respect when I took it out. When it was possible to have a bath some prisoners carried water in jugs into a tin bath which was free-standing in a field with a canvas screen around. This meant that the water cooled very quickly. One of these chaps stood there and added hot water to keep the temperature steady.

The other side of all this comfort was that we often had to work long hours, sometimes twelve to fifteen hours a day because reports had to be completed when urgent matters were concerned.

At a later period dances were organised in the sergeants' mess. WAAF girls were brought in from a nearby Air Force camp which meant very nice and relaxing evenings. No need to mention that many of these girls were very good-looking and quite a few romances developed.

During 1946 when I was stationed in Belgium it became possible to go out into the nearest town and see the local sights and of course pubs and cafés. The currency was often cigarettes. For one weekly cigarette ration we could all buy the drink that we could consume in the evening, have as many local cigarettes as we could smoke and probably buy some supper as well. In Bruges there were two patisseries. One served the most delicious cream and chocolate cakes in spite of the rationing which was still in force. The other patisserie was closed and had a notice in the window: 'closed for black-marketeering'. One afternoon we found the same notice at the patisserie we had been visiting. We went to the one that had previously been closed and found that the notice had disappeared and that we could now get the delicious cakes there. Rumour had it that both places had an agreement to share the losses. In this way nobody suffered seriously, the citizens of Bruges had their delights and the law was also enforced.

After a spell when we had to work for a fairly long period for long hours my commanding officer arranged a special leave in Amsterdam. The journey from Flanders to Amsterdam took a whole day. The railway track had been repaired so that trains could pass but at certain sections the speed was restricted to almost walking pace and certain parts were still single track. Today the TGV can do this journey in well under two hours. We were welcomed on arrival by the equivalent of the WVS and given a great deal of help to see as much as possible in the few days we were there. The warmth of the welcome was quite surprising after the treatment in Flanders where the population was very much more reserved. The population of Amsterdam had obviously suffered much more during the occupation than the rural areas in Belgium. There were still much greater shortages and many essentials could only be bought with cigarettes, which was the real currency and only non-essentials could be bought with guilders. This situation was at first surprising but I soon realised it was economically very sound and therefore gave very satisfactory results. For a currency to be stable it is necessary that the number of units available remains roughly constant. This had ceased to apply to guilders where the amount of currency available could not be controlled owing to black market money and the deliberate issue of excess notes by the Nazi authorities giving inflationary factors. The number of cigarettes was more or less static, controlled by the number of Allied troops in the area and their rations. No Dutchman or for that matter anybody else on the Continent would think about smoking English or American cigarettes. It would have been like smoking pound notes. If you wanted to smoke you bought local cigarettes obtainable for a small number of British or American cigarettes, at times two to four cigarettes for a packet of twenty. The Dutch and particularly the citizens of Amsterdam who were not only extremely honest but also very well up in financial matters, soon found a way of establishing a kind of Stock Exchange which operated in the following way:

The main body of troops in the area were Canadian. Each morning at 11 a.m. a lorry arrived on the main square of Amsterdam, the Dam, and the Canadians offered cigarettes for sale against guilders. Within minutes a rate of exchange had been established for the day and by an unexplained method this became known in the area within the next quarter of an hour. As this trade was, at least theoretically, illegal, military police would parade up and down the square and soldiers trying to sell cigarettes were arrested and punished. In practice, if you observed 'the rules' this trade was tolerated. The exchange was done like this: you put a packet of twenty cigarettes into the hollow of your hand and a passing local citizen would take the packet and slip the guilders into your hands. There was no possibility of checking the amount received until you were well out of the area of the military police patrol, but I remember not a single occasion nor has any other soldier I talked to ever mentioned one, when the amount received was anything else than the correct 'rate of exchange' for the day. This honesty becomes all the more impressive when one realises that the citizens of Amsterdam were still suffering great hardships and food was still scarce.

The ravages of the war were still clearly visible. Although Amsterdam escaped any severe bomb damage the shortage of fuel was such that towards the end of the war whole buildings had been demolished to obtain firewood and the rubble that remained was still left in place. The WVS ladies arranged some sight-seeing tours for us to the Zuider Zee which was then still open to the sea (it is now called the Ijssel Meer because it has become an inland lake because the completion of the dam cuts it off from the sea). We also toured some cheese factories where we could see the machinery but very little cheese was being produced because of the shortage of milk. This visit left me with a special feeling of closeness with this city and its inhabitants. It so happened that in later life I had many occasions to return to that city and had many business dealings with its citizens. The impression and feelings I had received during this first visit never changed.

The HQ L of C was in Brussels and also for a time the place where my commanding officer was. This necessitated a fair number of visits to this town, which I got to know reasonably well. There were some interesting old buildings the well known Grande Place, a French Theatre (the Flemish one I could not understand), an Opera and innumerable cafés and restaurants although at that time there was not very much to eat. The special treat was egg and chips which was a change from Army rations. There were also occasional visits to the coast at Ostende and Blankenberghe. There was a PoW hospital where I had a number of interrogations to do at Den Haan (Le Coq) which could be combined with an hour on the beach. I was following the problems that arose between the Vlaams, the Walloons and the Bruxellois with great interest. There was a certain similarity with the Czech-Sudeten German problems that I knew from my youth, but it was all much more complicated because of the questions involving the collaborations of various groups with the Nazis during the war and the somewhat doubtful position of the King. All these happenings also helped me to understand the different type of monarchs in Belgium, the Netherlands and some Scandinavian countries. The title of the King is 'King of the Belgians'. He is thus the king of the people and not the king of the country. The King is therefore responsible to the people and the deity aspect has no meaning. The British Coronation ceremony on the other hand has a reference to King David, i.e. it links with the Divine appointment of the King by God and therefore the Monarch's responsibility to eternal laws, which are different and not changeable by man. If the population in Belgium were dissatisfied with the behaviour of the king they could therefore ask for his abdication without in any way affecting the institution of the monarchy as such.

During a visit to the castle in Gent, I suddenly realised that when the guide spoke about the enemy he meant Spain, who had occupied the Netherlands and Belgium centuries ago, and not the Germans and the Second World War which had just ended. After my attention had been drawn to this attitude I found that some of this feeling had lingered on in the national memory in general both in Belgium and in the Netherlands. When a Spanish Princess was to marry into the Royal Family a generation later, I could therefore understand the fears of some reaction by the people to this event.

A friend of mine in Huddersfield had located a young relative of a friend of his who was still in the former concentration camp of Bergen-Belsen and had asked me to bring her some extra food and clothing, as I was stationed not far away. So on the eve of the Jewish New Year's Day 1946 I went with a friend in my unit to visit her and bring her a parcel. She was a girl who had been about eighteen years old when war broke out. She had lived somewhere in central Europe before the war and managed to escape to Belgium. She had lived there in the early part of the war and towards the end was sent to the camp at Belsen. Her parents and any other relatives she knew about had perished as 90 per cent of all Jews in these circumstances had done. She was not very willing to talk about the details and we obviously did not ask further questions. She had no relatives anywhere and the

Belgian authorities would not allow her to return to Belgium as she had no Belgian nationality and there were no papers to show any other citizenship. So she had to live in the camp another year and a half, hoping that somebody would eventually give her a permit to live in some country and become an ordinary human being again. There were several hundred people still living in the camp in a similar situation, a number of them because they had contacted TB or another incurable disease which was a reason to refuse a permit to any country in the world. The people were housed in the former SS barracks, which were solid even if cheerless buildings. They told us that the food was good and adequate. The guards at the gate were mainly there to keep any unwanted elements out rather than the people in. They were allowed out but had to report back in the evening. This particular evening there was a particular feeling of expectation and anticipation, replacing the usual feeling of depression and hopelessness, because there was to be a religious service in the evening of the Jewish New Year held by some rabbi who was specially coming to the camp for this occasion.

The service was held in the open in a field within the camp area as there was no hall big enough to hold all the people. It was a rather emotional occasion for me as well as for the occupants. These were also the first high holidays I had celebrated since I had received official confirmation that my parents had perished at Osvečín (Auschwitz). I was therefore not an objective observer, and I could hardly feel proud about the efforts of all the Allied institutions who allowed these people still to be here eighteen months after the end of the war, stateless, without the rights of ordinary human beings to pursue a normal way of life, when they were the pitiful remnants after six million of their people had been killed by the Nazis, and many more had suffered great hardships even if they had escaped with their lives. It was clear that nobody had planned the suffering and hopelessness of the people in this camp, but that this has happened because it had not been foreseen and no authority was charged with the solution of these problems or had been given any power to take effective action.

During the course of 1946 the emphasis of our interrogations moved towards investigations of historical importance, the possibility of preventing any subversive movements within the new Germany and later the pre-selection of possible war criminals. There was of course no strict dividing line between these different tasks and they overlapped all the time.

Our unit was now in central Germany and had expanded so that the captain in charge of our unit had been promoted to major, which entitled him to a batman, and the interrogation teams received the help of some secretaries attached from the Control Commission in Germany. We were billeted in a former German *Gasthaus* and for security reasons had a special mess where all ranks were together in one mess. This led to some extraordinary and extremely unusual moments by Army standards. We ate at little tables for four people. On one occasion I sat with a chap of Italian background and the rank of lance corporal at one table. I held at that time the rank of 'acting company sergeant major'. In the middle of the meal a brigadier entered, the highest-ranking Intelligence Corps officer I had ever seen. Seeing that the only empty place was at our table, without batting an eyelid he sat down with us. The conversation between the Corporal P. and the brigadier discussing the whole course of the war in Europe and what plans should be followed for the organisation of post war Europe was one of the most extraordinary events anybody could imagine taking place in a British Army mess.

There were few Army units in the area at the time but there was a military hospital and on one occasion we were invited for dinner by the officers' mess of that unit. How to reciprocate? We discovered that one of the prisoners in one of the camps had been a chef in the Hotel Adlon in Berlin. This was *the* five star luxury hotel in that town. He was 'seconded' to our mess as 'assistant to our Army cook' and charged with the task of producing a meal worthy of reciprocation for the hospitality we had received from the medics. After three or four weeks of saving the relevant parts of our ration and the odd excursion under guard into a nearby village by our 'assistant cook', he produced a six course meal, which after years of Army rations tasted to all the medics and us as good as the meal at the Adlon must have tasted to their regulars. Everybody agreed it was a memorable occasion.

Our HQ was now in Hamburg which caused various visits to that city. It was a strange feeling coming back to the town where at the age of six I had come to meet my father from his journey to South America and where I had been when I was leaving the Nazi area in 1939. In 1944/5 I had to study the aerial photographs of the bombing in order to check interrogations about what had taken place. Now we were driving through the suburbs where the rubble had been piled up on both sides to clear a road through. The centre of the city was in relatively better shape and the various units we had to deal with were in that area.

The *Putsch* of July 1944: on 20 July 1944 Count Stauffenberg together with a number of officers and some left wing politicians made an attempt to rid Germany of the regime of Hitler and the Nazi party. The Count threw a bomb at Hitler at the headquarters in Eastern Germany and managed to escape in the confusion that followed the explosion. He managed to contact his associates at the Army War Office in Berlin reporting the success of his mission: the plan of taking over control of Berlin and subsequently the whole of the armed forces. In fact Hitler had not been killed but was only slightly wounded. It took well over twenty-four hours until the true situation emerged and Hitler's regime took over control again. For us the period until the details were established and the interrogation of any prisoners who had taken part in this *Putsch* and its defeat was of course very exciting, until finally we interrogated the officer who had in fact managed to put the revolt down. It was a Major Remer who was the Commandant of an Army battalion that had the task of guarding certain important buildings in Berlin, and his report was roughly as follows.

On the day in question he was arriving to take up his guard duty when he was told that the Führer had been killed and a group of officers in Berlin were taking over command. This sounded strange to him, so he placed his troops in such a way that he could control the building and went to a telephone and rang Goebbels whom he considered would be the 2nd in Command and asked him the following question, which I quote verbatim in German: *'Stehen Sie, Herr Reichsführer noch hinter dem Führer und kann ich mich auf Sie noch verlassen?'* Which translated means: 'Do you, Mr Reichs-leader, still stand behind the Führer, and can I still have confidence in you?' One has to picture the extraordinary situation when a major asks the 2nd in Command of the country whether he is still loyal to the leader. Goebbels answered that he was still loyal to the Führer who was alive and only lightly injured and he would arrange that Remer could talk to him. He talked to the Führer and received direct orders to put any rebellion down. He returned to his troops, arrested all the rebellious officers in the War Office building and took over until reinforcements arrived. By nightfall all was again under the control of the old Army command. Remer described the rebellious officers whom he had arrested as 'elderly incompetent fools'. What he felt against them was mainly a disdain for inefficiency and he detested the lack of plan and the fact that they were so unsuccessful. Remer himself had no 'Party' connection and I had the feeling that he held no other strong views than being a good professional officer and his desire to be faithful to the ideal of being a strong and obedient officer. He never voiced any preference for the Army but was only concerned as to who had given him the legal order which he was honour bound to obey.

He was considered a dangerous person who could start a resistance movement if he were released. I came to the conclusion that he was certainly capable enough to organise such a movement but would only do this if he became convinced that it was the 'honourable and right' thing to do.

Although most of the leaders of this *Putsch* were arrested by the Nazi Party security organisations and a large number of them executed, officers who were on the outer fringe of this movement or had played a role which had not become obvious on 20 July had escaped the investigation by the Nazis that followed. From them we could build up a good picture of the movement that had led to the attempt to take over the rule in Germany after the death of Hitler and the demise of the central leaders of the Nazi party. Apart from factual evidence of who had been arrested and executed objective evidence was very difficult to establish. Very much information was based on opinion of the officer concerned as well as hearsay and rumours. A great deal of the activities many of these officers had been involved in had been illegal at the time, in the early years as breaches of the Treaty of Versailles, and later against the legislation and the rules of the Nazi regime. I have neither had sufficient access to official records nor did the interrogations I was involved in make it possible for me to form an objective picture. I will therefore give my personal subjective view of events.

From the time when in the early part of the nineteenth century the various parts of the German Kingdoms, Dukedoms, Counties etc. became united, the officers of the Kaiser-Reich became an important force somewhat independent from other political developments of the country. In some mysterious way, rarely directly expressed, they felt themselves to be the successors of the 'German Order of Knights' of the eleventh century, the first heroes of the expansion to the east against the hordes of Asia. Valour and honour were the most important qualities and to achieve this, a great deal of discipline and strength was required. These particular obligations set them apart from 'ordinary people' and I think that this was the beginning of the idea of a *Herrenvolk* (master race), the idea of people having different obligations towards the community and therefore the *right* to rule. A substantial number of the officers of the late eighteenth and early nineteenth centuries came from the land-owning families of East Prussia and other eastern provinces of Germany who played similar roles to the Lords of the Manor in England. When at the end of the nineteenth century and the beginning of the twentieth the German forces under the Kaiser were organised into a very formidable and efficient war machine it was this officer class that was the backbone of the scheme. There was a corresponding difference amongst the industrial and administrative classes of the fast expanding armament production, shipbuilding and other industries preparing for war. It was politically supported by the Deutsche National Partei (German National Party). This name was in the inter war years always translated as 'Conservative Party' which was extremely misleading as the British Conservative Party shared none of the ideas of the *Herrenvolk* in the German sense nor did it ever subscribe to aggression and conquest by large military forces. British colonial expansion was an entirely different development.

When Germany was defeated in the First World War and the land owning classes of the Eastern areas suffered in the chaos that followed the Bolshevik revolution, the classes who had supported the expansionist views of this German National Party, together with the former officer class, turned in the direction of revenge for the defeats suffered. This group were far too intelligent to show any resistance outwardly against the centre and left wing parties, who genuinely supported the Weimar Republic and co-operation with Western Europe, but it was in this early period (1923) that the expansion and training of officers was arranged with the Soviets in contravention of the peace treaty of Versailles. They left the demonstrations and agitation to the newly formed NSDAP (National Socialistische Deutsche Arbeiter Partei) (National Socialist German Workers Party).

After the elections of 1933 the German National Party made a coalition with the Nazi Party and Hitler became Chancellor with von Papen as Vice Chancellor. The complete disregard of any democratic process soon brought the Nazi party into complete control of the political process and Germany became a dictatorship that had to rely on the paramilitary forces of the SA and SS to enforce the will of the party. The German National Party lost the control agreed upon after the 1933 elections. They still supported the idea of 'Gross Deutschland' which aimed at a Germany which would include the Rheinland which was then still occupied by the Western powers, the Saar area, Austria, the Sudeten area of Czechoslovakia, large parts that were Poland at the time and, at the right time, the rest of the Slav countries west of Russia. They opposed however the acquisition of these areas by war, if it led to the danger of a war on two fronts i.e. both with the Soviet Union and with the Western powers. The high ranking officers and many of the general staff were of the opinion right up to 1939 that Germany was not yet ready for a war for a number of years.

The Nazi Party gained more and more support in the country by playing alternately to various directions in the name of their party. They were successful playing the 'National' card by making people feel good by raising the self-esteem and the belief in the restoration of the power of Germany in Europe. They got the support of the workers by the employment situation, which became possible owing to the re-armament that was taking place, and the support of the middle classes by their strongly anti-Communist line. This was supported by more and more unconstitutional arrests and the sending of political opponents to concentration camps. The cost of all these manoeuvres was assisted by the confiscation of Jewish property which followed each campaign, raising hatred against minorities and increasing the feel-good factor.

Only the Army remained in some ways independent from the direct control of the Party. Hitler in the end gained the acquiescence of the Army by appointing less traditional officers to the command, who would obey even the most radical orders. After the great success of the German Armed Forces in the West in 1940 even the more conservative officers were inclined to feel that they had been wrong in opposing the war, that Britain would now collapse and their dream of the destruction of the Soviet Union with the help of the defeated powers of France and Britain would soon become a reality. This mood continued during the early part of the campaign in Russia which brought great advances of the German forces towards the North Caucasian region and their oil wells.

After the entry of the United States into the war and the large number of casualties due to frost bite during the severe winter, it became clear to many officers that victory could only be brought about by either a coalition with the Western powers or at least by a separate peace with the West. It was clear that this could never be brought about whilst Hitler was in power. A number of Army officers therefore made secret contacts about how this could be achieved and which like minded people could be brought into this movement. They were joined by a few liberal and left wing personalities, including the former Mayor of Leipzig and other people known for their anti-Hitler attitudes from the pre-war period. A number of Secret Service officers (*Abwehr*) were also interested in this move and contacted their opposite numbers in American intelligence in Geneva and Allan Dulles to take part in these talks. Major Remer was quite right when he said the revolt was very badly handled at the War Office in Berlin and the Nazi Party Security Organisations very soon had the situation in hand and ruthlessly shot any of the officers who had either been connected with the *Putsch* or were suspected of having done so. The head of the Abwehr, General Canaris, was one of the victims. The party now took detailed control of the Army Security Services. As they were rather inexperienced in handling the information service, it seemed that it became less efficient and contacts abroad were sometimes lost.

It would appear that these events made a separate peace an impossibility as there were no German groups left who could undertake such negotiations with any hope of being able to carry out any commitments made.

The result of this was that the danger of a split between the Western Allies and the Soviet Union was avoided at that time and thus the possibility of a third world war following immediately after the second.

The unconditional surrender of all German forces now became a likelihood and with that the possibility of building a new democratic Germany within the framework of a new Europe where no one power would again have the ability to force the whole of Europe and the whole Western world into a general and total war.

Perhaps this view of the importance of the events of 20 July 1944 is not the one generally held, but I have never found anything that caused me to change my view of these events.

Even the 'Cold War' that followed at least remained 'cold' and the tremendous destruction and loss of life that a hot war in the atomic age would possibly have brought was avoided.

CHAPTER 24

Preparation for War Crime Trials, and Return to Czechoslovakia

GRADUALLY INTERROGATIONS became more and more concerned with the Holocaust and the preparation for War Crimes trials. Our direct information came from German soldiers who had been at some stage drafted to guard concentration camp prisoners, largely those who escorted them daily from the camp to the place of work. Time and time again they described the process of starving prisoners to death in a scientifically calculated way to obtain the maximum of working hours for the minimum of food. The guards knew that this process was going on and became experts in telling the stages of starvation and estimating how many more days they were likely to escort a particular prisoner.

In one instance I interrogated a schoolteacher, then about forty years of age, who was directed to these escort duties. He remembered the names of a number of prisoners, their former professions and occupations and could in some cases remember topics he had discussed with certain people. He could describe the time when they collapsed on the march to or from the factory and how he had laid them down by the side of the road for a later patrol to pick up and bring into the camp. He showed no sign of emotion in making these reports. When he was asked later whether he realised that he had assisted in the killing of these people, his first reaction was genuine surprise. No such thought had ever occurred to him. When I saw him several days later he had begun to realise what process he had taken part in, his mind had become confused and he kept apologising to the people he had helped to kill, even though it was quite clear that they were dead. This state lasted for some days whilst he was in the same prison camp. Then he was moved and I do not know whether this condition was now permanent or whether he later returned to a more balanced state of mind.

From this and other examples we could establish that such marches of concentration camp prisoners was routine in all 'Labour Camps' and that these marches went along ordinary roads and were seen by the local population. They continued during the whole period of the war. The people in those areas were aware what was going on, even if they did not know any details. Had they spoken about it they would have probably themselves landed in a KZ (*Konzentrations Lager*, a word that had become a well known expression in the German language of the time and had been known from 1933/4 onwards). Any statement by

Germans that they did not know that concentration camps existed is therefore untrue. The horror that took place in these camps was so unbelievable that nobody who was not an eyewitness could believe it when he was told the truth. The enormity of the crimes was of such a magnitude that any more or less normal person refused to believe it. As far as possible they tried to reject it and close their minds to it as it was nearly impossible to realise the magnitude of these crimes and remain a sane human being.

When one takes into account that from 1933 onwards the population was under ever increasing propaganda that the pure Germanic dream race was essentially good and could or would do no wrong whilst the minority races, be it Jews, Gypsies or some Slavs were essentially evil and were therefore always criminals and wrong, one begins to realise how it was possible that the knowledge about the camps and the atrocities remained 'secret'. It was part of the dream that had spread so effectively. The combination of fanaticism, a kind of hypnotic-religious belief in the Führer, the wishful thinking that everything might be put right by eliminating the culprits, and the impossibility for any human mind to accept the reality of such inconceivable cruelty made this disease almost universal. This was the only way I could explain to myself this phenomenon of such extreme cruelty so obvious to any more or less normal person.

It was a quite different problem with the people who planned the genocide. This appears to have been done in a cold calculating way that defies any normal human reaction and way of thinking. If one met any of these planners they appeared very ordinary people, very often without any personal courage. I am of course not talking about the people on top whom I never met. It was the 'ordinariness' of most of these planners of the mass murders that made the War Crimes Trials such a difficult process. There was no law to deal with this situation. It all had to be dealt with under the ordinary law of murder. Only in exceptional circumstances did any officer with real authority in concentration camps carry out these inhuman crimes personally. In the vast majority of cases the planners of the genocides were a kind of 'bureaucrat' behind the scenes, whilst the actual murders and other crimes were carried out under 'orders from higher command'. Any disobedience to military orders in wartime was punishable by death. Fear and the 'disease' that I have described earlier brought about the situation in which some six million Jews, a large percentage of the Gypsies and other minorities as well as many Russians and political opponents of the regime were slaughtered. It was estimated that more than 20 million people lost their lives in other than military actions. It is of course impossible to obtain accurate figures as in some cases whole villages and towns were wiped out and there were either no survivors, or they were scattered and fear prevented them from speaking up.

The pre-selection for the War Crimes Trials took place in a kind of 'court procedure' where interrogation officers submitted the 'evidence', i.e. the interrogation report, in writing, without being personally present. The PoWs were then questioned by the 'court' which consisted of officers generally of the equivalent rank of colonel, who had not been trained for the task, frequently had no knowledge of German, and often were unaware of anything that had been happening away from the battlefields. In one case where I knew the details, the officer in charge asked the interpreter after three days of proceedings: 'Tell me, what is this NSDAP they keep talking about?' In other words, the person in charge of the pre-selection of cases of genocide was unaware of the existence of the Nazi Party.

The result of this method therefore could not bring many real culprits to justice. Some relatively minor persons were convicted as long as one murder could be proven in court.

There seemed to me to be little correlation between atrocities where a murder trial appears appropriate, and the situation we were dealing with, the killing of millions of people by a central plan, where the 'murderers' were not the real villains, but the guilty were the planners behind the scenes. Although this problem was vaguely voiced at the time, no government was willing to propose a new legal system which would allow the real culprits to be brought to justice and also for justice to be seen to be done.

The War Crimes Trials that followed could deal with the people at the absolute top of the Nazi Party. Both the populations in the victorious countries as well as the average people amongst the Axis Powers could agree that these people were criminals, and deserved to die or be imprisoned for a long time. When it came to the military commanders of the Wehrmacht, it was already a question which was more difficult to define. 'Aggression' had never been legally defined as a crime equivalent to murder. How far had the military commanders exceeded the behaviour of a soldier? All German officers were of course fully aware that ever since Bismarck the professional Officer Corps had supported the idea of 'Gross Deutschland'. The exact establishment of the borders of this Greater Germany had never been defined and was in any case not a matter of basic principles. Most officers I spoke to detested Keitel and Jodl and when these two Generals were condemned to death these officers felt that the fate was deserved, but for rather different reasons than those put forward by the War Crimes Court. They considered them militarily second rate, and therefore responsible for the inefficient conduct of the war. The two Generals had given in to Hitler's demands even when these contradicted the code of the German General Staff and their actions were therefore unworthy of that of a German officer. They had agreed to co-operate too freely with the Party organisations that lacked the principles a German officer should follow. In this sense they condemned the atrocities committed by the Party organisations and their methods. I have never heard any officer condemn the 'Final Solution' itself, but only the methods employed, and perhaps the fact that this was achieved by murder. I probably discussed these questions with approximately one hundred officers from all three services, and this seems to have been their general view.

At the end of the war, a number of middle aged officers, beyond the age suitable for front line service, who had been stationed in the fortifications of the ports on the Atlantic Coast, were very upset that German forces were accused of war crimes. They collected evidence of similar actions committed by Allied troops in the heat of action. And from all the evidence I have seen, actions committed by regular German Army troops did not differ very greatly from actions taken by any other army in front line engagements. It was of course a quite different situation when the Nazi Party organisation, particularly the SS, was compared.

Owing to the legal situation it was very difficult for anybody who had not specially studied the Holocaust to distinguish between just ordinary breaches of the Geneva Convention and the mass murders of the Holocaust.

During 1946 we were daily investigating people who were suspected of thousands of murders in concentration camps and during 'transport' of concentration camp prisoners. I was given a memo from Churchill's office concerning the treatment of eight Canadian officers who allegedly had been manacled at some time when they were PoWs in contravention of the Geneva Convention. I took no action and a short time later I got a second memo asking for a report on the first request. I answered that when we had completed the investigation of millions of murders we would deal with the complaint of the eight Canadian officers. I wondered whether I would be taken to task and perhaps a court martial for disobedience would follow. This however was the last I heard of this request. Somebody at HQ obviously realised that these two matters were of a different level and that genocide could not be dealt with in the same way as some infringement of a convention, however regrettable the latter might be.

An interesting investigation took place in a PoW camp in Belgium some time during 1946 when the German other ranks PoWs were employed in clearing the mines along the coastline which their army had planted there during the war. They were driven by lorry to the coast in the morning, worked an eight-hour day and returned to camp in the evening. It was rather strenuous physical work. They were generally in good health, and on the whole were putting on weight, being given the standard PoW rations.

In another compound of this camp were officers with an average age of fifty to fifty-five, generally of the rank of lieutenant colonel and upwards. Almost every day one or two of these officers reported sick showing signs of starvation. They were on exactly the same allocation of rations as the other ranks.

The obvious first thought of the camp commandant was that some rations were somehow disappearing into the black market and that some prisoners were being deprived of the right amounts. An Intelligence Team was therefore sent into this compound to check the amount of the food actually handed out and to talk to the prisoners to see whether any reason for this could be found. The medical officers confirmed that the signs of starvation were genuine but that they had observed the German senior officers eating the allocated quantity of food.

It was from a very senior German medical officer who we traced in another camp in the area, that we got the pointer to the answer to this question. As Major General he had been in charge of the medical services of a large area on the Russian front from 1942 to 1944. He put it to us that the reason could be as follows. Most of the other ranks who were now clearing the mines had served for long periods on the front line in Russia and had undergone great physical hardship. Owing to the supply difficulties they had often had to survive on meagre and irregular rations. There was of course the factor that only the really fit ones had survived to be now PoWs in the West, where with regular and adequate food they could not only work a full day but even put on weight under these conditions.

A large number of the senior officers in the other camp had spent the same period of time working in headquarter establishments behind the front line in far less strenuous physical conditions with regular and full rations as the supplies there posed few problems. Their bodies had therefore never become accustomed to subsisting on insufficient food. He had in his time at the Soviet Front also had to investigate problems relating to lack of food for Soviet PoWs in German camps and he was of the opinion that a young and healthy body can learn to digest 'with greater efficiency'. He compared it to a steam engine. Efficient ones will convert about 40 per cent of the energy, whilst inefficient ones will lose more and only convert about 30 per cent. In the same way a young and healthy body will learn to convert more calories from the same amount of food, particularly if the process goes on for a long time and the reduction is rather gradual. He had investigated this problem in the East as the German Command wanted to know why Soviet soldiers fought well in spite of very small rations. This applied particularly to the people in the east of the Soviet Union such as Khazaki, Turkmeni and Kyrgysi, where the normal standard of living was very low. These investigations came to the conclusions that this 'efficiency factor' could be increased in young recruits (normally between the ages of eighteen and twenty-one).

Concerning the older officers he suggested that after the age of about forty-five this 'change of efficiency' was no longer possible. And this difficulty was aggravated by the fact that most of these officers came from social classes which could afford any amount of food and had been over-eating for many years. Their metabolism had, at their present age, become permanently 'inefficient'.

We made these suggestions to the Medical Officer at the camp infirmary, who established in controlled experiments that these officers needed nearly double the normal PoW rations to keep a balanced healthy weight.

One consequence of this investigation was that I could never believe again in any of the 'health' theories' recommendations that you should eat so many calories for breakfast and so many for lunch. The question of the natural 'efficiency' of a person is probably one of the most important factors in establishing a healthy diet. This efficiency can only be altered gradually in young people and not at all after the age of forty-five. In the half century since this investigation I have found nothing to contradict this, and we have brought up four healthy children with differing but always healthy eating habits.

In the course of these talks this General also spoke about various other questions where this combination of military and medical responsibility gave his views a special value. One of the interesting discussions was about homosexuality. In an army that was far away from home with very limited possibilities of home leave this was bound to become a problem. The Nazi Party doctrine in this matter was that homosexuals were criminals who should be sent to concentration camps and preferably exterminated. This caused of course a lot of fear and anxiety, which was bad, both from the human angle and for the efficiency of a fighting force. He was therefore of the opinion that it was best to take as little action as possible whilst the unnatural conditions of an army away from home existed. On return home the possibilities of normal heterosexual behaviour should be supported and helped by suitable lectures. In his experience the vast majority of soldiers very soon returned to normal behaviour. In the small minority who persisted in homosexual behaviour this should be treated as an illness to which anybody could be prone but which did not require punishment. In this way it could be avoided that this problem became an emotional issue.

Thinking about these talks during the following fifty years I have often thought that, had this become the general view of the Western world, a great deal of suffering on the one hand and a wrong type of 'self expression' on the other hand might have been avoided.

During 1946 I had been officially informed by the Red Cross that my parents had not returned and that the last official record was their arrival in the concentration camp Osvěčín (Auschwitz) in 1942 and that they must therefore be considered to have perished in that camp. This news was hardly unexpected after all the information I had been in contact with, particularly from the second half

```
BRITISH MILITARY ATTACHÉ
COLONEL G. J. de W. MULLENS, OBE.
```
                                                    BRITISH EMBASSY,
                                                    THUNOVSKÁ 14,
                                                    PRAGUE III.

                                                    10th January, 1947.

TO WHOM IT MAY CONCERN.

    THIS IS TO CERTIFY that 13117689 Sgt. A. HAAS is on compassionate leave in Czechoslovakia.

    It is requested that local authorities will give him assistance and that ration cards may be issued for 16 days.

                                                    Colonel,
                                            Military Attaché,
                            British Embassy to Czechoslovakia.

POTVRZENI.

    ze Sgt. A. HAAS se nachazi v Ceskoslovensku na dovolene.

    Zadame urady, aby mu vychazely laskave vstric a aby byly vydany potravinnove listky na 16 dnu.

                                                    Colonel,
                                            Vojensky Attache,
                            Britske Velvyslanectvi V ČSR.

Certification of compassionate leave.

of 1944 onwards. It was obviously a shock and I felt at that moment particularly alone in this world. In another way I felt very strongly that there was no change in my real relationship with my parents and this feeling has in no way changed in the half century that has elapsed since then.

I was of course very interested to find out what I could about the last years of my parents' life and get to know who of my friends and more distant family had survived. When it became possible in the last quarter of 1946 to obtain compassionate leave to go to Czechoslovakia I obviously applied and very soon received my leave pass.

The train journey along the bank of the Rhine which was one of the unfulfilled dreams of my childhood was all the more beautiful because so unexpected. The stay in an American transit camp in Nuremberg highlighted once again the different attitudes of the American and British forces: syrup and waffles for breakfast, white sheets on your bed, but had I been a member of the US Forces I would have had to pay $3.00 for all this. Then came the train from Nuremberg to Prague, which took nearly twice as long as it had taken before the war. In the compartment with me were two English girls who were teaching English in Prague at the time and were returning from holiday, and an officer of the Czech Brigade who had been recruited in Britain during the war. The conversation was therefore in English all the time and the only reminder that I was going 'home' was when we came to Plzeň (Pilsen) and I heard the cry of the vendors of hot sausages (*párky*), a form of small frankfurters which were always sold on station platforms. Naturally I bought a pair.

On arrival in Prague the officer, who had been to Prague a number of times recently, said he knew a hotel where we could get reasonable rooms for the night and he made all the arrangements. The next morning at breakfast the waiter, seeing a British uniform, addressed me in English. I then had to report to the Ministry of Defence to get my leave pass stamped, which meant a tram ride. When the conductor came, I suddenly realised that I had been in the country for half a day and had not uttered a word in Czech and I found myself unable to find the words for asking for the ticket. As I was in British uniform and any foreign soldier had to report to the same place, the conductor immediately guessed where I was going and handed me the right ticket. I suppose this whole event must have taken place within two or three seconds but the agony of not being able to say this short remark in my own language appeared as a very long agony and left me stunned. I managed of course soon to make contact with my 'Czech brain' and was able to speak the language again, but this moment has remained absolutely in my memory in all its physical and emotional aspects.

I stayed for several days in Prague with an old friend who had a flat in a very central area which enabled me to re-visit some of the beautiful sites of this city,

BRITISH MILITARY ATTACHÉ
COLONEL G. J. de W. MULLENS, OBE.

BRITISH EMBASSY,
THUNOVSKÁ 14,
PRAGUE III.

25th January, 1947.

<u>MOVEMENT ORDER for 13117689 Sgt. HAAS, A.</u>

The above named N.C.O. is returning to his unit in B.A.O.R. from compassionate leave in Czechoslovakia as authorised by BAOR/3747/114/A(PS2) dated 31 December 1946.

It is requested that all military authorities will give him assistance to enable him to return to his unit.

Colonel,
Military Attaché,
<u>British Embassy to Czechoslovakia.</u>

Movement Order for my return to my unit.

enjoy the good food and experience once again the atmosphere even if things were a bit more subdued than in the old days and everything was more poverty-stricken.

With a certain apprehension as to what I would find I then took a train to my home town Olomouc in central Moravia. During the four hour journey I had some very interesting discussions with a clergyman of the Church of the Czek Brothers of Bohemia and Moravia, a group derived from the Protestant teaching of Jan Hus, who lived in the latter part of the fourteenth and beginning of the fifteenth century. The events of this reformation and the counter-reformation that followed have played a major part in the shaping of the development of the Czech nation, both culturally and politically. The history of the Kingdom of Bohemia, with the counties of Moravia and Silesia which formed part of it, is incomprehensible without some grasp of the events caused by the forces that shaped the events of that period and were very important in the development of the Czech language and the way of thinking that lasted and continued to dominate the attitude and actions in that Kingdom. The creation of the Czechoslovak Republic was based on this thinking and way of life.

We talked about the fact that although only about 5 per cent of the population now belonged to this church, it was the dominant factor in the way of thinking of the nation. In an amazingly clear way he was able to put before me the whole development of the revolt against the tyranny of the Church and Pope and the movement towards tolerance and what we would probably call 'democracy' today. The Pope and the Emperor were able to defeat this movement which in turn led to the next revolt which forced the revolutionaries to be as intolerant as the 'forces' of the counter revolution. Somehow this spirit of tolerance managed to reassert itself and finally bring the forces of humanism to the fore which so dominated the thought and teaching of T.G. Masaryk, the founder and later president of the Czechoslovak Republic. This clergyman maintained that whilst the resistance against Hitler and the suffering of the war years had brought a hardening of attitude he felt that the spirit of the country had not died and would reassert itself. Perhaps events in the fifty years that followed this discussion have not extinguished the hope that he may have been right. The suffering of the Czech people in the fight against Soviet oppression seems to have brought out once again the fact that the forces fighting for survival are no more tolerant than the forces they are trying to defeat. But perhaps the deeply ingrained spirit of tolerance has not died, as personified in the writer and President Václav Havel, and the way the Czech Republic was formed without any bloodshed in the parting of the ways between the area of the old Kingdom of Bohemia, and Slovakia, the former Hungarian province of Upper Hungary.

★   ★   ★

But back to the events of 1946; I arrived in Olomouc in the early evening and went to the only hotel I knew, the Národní Dům. I went into the dining room for dinner and discovered that, allowing for the shortages and difficulties of this early post war period, the food was as good as it had always been.

On the way out of the dining room I met somebody whose face was familiar, but whose name I could not recall. I was vaguely aware that he was one of the members of the Jewish community of the town. He shook my hand and spoke in a tone of voice as if it were the most natural thing that I was there, and as if it had been yesterday that he had last seen me. He said: 'Come up, we are all upstairs.' Somebody handed me a ticket, I paid a small amount of money and found myself at a masked ball. Immediately some of these masked people rushed towards me and shook my hand, embraced me and welcomed me. It took them some time before my puzzled look made them realise that I could not know who they were. And one by one they took off their masks and the real welcome started. It turned out that this was one of the first occasions when the survivors of the Holocaust were able to celebrate together and nearly all the young people who had survived had come. I guessed there were about 120 people present. The community had numbered about 3,000 in 1939.

A number of people thought my British uniform was a form of fancy dress and asked me why I came dressed up as a sergeant major. This misunderstanding was soon cleared up and the welcoming and greeting continued. One of the people who embraced me was one of my best friends, Kurt Engelmann. I had heard nothing from him or about him since I had left in 1939 and no rumour of his survival had reached me. He told me that he had a flat near the centre and that he would come the next morning to collect me at the hotel and I had to stay with him. I gladly accepted and after shaking some more hands and hearing more stories of survival, and also about those who had not come back, I left to go to my room, my head spinning with this unexpected event, wondering whether this was real or a dream.

The next morning Kurt came to fetch me and for the next two days we told each other our life stories from the days when we had last met.

Very shortly after I had gone west he started his journey east. He took a train to Slovakia and crossed on foot over the Tatra Mountains, an inhospitable mountain range reaching up to 2,600m on the border between Slovakia and Polish Galizia. He first stayed with a family whom we all knew who had come to Olomouc in the previous century when all was part of the Austro-Hungarian monarchy, and who had managed to return to this part of western Poland when Hitler occupied Bohemia and Moravia. When the war broke out and Poland was divided between German and Soviet areas he managed to escape to the eastern part. He soon acquired the necessary knowledge of Russian and joined the Soviet forces. He had studied medicine in Prague before the troubles started, and on joining stated that he had attended Prague University for five semesters. They required metallurgical experts at the time and the reason why he had been to University was considered by the Soviet authorities to be a minor detail, as long as he had attended tertiary studies. He was therefore sent as an expert to a munitions factory. I do not remember what they were producing but Kurt managed somehow to acquire the necessary skills and for a time things went on very pleasantly. The factory was somewhere in the Crimea. When the German troops were advancing and getting to south-eastern Ukraine, it was decided to evacuate the whole unit and on the journey across the sea of Azov the ship was bombed and he was wounded. He spent some weeks in a hospital somewhere in the Caucasian region. When his health was restored he was sent to a 'munitions factory' in Siberia.

The description of his life there was the most fascinating part of his report. It must be very rare that you could hear about life in that time and place from somebody from whom you can judge the meaning and significance of what is said because of your common background. We had lived as children in the same block of flats and I can remember no time when we did not know each other. We went together to primary school and the lower part of the grammar school. We experienced the pleasures and traumas of growing up together, shared the experiences of the first innocent adventures with girls and went skating, skiing and swimming. After our matric we travelled round Eastern Europe and the Mediterranean together and saw the world from the same point of view. Before I went into the forces we 'did Prague' together, the way young men did in that period. In view of this we had a very rare opportunity of sharing our experiences as much as this is ever possible and I could take part in life in Siberia as much as one ever can in a description.

Life must have been very primitive and food was always scarce. There was however a conviction that the government, in short 'they', were always doing the best that was possible and that everybody had to serve and sacrifice in order to defeat this terrible enemy and make a better life possible in the future. If the train carrying the food did not arrive because the engine had broken down, this had to be accepted. 'They' were doing their best, and if somebody suffered this was unfortunate but nobody was to blame. This attitude however did not stop them using their cunning to gain a personal advantage as long as this was done within the rules of the game. My friend managed to have an affair with one of the kitchen maids. This enabled him to scrounge a bit of extra food, which enabled him to get a better job. This new job entitled him to a ration of vodka. This vodka he did not drink but bartered it for more food, which enabled him to climb further on the ladder of more important jobs, which in turn carried a bigger vodka allocation. This enabled him not only to keep up his strength but eventually save enough roubles to obtain a train pass to the west of Russia and so he arrived by early 1945 in an area where it was possible for him to join the Czechoslovak Legion which had been formed in the Soviet Union and thus return home after the end of hostilities.

He conveyed to me, probably more by his own way of thinking than by any words, what a different world he had lived in during the past seven years and how in a certain way it had become his own world. I could experience with him the way of thinking and reacting of the people, how such words as 'democracy' or 'equality' had simply no meaning if these concepts were used in a Western sense. As propaganda slogans these and other words existed but bore no relation to the meaning of such words in the West. The Tsarist oppression which was the government by an 'enemy class' was followed by a regime which intended the right things, even if the practical improvement had been slow and was now in danger of being destroyed by the onslaught of the wicked 'Western Power'. The differentiation between the Western Powers of the US and Britain who had attacked the Soviet Union in their early struggles (1921-22) and the present attacker, namely Hitler, were rather blurred by the thirty years of propaganda that the people had been subjected to during the period in question. The relatively small number of intellectuals who had absorbed Western thought in the period before the First World War had by the time in question in any case been killed or died from natural causes and did not influence the thinking of Siberian factory workers in the last years of the war to any large extent. Both my friend and I were two years old when the Russian Revolution had started and our knowledge of the Tsarist period therefore comes from descriptions influenced either one way or the other.

We had of course both lived in a free society until 1938 and we had both experienced the betrayal of Czechoslovakia by Britain and France in 1938, and had both had access to the facts leading to the handover of the well fortified borders of that republic to Hitler, which gave the Germans unrestricted power over the whole of Central Europe. Our sources of information during the 1939-46 period were entirely different but we both came to the same conclusion about the future of Czechoslovakia. We both had decided on the basis of opposite sources of information that the Soviet Union would in the end occupy Czechoslovakia, or find another way of making it a vassal state. We both agreed that if the Western Powers were unable to help Czechoslovakia in 1938, there was no possibility that they would be either able or willing to come to its aid in the late 1940s or 1950s when the balance of power was so much worse. This assessment proved absolutely correct in following decades.

What was absolutely opposite was our personal decision about our own future.

I found more and more, as my visit proceeded, that my country of birth had become a foreign country for me, as my way of thinking had gone in a new and different direction whilst the people I was now meeting had in turn been under very different influences for seven years and thus the gap had widened from both sides.

My friend had decided that after living for all the war years in the Soviet Union and having fought part of the war in the Soviet Forces, the Western capitalist world had become strange to him. He was just finishing his studies in medicine and, once qualified, a job in the local hospital was assured to him. He had a nice flat; health service and pension were assured. He had no desire to uproot himself and suffer all the hardships of emigration and the uncertainty of a competitive life in the West.

I could understand his point of view and we decided that as soon as Czechoslovakia came under Soviet domination or occupation we would stop writing to each other in order not to cause him any difficulty. Things turned out as expected. I heard later from third parties that his life went on as he had expected but that he got married in the early sixties and that this marriage turned out to be a very unhappy one. He became a very heavy smoker and drank more than was good for him. He died in the mid 1980s, a respected member of his community.

CHAPTER 25

Back to Civvy Street

AFTER MY RETURN from compassionate leave in Czechoslovakia our work continued to be partly concerned with the preparation of war crimes trials but it became gradually clearer that emphasis was shifting gradually from the events of war to the building up of an intelligence organisation concerned with the gathering of information of happenings in the Soviet Zone of Germany. As far as we were concerned the recruitment of German Army PoWs for gathering information about the Soviet activities became our main purpose. As there was no peace treaty, the Germans were still technically the defeated enemy, and the Soviet Union was our ally, who had so importantly contributed and suffered in bringing about the defeat of this enemy. I could hardly bring a lot of enthusiasm to this task that I was now asked to assist in. I had of course learned by now that every country gathers information on all other countries whether friend or foe and that these activities are necessary. I was grateful that my task was confined to introductory interviews and that I was not asked to take any decisions.

One of my last duty journeys was to report to a colonel in Hamburg who had to interview me concerning the possibility of obtaining British citizenship. There was something rather absurd in this situation as I stood in the uniform of a sergeant-major of His Majesty's Forces in front of this officer; after all, I had dealt for years with secret matters; had held a King's Commission in the Home Guard and sworn an oath of allegiance six years earlier. I had the feeling that the interviewing officer felt about the matter exactly the same way as me but the bureaucratic formalities had to be gone through. I can not remember anything about the questions I was asked but I remember very clearly the journey from the Hanover area to Hamburg and back. It was early 1947, the coldest winter on record for very many years with plenty of snow. At one point the road was blocked for what looked like several miles with stranded vehicles. We were in a four wheel drive vehicle. The driver simply turned off the road and we drove across the frozen fields by compass as if we were at sea, to join our road again several miles to the north.

Once again I found myself in the town of Hamburg at a moment of importance in my life. The first time was in 1921 when I met my father in Hamburg on his return from South America, when I became aware for the first time of the 'world outside', particularly outside Europe. The second was in 1939 when I escaped from Hitler's clutches via Hamburg. Now my future citizenship was being decided in Hamburg and about two months later, on my demobilisation, I travelled via Hamburg. This journey was proof for me that I would never have made a sailor. It was on one of those American built 'utility' ships, which had transported the troops across the Atlantic in 1943-45 and although technically perfectly sound, lacked any luxury or unnecessary fittings. As I have already mentioned it had been one of the coldest winters for many years and the river Elbe had been partly frozen over. Now in March the ice was breaking up and floating downriver. We were billeted near the bow of the ship and the bunks were very near the hull. As we hit the blocks of ice on the journey to Altona, at the mouth of the river, we had the impression that we were hitting icebergs all the time. This shattering noise and the vibration made any sleep quite impossible and as we entered the North Sea a healthy gale was blowing. I spent the rest of the night being seasick and when we landed in Hull the next morning in thick fog and bitter cold, this was not at all the way I had pictured the end of my military life. This had started nearly ten years earlier, in October 1937, and now it was March 1947. It was nevertheless a very exciting and emotional moment when I handed in my uniform and my rifle, received my pin-striped 'demob suit', and boarded a very slow and dirty train, which after two changes took me to Huddersfield and to 'Civvy Street'.

I took a room in a boarding house in the same area where I had stayed when I first came to Huddersfield in 1939, before the war had started. Two months later my naturalisation came through and I once again had rights like anybody else and was no longer a 'refugee'. Although I had always been treated fairly during these nearly eight years as a refugee, it was nevertheless a degrading experience to be a person who is only tolerated, has no rights, has to ask for permission to stay in the country and to be allowed to earn a living. In war-time, to get permission to travel about the country and be away from your place of residence during the night was demeaning. The authorities were correct, but the individuals I met showed compassion and understanding which made it possible to overcome this feeling of degradation and helplessness. These started with the police officer with whom I had to register on arrival in Huddersfield, and included the lad with whom I had to carry cases of yarn at the mill and who bought me half a pint of bitter when I could not afford the three ha'pence; the salesman of bathsalts at the boarding house who took me out to the Palace Theatre during the first week; the boilerman who asked me for 'high tea' on Sunday; and many more actions of this kind. Now this had suddenly changed and I was a person in my own right again. Gradually over the next years my general attitude changed. In the early years I had tried, largely without realising it, to become more English than the English. Now in an equally unconscious process I could become myself again, a person who was 'in between' all the cultures that had influenced me in this process of development and growing up.

Whilst I was still in the forces an expatriate friend of mine had offered me a job as technical manager and designer in a woollen mill which was just starting production. I gladly accepted, as this was a job that interested me very much as it entailed the organisation of all the departments of the mill and the record keeping, costing and the general flow of production. It was exactly what I had been trained for and what I had assisted with in two different mills in Huddersfield in the period between the beginning of the war and joining the forces in 1943. I started immediately on my release from the forces and threw myself into the task with great enthusiasm. There were still shortages in every field, wool was still rationed and most materials in short supply. To get things moving was therefore quite a challenge, which I enjoyed very much.

Gradually things in ordinary life became more possible, petrol rations became somewhat larger and it was possible to see the local countryside even away from bus routes. I could afford to go horse riding on Sunday mornings, an enjoyable activity which I could do for the first time since my days in the Czech Dragoons. The contrasts I had lived through during the last eight years gave life still a dream-like quality but also a *joie de vivre* of an intensity that life rarely provides. The awareness of the horrors I had seen and the feeling of helplessness which had accompanied the time when I had to decide people's fate in a few minutes' interrogation were still very much alive in me.

After about eighteen months in this job production was running smoothly, the organisation I had helped to create was beginning to go well and the workforce had become very co-operative. Each valley in the Huddersfield area had traditionally its particular trade. To make different cloths of the types that were 'native' in that particular valley or district meant, therefore, a certain amount of re-training. This mill was in Elland in what had traditionally been a blanket-producing district. We were making woollens which had originally been made in southern Moravia, now Czech Republic, and were better quality woollens than were generally produced in the Colne Valley but lower in quality than the cloths that were made in the Holme Valley. Huddersfield stands at the point where these two river valleys meet. We were also making some cheaper worsteds which were nearer to the types normally produced in parts of Bradford, where I had also worked during the war. Each district even had technical terms which were different in each area, and it was very useful to be familiar with these expressions. One of my successes was that I managed to 'import' a pattern weaver from the Holme Valley five miles away and made him feel at home amongst people in this 'lower grade' industry and weave designs which were 'foreign' to this valley. Now over fifty years later these distinctions have long disappeared and the whole industry has been very much destroyed. What survives now seems to me to be either museum pieces which are attractive for the tourist industry, or very automated modern units which seem to vary little in whichever country they are situated.

At that time in 1948 the problems were still rather different and the main question was to overcome all the various shortages and produce the best that was possible under the circumstances. We had been able to purchase some Italian worsted yarn and I had managed to produce a range of cloths which looked almost as good as the variety which was made from much more expensive English yarn. When I submitted this range to the senior partner of the firm he showed no interest in the quality of the product but declared that he was solely interested in the profit margin he could achieve. It was at that moment I realised that our basic outlook on life was different. I had been brought up to produce the best quality article for the price, and for me the profit margin was an indication of the technical success and not an end in itself. It was then that it became clear to me that I would not stay permanently with this firm even though I had enjoyed the work I had been doing so far.

Having made this decision I took no action, but, as seems to be the pattern of my life, a few weeks later I received an offer to manage a mill in Galashiels with such tempting conditions that I simply could not refuse. With hindsight I know that it was a blessing that I left this firm in Elland as a few years later the partners of that firm sold out and moved to the United States. Had I stayed I would have lost my job at a time when the textile trade was in one of its regular recessions and crises and it would have been rather difficult for me to find a new job.

The job in Galashiels turned out to be very far from what I had expected. I learned a lot about 'the rat race' and 'in-fighting' within the firm and I was very pleased when it came to an end after six months. The highlight for me had been the Sunday morning rides over the moors, in the early autumn. I began to understand that the marvellous colours of Scottish tweeds all came from the colours of nature in the area. Scotland has no trespass laws and you can therefore ride across any field or wood in any direction you wish, which gives a colossal sense of freedom.

Although all the local people were extremely nice and helpful I have never felt so much of a foreigner than at that period in Scotland. The climate certainly must have played a part in this. Even on a clear day the sun seemed very far away and daylight at midnight was never a phenomenon that was other than strange.

Shortly after the outbreak of war, when I was in my first employment in Huddersfield, I was given the duties of 'greasy percher', that is to examine the pieces of cloth after they had come off the loom for any faults during weaving. I was given an assistant, who was also a refugee, whom I had known vaguely in

Brno. We came from the same background and had many common friends and acquaintances and our families had known each other for generations. He had spent the last two years before emigrating studying law at the University of Prague and had no textile experience. His job consisted largely of carrying pieces of cloth from the weaving shed to the 'perch' and fetching the weaver when I had found any faults or careless work. Not surprisingly, he did not find this a very inspiring occupation, and as soon as possible he found himself a more interesting job in Bradford.

About a year later when I had become a designer in a mill in Bradford we took lodgings together in the same boarding house and our friendship continued. Before joining the forces we went on a cycling tour through Scotland, travelling for several weeks through the Highlands from Glasgow to Aberdeen. This experience brought us rather closer. At that time the vehicles which we encountered on the road were mostly Naval lorries and cars. We had been living in the polluted atmosphere of the industrial towns of the West Riding of Yorkshire for rather a long time now. Owing to lack of money and the severe petrol rationing it had been rare that we got out of any built-up areas. To find ourselves in nature, in conditions which were the nearest to Victorian Britain that could be experienced in the mid twentieth century, made a very great impression on us. One day in Fort William we visited a Catholic monastery and were shown round by a monk who was probably more or less our age and soon we were exchanging experiences of our rather different lives. We happened to arrive at a very beautiful round mosaic table and we were asked to sit down and continue our talk, which in the end lasted for several hours. Our discussions ranged from Old Testament Law to Church Law, Roman Law and its acceptance in modern European countries and finally to English Law. It was surprising that our clerical friend knew rather more Hebrew than we did and naturally much more Latin. He told us a great deal about his training which we found fascinating. The early studies concentrated on the various rules and rituals that had to be obeyed. At a later stage his education became much wider and they were allowed to read 'forbidden books' and finally had to read and discuss them. From this discussion emerged a picture of the Roman Catholic clergy, which indicated a division into three levels: the ordinary village priest, who had to know all the rituals and rules and tell their flock how to behave; the next grade which included a large part of the monastic orders, who had to learn to ask questions; and finally those who had reached real understanding.

This was surprisingly similar to what we had heard about the method of teaching of one of the great Rabbinic teachers of the second century, Rabbi Akiba, of whom it was said that he had three kinds of pupils: the general followers whom he taught the Law and the Commandments; the special pupils whom he taught to ask questions; and four special disciples with whom he ascended into the Garden of Eden.

The next day we climbed Ben Nevis (without bicycles) and then started our return journey to England. It was during our return journey that we discussed our plan to start manufacturing woollen cloth together after the war, if and when circumstances would allow this.

In early 1946 I was stationed in central Germany when one of our duties was to interrogate prisoners who had possibly been connected with war crimes. If such a possibility was established those prisoners were then handed over to a special kind of court, which had to establish whether they should be sent for War Crimes Trials. Such a pre-selection court was set up in our camp and to my surprise one of the interpreters in this court was my friend Felix. We now spent several months together in the same quarters.

After we had both been demobilised, I became manager in the mill in the Huddersfield area and my friend had started a wholesale business selling knitting wool in Bradford.

Felix had an accident, being knocked down by a bus, and had to spend a rather long time in hospital. I went to see him frequently which led to a deepening of our friendship and we discussed again our plans to start manufacturing together.

When now my job in Scotland was coming to an end Felix and I decided that this was the moment we had been planning for and we started to get things in motion.

He was running a small wool merchants' business in Bradford and suggested that whilst we were making our preparations to start production I could help him a bit selling wool. We could keep costs down in that period by me moving into his house, which in any case was too big for him at the moment. This I did. For a week or two I was very busy making all the arrangements for the start of production. Having taken all these steps, I now had to wait for delivery of the raw materials and the processing of the first samples to be done. My friend's business did not require much help, so for the first and only time in my life I had time on my hands, reading newspapers in great detail and accompanying my friend to parties where he was invited.

Thus I found myself one evening at a cocktail party at a house of some people I knew vaguely but I had never been at their house before and as far as I remember never after this occasion either. We were standing in groups and making useless conversation as is usual on such occasions, when I suddenly heard the word Gurdjieff mentioned by somebody in the group of people standing next to us. That very morning I had read a letter in the *Manchester Guardian* where the writer expressed his opinion that the person of this name, who had just died in Paris, had been a Tibetan spy. It was only just over two years since I had left the Forces where I had a lot of contact with Eastern nationals who for some reason had found themselves in German uniform, including people from Turkestan, Tibet and Indochina. At that very time the French were just concluding the first negotiations with Ho Chin Min and what later became Vietnam, and the invasion of Tibet by China seemed to me a distinct possibility. Hearing about a Tibetan was therefore red hot news for me, and when I heard the name mentioned that I had read in the papers only that morning, I must have turned rather sharply in the direction of the speaker. I was facing a gentleman whom I had never seen before. He looked at me calmly and asked, 'You know about Gurdjieff?'

'Yes,' I answered. 'He was a Tibetan spy and I am very interested in spies from that region.'

The gentleman nodded seriously, and made no further reply. I turned back to the group I had been chatting with and the conversation continued.

Just before we were leaving the gentleman who had mentioned the name Gurdjieff put a little piece of paper into the palm of my hand and said, 'If you are still interested come to this address next Wednesday at 8 p.m.' In typical 'Intelligence' manner I did not look at this paper until I was by myself. I had been given the address of a doctor not far from where I was living.

Having plenty of time on my hands it was easy for me to keep this appointment. I was ushered into a room where about fifteen or twenty people were assembled. The majority were middle aged and rather respectable looking. There were also some people my age and younger, about equal numbers male and female. I was told a Dr Foster had come up from London. He proceeded to read to us from a typescript. It was a story about a Kurd walking over a mountain, obviously somewhere in the East, and coming to a place where he bought some red peppers which he proceeded to eat. An obvious beginning of a spy story, I said to myself, and continued to listen with great interest. The reading continued for about an hour and by the end of it I had forgotten about spies and had figuratively eaten the red peppers myself. I was told when the next reading would be and on the way out I was offered a book called *In Search of the Miraculous*, which had just been published, and was told that on one of the next occasions I would be able to buy another book, which was the one from which tonight's reading was taken. As I have mentioned before, this was the only period in my life when I did have leisure to read books, so I thought it would not be too great a risk to buy this book, particularly because it was written by a man called Ouspensky who, judging from his name, must also come from the East.

It was still relatively early when I came home and started to read. I normally read books very systematically from the first page to the last. But in this case I was so fascinated by the unexpected content of these writings that I started reading bits here and bits there, each more interesting than the bit before. Then I came to the diagrams on pages 127 and 128 which describe how in an automatically flowing process, owing to the deflection at the intervals, each process would eventually turn into a movement in the opposite direction.

Here was suddenly an explanation of the events I had experienced in the Forces, when together with a lot of other well meaning people we had tried to build the perfect future for the new post war Germany, but where unaccountably these processes took a different direction, sometimes even achieving the opposite of the original plan. Here was finally the pointer to how such processes flowed and saying that there were laws which could explain the depressing chaos which I had witnessed over the previous ten years.

In a flash I realised that by a 'miracle' I had come across a teaching led by a man or perhaps group of men with real understanding. I had not knowingly searched for anything and if anybody before this night had mentioned the word 'esoteric' to me, I would probably have run away avoiding it.

It was now early morning, so I went to bed and started more systematically reading the next morning.

I went of course to the next meeting and bought *All and Everything* by G.I. Gurdjieff that had just arrived in 'Mr Brixley's bookshop' in Leeds. That was the name of the man who had sold me the copy of *In Search of the Miraculous* by P.D. Ouspensky on the previous occasion. He had been in touch with Mr J.G. Bennett, who ran a group at Coombe Springs, near Kingston, for some time and always stocked all the books connected with Mr Gurdjieff's work as well as all the books by P.D. Ouspensky.

I went home and immediately started reading this book. For the time being I stopped reading *In Search of the Miraculous*, explaining to myself: 'Why should I read the book written by the pupil when I can read the work of the master?'

Gurdjieff explains on the first page of the book the purpose of the first series of his writings, namely: 'To destroy mercilessly, without any compromise whatsoever in the mentation and feelings of the reader, the beliefs and views, by centuries rooted in him about everything existing in the World.'

I have no memory of reading this and therefore exposed myself to the effect of sense; I was submitting myself to writings entirely unconscious of the aim of the process. Perhaps this made the effect of these writings even more powerful than they would otherwise have been. And so in succession I experienced a great many contradictory feelings: complete agreement with what was said, disagreement of the same intensity, admiration and repulsion, doubts and certainty, and so on. When I came to the 'Ape question' (pages 271-3) I became so furious that I threw the book right across the room into the far corner, determined never to open it again; only to pick it up the next morning and continue reading. The book still shows the signs of this ill treatment today.

I continued to attend these meetings which apart from the readings included some talks about physical sensation, and the possibility of 'change'. This was all rather vague and I could not understand the connection between on the one hand these fascinating descriptions of the basic laws of the universe, the wisdom and truths which were obviously in the writings even if I could not understand them, and on the other hand the exercises which we were asked to try and which were meant to 'change' me from an 'automaton' that I know I am, into a 'conscious being' which I would become.

I was told that the person who was leading this group was a Mr J.G. Bennett, who would shortly be visiting Bradford, and that all the people who had not yet met him would be able to talk with him. I was gradually told more about the organisation in general and how it had come about that it was possible to have contact with this teaching in Bradford, which was one of the few places outside London and Paris.

A certain Air Force commander, at the end of the war, found himself in charge of a young flight lieutenant who produced energy surplus to Service requirements. In order to keep this young man out of mischief he lent him some interesting writings which kept his mind occupied. It turned out that this young officer was the same man as the gentleman who had mentioned the name Gurdjieff at the cocktail party and had given me the mysterious piece of paper at the end of that party; his name was Alex. He became very interested in the articles Commander L. Thompson had given him and continued the contact after Alex had left the Forces. It emerged that Leslie Thompson had been a follower of Ouspensky and J.G. Bennett and what Alex had been given to read was largely unpublished writings of Ouspensky and some notes about meetings of Bennett with Gurdjieff. Mr Bennett asked Alex to organise a place where he could give some lectures and in the early autumn he gave six lectures at the YMCA in Bradford, as a general introduction to Gurdjieff's teaching. A total of about three hundred people attended these lectures and some sixty came to the readings that followed; by the time I attended the list had shrunk to some thirty to forty people.

In the early spring of 1950 Mr Bennett visited Bradford and spoke to all the 'new' people. He was physically a very tall and strong person and he somehow seemed to use his whole physical weight to give power to his words, and his 'leader personality' together with his intellect and command of language made this a very impressive encounter. He managed to give me, during this twenty-minute meeting, what at that moment seemed to be a clear description of the purpose of the efforts which were required to follow this teaching and to set it all within the framework of the history of the last 3,000 years. He also illustrated the dangers of the present situation in the world, with the possibility of atomic, chemical and biological warfare. He had just written a book called *The Crisis in*

Human Affairs, which set out his opinions on the present situation in the world, which in many ways used the language of Gurdjieff and talked about the importance of 'schools' in relation to the need of guidance that was required from a different level. I now had yet another book to read.

I was getting a bit nearer in making the first pattern lengths for our planned production and also the selling of raw wool, which was intended to keep me going until our production started to move a bit. The most interesting part of this was that we discovered a supplier of karakul wool in South-West Africa (Namibia). In 1947/8 I had used karakul wool for making tweeds which had rarely been done before. Karakul wool is coloured brown or grey and by purposeful sorting can be supplied in definite and repeatable shades. This saves dying the wool and either in combination with white yarn or with other dyed shades can therefore produce cheaper cloth because only some of the wool needs to be dyed. It was quite unusual how this trade operated. Mr Pupkevitz, our supplier, would receive a cable from us that there was an interest in such and such a quality and colour of karakul wool. After a day or two a reply with price and delivery date would arrive. One day, when there was a delay in an urgent reply, we rang up and were told that Mr Pupkevitz had left on horseback yesterday when our enquiry arrived and was just riding to the tribe where the required wool was likely to be available. He was expected back in two to three days and would supply us immediately with price and delivery date. In spite of this primitive method of trading I do not remember a single consignment that was not exactly to type; and delivery dates were always kept. Mr Pupkevitz had also heard that some electric sheep-shearing equipment was now on the market, which was battery operated and could therefore be used in areas where electricity was not available. These could replace the hand clippers which had been in use for many centuries. As currency exchange at that time was under strict control we were able to speed up the process by arranging barter deals where we exchanged sheep-shearing machinery for bales of wool. This was very satisfactory for us, Mr Pupkevitz and the natives whose methods of shearing were suddenly brought into the twentieth century. In relation to the general Bradford wool trade this was of course an infinitesimal part of general trade.

Just at that time (May/June 1950) the Korean War had started and wool prices began to rise rapidly. During the whole of the period of the Second World War wool had been strictly rationed. Britain, Australia, New Zealand and South Africa had maintained a large strategic reserve of wool. By 1948, it was considered that these large reserves were no longer necessary, and the strategic reserve was gradually reduced. Now suddenly all this had changed and the US in particular required large quantities of wool for the troops in Korea. There were fears that this war could spread and that the reserves would be insufficient. Wool now started to increase very rapidly in price and by the end of 1950 wool prices had doubled.

Our plan to start a cloth production would now have required twice as much capital compared to the time when we made our original calculations. We simply did not have that amount of money and there was also the danger that if the war ended wool prices might suddenly drop to such an extent that it would bankrupt us very quickly. We therefore decided to complete our samples, but shelve our plans to start any production and keep our heads above water as raw wool agents and merchants.

I found this pure selling activity extremely depressing. You basically required little skill, and work consisted mainly in taking a wool sample received from abroad to a possible buyer in Bradford or the West Riding districts. Whilst a certain amount of bargaining took place it was fairly unimportant as both the buyer and the seller knew the market value of the day.

I therefore looked forward to the evenings when I could go home and read the books, which became more and more interesting; and attend the meetings.

CHAPTER 26

The Gurdjieff Society and my Family

IN JULY 1950 I was invited to Coombe Springs for a weekend and I was also told I could watch a movement demonstration, at Colet Gardens.

Alex and one or two other people from Bradford were also invited. We were shown round the place which was quite impressive, particularly the well that dates from the days of Cardinal Wolsey. And Mr Bennett told us that it was the tradition to have a dip in this rather cold water every morning, which was a marvellous way of waking up in the morning and to start the day.

After our tour we were then shown into the dining room. I estimated there were about sixty people present. It was usual for people who came for the first time to sit at the table with Mr and Mrs Bennett, so I found myself sitting opposite Mr Bennett and next to Mrs Polly Bennett, his second wife, and Luba Gurdjieff, Mr Gurdjieff's niece who lived at Coombe at that time and seemed to have the job of chief cook. Both Mr and Mrs Bennett were just praising Luba's excellent cooking when the sweet was placed in front of me. It had some raspberries on top. Just as I was joining the praise some maggots crawled out of the raspberries. To this day I do not understand how I managed to find the agility to remove these wriggling things, smother them with cream at the side of the plate and continue to eat and praise the quality of the food. Nobody had noticed anything or at least did not remark on it. I do not remember ever feeling so hot after eating a cold sweet.

The next morning we got the first taste of work on sacred dances by doing some preliminary exercises and later 'activities', which in my case consisted of moving some soil in a wheelbarrow from one end of the garden to the other trying to 'remember myself' on the way; we then assembled in the house to talk about our experiences.

In the late afternoon we were driven to Colet Gardens where there was a large hall that had been hired or leased by the pupils who had originally started with P.D. Ouspensky. It had a stage where the movements were going to be shown. It was difficult to guess how many people were present but I thought possibly around two hundred. Mr Bennett made a speech saying that movements were a language which could be understood precisely. The words meant very little to me but the presence of all these people sitting quietly gave me a much stronger experience and a great sense of expectation. After the introduction about the language, which would explain the laws to me, I expected that somehow miraculously I would now understand the laws I had been reading in the books. Nothing of this kind happened, of course, but just as at my first attendance in January, when I had gone to hear a spy story and had experienced something that made the spy story quite unimportant, so also now I forgot about a mysterious language and experienced something quite unexpected which I hoped strangely I would have the opportunity to try.

During the interval, Alex took me into the basement and we were offered a coffee. Suddenly Alex said, 'I must introduce you to Miss Hands,' and he took me across the room to a lady who I guessed was probably in her early forties, who asked me what I thought of the movements. It was of course quite impossible for me to answer this question truthfully and I mumbled some conventional reply of approval.

'Would you like me to come to Bradford to teach the movements?' she offered.
I simply said, 'Yes.'

With that the conversation ended and we returned to our seats.

I did not think about this casual conversation any more, and was very surprised when Miss Rina Hands appeared in Bradford some weeks later.

It was obvious of course that my conversation over coffee was purely coincidental and that Mr Bennett had decided long before to send Miss Hands to Bradford as his assistant. He himself came to Bradford at fairly regular intervals for the next three years.

The next big event in my life came when in December of that year some of us were told we could come to Coombe Springs where we would meet Mme Jeanne de Salzmann who was now in charge of the 'work' world-wide, and Mme Lannes who would look after all the groups in England. A number of us took the train to London. I remember in particular the family of the gentleman in whose house I had attended the first meeting who travelled with his wife and a baby in a carrycot a few months old. There was also a young lady called Jean Rennie. My main contact with her up to that time had been that at every meeting she had collected one shilling from me which was the contribution required to pay for the people who came from London to direct our meetings.

This meeting with Mme Salzmann and Mme Lannes turned out to be a very important turning point in our lives. It was the first occasion that I experienced the presence of people who for such a long time had worked so closely with Mr Gurdjieff. What impressed me most was the absence of any emotional words and the absence of all sentimentality. I also remember very clearly that it was possible to scrutinise and analyse the appearance of these ladies as I had been trained in the fashion world, and in terms of the factors I had learned during interrogations. This however did in no way affect the real impact this meeting made and these

Jean at the time of our meeting.

two experiences were so separate that I did not become aware of the contradiction until very much later.

The return journey from this meeting has remained very clearly in my memory and I can recall many details. When we had occupied our seats the other members of the party decided to go back and purchase an evening paper. The train started moving and nobody had returned. I was alone with that little baby and suddenly I saw the possibility of being alone with this baby in the carrycot. An absolute panic gripped me. I had never dealt with such a little baby and the journey was over four hours. I can still see clearly all the details of the compartment and the baby in the carrycot. Would this baby starve before we got there? Just then the others returned. They had got on at the rear of the train before it moved off and had walked through the carriages. This possibility I had not contemplated in these moments of panic.

This journey was also of great significance in my life, because, standing in the corridor of the train, I arranged with Jean to meet her at the Great Northern Railway Hotel in Bradford, so I could explain to her all the details of the 'Law of Three' and 'Law of Seven' which Jean had not understood. A great deal of Mr Gurdjieff's teaching is based on the operation of these two basic laws. We continued these meetings with increasing frequency over the next few months. The Great Northern Hotel was probably the least romantic place in the British Isles but that did not seem to be a deterrent to us. When Jean's birthday approached we booked a meal in a restaurant. I believe it was at Heckmondwyke, a small town in the West Riding. The owner had had a good idea to get around the rationing restrictions which were still in force, under which no meal of more than three courses could be served. By booking for four people and receiving two bills, you could consequently get a six course meal. Under the circumstances this was considered a real feast, and for the next forty years I had to hear the story that this was the only time in our courtship and subsequent married life that I had really taken her out on such a grand scale.

In relation to the times and our circumstances there was some truth in this. Apart from the romantic angle, this day was also important for the fact that wool prices, which had been rising fantastically because of the Korean War, showed the first reduction because of the likelihood of a settlement. Within the next few weeks wool prices decreased with increasing rapidity and soon were less than half of what they had been on Jean's birthday. The result was that when I proposed to Jean, on platform 5 of Leeds City station, the Bradford Line, I had to warn her that on the morning of that fateful day, her birthday, we had sold a large amount of wool at the high market price of that day. The consignment was due to arrive shortly and as the market price was now well below the contract price the buyer would almost certainly find fault with the delivery, and therefore go to arbitration by the Bradford Wool Secretariat, which was a normal condition of sale. If the Arbitration Board were to find against us, the loss would far exceed our total assets and the bankruptcy court would then be the most likely outcome. The buyer did complain. The case went to arbitration, but the decision went in our favour. Jean somehow had never taken the talk about the bankruptcy court very seriously and after due consideration decided to accept my proposal. It was just Whitsuntide and we went to Coombe Springs for a 'work weekend'. Somehow Mr Bennett had got to know of our intentions and announced our engagement publicly.

In the spring of 1951 wool prices had fallen to about half the price they had been at the end of March. As this followed a year of continuing rise combined with the fear of a world shortage due to the Korean war, everybody now suddenly discovered that they had too much stock. This was largely bought at prices above the present level, and wool merchants were well aware that sale of stock now only meant a loss. Nobody, therefore, wanted to buy at this moment and trade came to a more or less complete stop.

With our arbitration difficulty behind us and little prospect of any major trade in the near future I could focus my attention on my forthcoming marriage.

It is now, in the 1990s, with vast choice and an abundance of goods available, difficult to cast one's mind back to the period of our marriage when bread was still rationed, and all clothing and household goods were only available on coupons, and although the quantities of petrol allocations had increased since the end of the war, it was still rationed. The delivery period of a new car was about two years and the foreign exchange allowance, other than on business, was £50 per annum.

People were grateful for any goods and the attitude of not complaining was very widespread. Thus our purchase of two hand towels with the number of coupons we had allocated for this purpose became a memorable event. They were 'utility towels', which means they were manufactured to strictly controlled specifications which gave the most efficient result for the amount of material used. Being in the trade I gave the towels a thorough examination and found they were both faulty. With my continental upbringing I did not share the prevalent attitude of not complaining, and promptly rejected them. By the time six towels had been produced to find two perfect ones Jean was absolutely red in the face and was embarrassed to such an extent that this occasion has clearly remained in her mind. Over the years it has been discussed by us as an example of a basically different attitude, which in itself is neither good nor bad but which can have very important consequences. This British attitude of not complaining and accepting second grade merchandise was undoubtedly a major cause of the shoddy production of goods in the early post-war years and the consequent drop in exports of all types of industrial production. On the other hand this attitude helped to bring it about that life in Britain was so much more tolerant and agreeable than in most other countries.

During the months after our return from honeymoon it became increasingly clear that the general situation in the textile trade would not allow me to carry out our plan of manufacturing for a considerable time. I decided to look for a suitable job in the woollen and worsted manufacturing trade again. Through some connection with the Czechoslovak Selling Organisation in London it became possible for us to act as selling agents for the Czech chocolate industry. Chocolate was still on ration in this country but certain specialities could be imported without being subject to the quota. The Czech industry was producing chocolate figures, mainly Father Christmas figures and similar articles for the Christmas trade. The initial marketing exercise to establish which wholesalers would buy such articles was still quite interesting, but the actual selling was probably the most depressing activity I had ever carried out either before or after this time in the efforts of making a living. It involved extremely little skill. Goods were in short supply and once you had established that a firm dealt in these particular goods you had simply to ration out the quantities available. As petrol was still rationed, the travel had to be done by train and bus and entailed a fair amount of walking. The area I covered was Yorkshire, Lancashire and other northern counties. Although British Rail, as a single entity, had already existed for some years, timetables had not been brought under one scheme and were still operated as if there were separate companies who did not exchange information. I therefore spent long periods of time waiting at smaller stations for connections. This activity, however, helped to keep us solvent, which was particularly important as our first baby was on the way.

After Christmas I was offered, through a friend, a job in the textile trade. It was with a fairly large worsted weaver making gabardines and other coatings. My official capacity was 'yarn tester', to ensure that all materials delivered were to specification. As the firm had grown rather rapidly recently, a lot had to be organised and adjusted to the new enlarged volume and I soon found myself doing the job of an unofficial assistant to the general manager. It was very much better than the stop-gap occupation that I had at first accepted. It was clear, however, that once the short-term difficulties in this firm had been overcome, there was not much likelihood of a long-term career.

Once again an acquaintance had suggested my name to a manufacturer in Huddersfield and so I was approached for this position. It was now clear that somehow my career opportunities always appeared through some friend or acquaintance suggesting my name. However many job applications I made, however many interviews followed, the actual jobs were always mediated or

Our wedding photograph.

assisted by some person more or less closely known to me. In no case had I asked this particular person to help me, and it always happened at an unexpected moment. There seems to be some kind of pattern behind this for which I have no explanation.

The task was to manage a small woollen mill, which was making products that required exactly the knowledge I had acquired in my early training in Brno. It also required the skill of organising a production and its expansion, which was something I had done twice before.

We soon came to an agreement. Now the most interesting and satisfying part of my career followed.

My responsibility started with the purchase of the wool, waste or other raw material required. These materials had to be dyed, blended, spun, woven and finished. To a large extent we were making scarves, stoles, travelling rugs and blankets where all the processes of making the final article were also included. When I had set out on my career in 1933, in the middle of the biggest recession in recent history, it seemed an unattainable aim to be in charge of a production of woollen cloth. And now nine years later it had miraculously come to pass in spite of Hitler, emigration to Cuba, where I never wanted to be, the difficulties of being a refugee, five years of World War and the failure of the previous attempt to start my own production during the Korean War. Perhaps it was not as grandiose as it had been in my dreams. There were always plenty of difficulties, doubts and uncertainties. It was very obvious that some circumstances or forces which had prevented me so decisively and powerfully to carry out any plans for my future had suddenly, and equally beyond my 'control', placed me in exactly the position where I had always wanted to be.

The parts of the work that I always found most satisfying were the processes, which could not be defined precisely and scientifically. The wool merchant brings a sample of wool and as you handle it you know in your fingertips whether it will make the cloth that you require. Your head has, of course, no idea at that moment whether you are right or not and there is therefore the problem of how to listen rightly to the 'feel' in your fingertips. When buying greasy wool, before the wool is scoured, one has also to assess the likely yield since some greasy wools contain more than 50 per cent of grease (lanolin) and impurities such as thistles that the sheep pick up during grazing, so it is therefore not easy to estimate the 'clean' price.

In cheaper cloth, where you use waste and re-manufactured fibres, which are of course much shorter, the blending of the right lengths of fibres to spin to the fineness of count that you require is also a very exciting process done with your fingertips.

Another process that always fascinated me was the feeling for the colours that are going to sell. I am not talking here about high fashion but the feel for colour that makes people choose household articles like blankets, carpets and rugs where on the whole they do not think of 'fashion' and yet the choice is made according to some impulse that is 'in the air'. One had to know for instance that certain colour combinations and tones could be offered in Belgium, northern France and northern England but not in Paris, Vienna or Sweden. In New York the ranges were different from California. When offering ranges during the main selling season when one saw one buyer after another one had always to take out certain designs and add others according to the place and type of trade of the buyer.

No designer and manufacturer can of course always be right so the time of showing a range was always very exciting. As most of my selling was done to wholesalers or large store groups I was often required to change the basic construction of a product, for instance: 'Can you make it lighter or heavier in weight?'; 'Can you bring it to such and such a price level?' If you could do such a calculation on the spot it gave a greater chance of a larger contract to be signed there and then. This was done in those days by means of calculations on a slide rule. Pocket calculators and desk top computers did not yet exist or were terribly expensive. I remember the thrill of sitting in the buyer's office and calculating such a change of specification which was then accepted at the price I quoted, and then actually delivering on time the new article, and making some profit in the transaction.

During the 1960s our firm had grown and was taken over by a Public Company. More time had to be spent in board meetings and other discussions and the type of activity that I really enjoyed diminished. Because of my knowledge of languages I became Group Export Manager which was quite interesting, as I travelled all over Western Europe. Owing to the 'rat race', as is so usual in large companies, the work became less enjoyable and when in 1968 the opportunity arose to change my occupation, I took it. This turned out to be a very timely move, as the textile industry started to shrink very soon after my departure. It would have been very likely that I would have had to take early retirement or would have lost my job at a time when the family was in their greatest need of financial support.

During the period of my selling activities in Western Europe I had the very interesting experience of meeting a new generation from the one I had known before and during the war. Whilst my experiences were of course confined to a relatively small number of people I nevertheless got a feel of the atmosphere of these countries and some of the changed attitudes. Naturally I could not look objectively at the people I now met and my own prejudices must have coloured my impressions so as I was forced to generalise my views, they would be still more subjective.

The biggest change I found was in what was then the Federal Republic of Western Germany. The new generation I met who had been brought up after the end of the Nazi regime had a completely different outlook on the world. Most of the people were of course middle class and in some way connected with trade or travel. Nearly all spoke reasonably good English, many with American accents, and were familiar with Western hit tunes, football and sport in general. They were, on the whole, physically very much more relaxed and their movements had lost the stiffness of so many pre-war Germans. I once found myself on a train taking football supporters back to Frankfurt from an important match in some other town. The amazing difference from the equivalent English crowd was that hardly anybody was drunk. They all looked 'middle class' although most of them were factory workers, as I discovered during the journey. They were naturally discussing the events of the match rather excitedly, which I could of course not follow, as I knew nothing about German football.

When I saw groups of young people of 18 to 25 the striking thing was that they both dressed and moved like any group of English or other Western European youngsters and even their 'square' physical build which I remembered from my childhood stay in Germany had been replaced by a new 'international' shape.

That the old type of German had not completely disappeared I witnessed in a small town in Southern Germany where in a pub a reunion of ex-soldiers was taking place and the familiar old atmosphere prevailed.

I do not remember any occasion during these business meetings that any wartime events were ever discussed. The young people did not seem to know about it and with the older people there was always a strong silence followed by a change of subject.

In Austria it seemed rather different. The Austrians on the whole have a special ability of sensing what you wish to hear and telling you just that. Meetings are therefore generally very pleasant. They have a good sense of humour, and truth is a necessary evil to be avoided if possible.

In Vienna I found an atmosphere that somehow pretended that both the inter-war years and the Nazi period were just a short unimportant interlude between the Great Imperial past and now and that as the restaurants and pubs still served the same speciality dishes the rest was really unimportant. In the industrial towns in the provinces the sense of reality was much stronger. The thing that struck me was that once you had left the factory gates, there were no workers but only middle class citizens. The 'cloth cap' attitude did not exist.

My experiences in the Netherlands were concentrated in Amsterdam, a city that struck me as particularly honest and open when I was there at the end of the war. I came here very frequently in my selling period and always felt very free and at home.

In Belgium, which I had known very well at the end of the war, a tremendous amount of building seemed to have taken place and the country gave the impression of being very prosperous. Brussels had built a very modern underground ring road around the inner city, a train service from the airport right to the centre of town, new fast trains to provincial cities and motorways, and well designed office buildings in the city. Even if the relations between Vlaams and Walloons had not improved very much, that did not affect business relations.

Returning from Brussels to Britain always seemed like a journey back in time.

The France I met now on my business trips was a very different country to the one I had known in earlier times. There was none of the dilapidation I had seen in the early thirties, and all the destruction that was so visible immediately after the war had been re-built. The trains ran on time and everything was much cleaner. In business absolute adherence to delivery dates was essential and quality had to be absolutely perfect. At one time I was at a 'British Week' in Lyon. These British Weeks were efforts to sell British goods, organised by the Board of Trade, the various Chambers of Commerce, the Foreign Office and various specialist trade organisations. I had been to such British Weeks in Amsterdam and Brussels. What struck me here was that in this part of France, Britain seemed to be a very unknown country, and during some non-business conversations I had during that week the period of Eleanor of Aquitaine seemed to be more familiar than present day England. Relatively few people spoke English, and in view of the strong local textile industry, interest in English textiles was limited to the world famous items. What I heard about the machinery industry seemed to give a similar picture.

My business life after 1969 turned out to be fairly uneventful. It was mainly concerned with administration and compared to my previous occupation rather humdrum. It allowed me however to support the family financially.

Our eldest son David went to an agricultural college and qualified for an OND. He went to Queensland to work on a farm in connection with artificial insemination but shortly after his arrival circumstances altered and the scheme came to an end. He had to find various sometimes rather menial jobs, including work on Queensland Railways and working in a meat factory in tropical Townsville. He met a friend from home and made new ones and eventually together with these lads bought a car and drove to Ayers Rock and through the centre of Australia to Adelaide and later to Sydney, where he passed a test on local knowledge and became a taxi driver. He eventually managed to get a job in the seed trade and ultimately became manager of a firm selling chemicals and fertilisers in Perth, Western Australia. There he met his future wife. He brought her home to meet us and during this visit decided that he preferred life in Australia. After some years he decided he wanted a degree in order to have a better career. He studied for several years, very much supported by his wife, and

John's wife Giselle with their children.

obtained a degree in Horticultural Business. This enabled him to work for a firm dealing with the reafforestation of desert land, a trade that seemed to hold good prospects in the Middle East. When the Iraqi war broke out these exports became impossible and he had to start something new. By that time he had learnt enough about computers to start a business on his own, advising firms how to organise their computer systems and help them over all technical difficulties. It turned out that he had a flair for this sort of work and this business is keeping his family going. He has three children, and since my retirement we have been able to visit them every two or three years which is always a great pleasure.

Our second son John who was eleven when we moved to London got into a grammar school and did his 'O' Levels. His form master wanted him to continue to 'A' Levels and like any ambitious father I supported this, but John had applied behind my back for a training course with GEC as electronic engineer and had been accepted. Seeing that he really wished this, I was pleased that he had won this fight against me, and I think it has helped him in his self-reliance. When he had completed his training he changed to a job with Rank Xerox. He saw on the notice board that some engineers were wanted for work in Sydney, applied and was accepted. So we ended up with two sons in Australia, alas four or five flying hours apart by the fastest jets. When I retired John and his girlfriend invited us for a holiday in Queensland, and in this way we got to know our future daughter-in-law. This was the beginning of the second happy family in 'Aussie' land. They

John and Deborah.

now have three lovely daughters and John has a rather responsible job in a firm making computerised printers.

Our elder daughter Ruth had just started primary school when we moved to London. She did not particularly shine at her local comprehensive but one of her teachers remarked one day that she was good at sewing. So we bought a sewing machine and Ruth discovered an ability to make clothes. A friend gave us the right advice and she applied to and was accepted for the London College of Fashion. This led to a career in the ladies' fashion trade. Starting with pattern cutting she managed to become a successful designer because she could approach things from the technical (or craft) angle and her designs would therefore fit and be wearable. As her great-grandfather had been in the textile trade I felt that she was continuing an old family tradition and I was very pleased when I sometimes could give her some technical advice. Ruth ended up as an important wedding dress designer which she gave up only when she decided that being a mother was a more important career, and her husband and we supported her in this decision. Ruth and her husband are into Gurdjieff's work, which adds an additional 'family' tie to the existing one.

Our younger daughter Deborah was three years old when we came to London. Her school reports were very much of the 'could do better' variety until she suddenly decided that she wished to go in for a degree. As she had decided this herself she found the determination and strength to make up for the earlier

John Hare 15.12.57 - 7.9.98

John Hare, National Support Manager for Printing Systems, died suddenly of a brain aneurysm on September 7, while attending a training course in Melbourne.

John joined the company in March, 1996, when Océ acquired Siemens Nixdorf Printing Systems, and was based in Sydney.

John was instrumental in the successful integration of Printing Systems into Océ. He had been with the Printing Systems Division for ten years.

For those who knew John, he was kind, caring, calm, always ready to help others and was liked and respected by colleagues, customers and suppliers alike.

John is survived by his wife Giselle and children Laura, Amy and Rebecca.

Above: John Hare

John Hare 15 December 1957 to 7 September 1998.

All the present family except three grandchildren from Sydney.

shortcomings and ended up with a degree with distinction at Leicester Polytechnic. She found work with a credit card company doing a computer related job. Working for this company she met her future husband, and after the birth of a baby daughter also decided that bringing up the child was the most important work for her.

We thus find ourselves in the almost miraculous situation that in spite of all our mistakes, doubts and uncertainties about bringing up our children we now find that there are four happy families which have sprung from the one started in 1951.

Since writing this description of our family a disaster has struck quite unexpectedly. Our son John died suddenly from an aneurism in the brain, whilst on a business trip to Melbourne. He was forty years old and only two years earlier had reached a responsible management position he had been aiming for. It gave us great satisfaction to learn what a place John had made for himself in the hearts and minds of the many people he was connected with.

This tragedy left everybody in the family completely stunned. I found that one's body took all the actions that were necessary, quite detached from the other parts. Corresponding processes seemed to have taken place in other members of the family. Our family in Perth went to Sydney and all possible arrangements were made. When we came to Australia shortly afterwards, we found a family more closely united than before, and the link with the English half strengthened.

For Jean and me there was clearly nothing to do, only to accept what 'is'. The cycle of life goes on. A boy has been born to Deborah and Miles, which means that there are ten grandchildren.

From my retirement in 1986 onwards I have had the possibility of spending more time in the various activities and studies connected with the pursuit of Gurdjieff's teaching and the questions of the purpose of my presence on this earth have become stronger. This has brought, on the ordinary level, a new experience of *joie de vivre*. Looking back now at the whole of my life it can perhaps be described by one Hebrew root *PaLaH* (פלא) which includes many meanings which all seem to apply: to be extraordinary, difficult, hard but also to be wonderful, marvellous and sometimes even miraculous.

PART II

Hebrew Study

Introduction

During the summer of 1953 I was at a 'work week' at Coomb Springs. One morning I happened to be at the front door when somebody rang the bell. When I opened it an elderly lady in a rather 'ethnic' dress with a straw hat with an enormous brim stood there, carrying a large bag exactly like the one worn by Mary Poppins in the famous film. When Mr Bennett, who was standing in the hall, saw her he rushed to the door and embraced her. She simply stated that she had just come from India and asked: 'What's happening?'

Mr Bennett replied: 'We are stringing up beans in the garden.'

The lady put her bag down, proceeded into the garden and commenced stringing up beans. I was told that she was Ethel Merston, a very old pupil of Mr Gurdjieff's. I was told that when she was in charge of the kitchen garden at Fontainbleau Mr Gurdjieff instructed her to plant rice; she refused and persuaded Mr Gurdjieff that in the climate of Fontainbleau this was impossible and Mr Gurdjieff relented. My reaction was that a person who had the courage to oppose Mr Gurdjieff and succeed must be a person to be taken note of. I later read about her in Fritz Peter's book *Boyhood with Gurdjieff* and read her memoirs which are available in the Kensington public library.

It is perhaps appropriate here to add a short summary of Gurdjieff's beliefs. With the gradual erosion of the influence of the great religions and traditional ways of living in the Western world, it becomes increasingly difficult for one to satisfy one's need to find the truth about oneself and the meaning of one's life. Gurdjieff undertook to gather the elements of an esoteric knowledge, in danger of being lost for ever, and to present them in a system of ideas, as part of a practical teaching to help the understanding of modern man.

In the autumn of that year I spent an evening at Coomb Springs, as I sometimes did when I happened to be in London on business. There were very few people there that evening. The only ones I remember were Mr Bennett's second wife Polly and Miss Merston. The conversation was about study in relation to the 'work'. After some more general remarks Miss Merston proceeded to question me rather directly about who I was, where I had come from and why I was in 'the work'. This direct approach reminded me very much of my first meeting with Mrs Bennett, when as a new person I was sitting next to her at dinner at the table of honour. After giving me a long piercing look and without any of the usual smalltalk she asked: 'Are you married?' and when I said I was not she simply added, 'You ought to.' After that she turned to the person on her other side and no further conversation took place. Marriage was very much on my mind at that time, as I had met Jean a short while before.

The interrogation by Miss Merston had somehow had the same flavour although the comparison came to my mind only very much later.

When Miss Merston had found out about my background and the fact that I was Jewish, she suddenly asked me: 'Have you *read* the Bible?'

I heard myself giving a very clear answer to this, 'No.'

'You should read it,' she continued. 'It is a very interesting book, we have been reading a lot of it in our study of *kabbalah* which we are undertaking this winter.'

I took it that 'we' meant her as well as Mr and Mrs Bennett.

With that remark the conversation ended and I left. Having returned home I bought a Pentateuch in Hebrew and English with commentaries by the late Chief Rabbi Hertz, and started to read this 'interesting book'.

I had to read it in English of course as my knowledge of Hebrew was confined to being able to identify the Hebrew letters and understand a few key words which I had picked up as a child.

From that time on a new aspect to the question 'Who am I?' was added to my search and just as there cannot be an answer to this question in general terms there can equally be no answer to this question from the Jewish aspect. I was very interested to read recently a book by the present Chief Rabbi Dr Jonathan Sacks where he discusses the question 'Who or what is a Jew?' and where he appears to come to the conclusion that he also does not know. He knows of course most of what can be known about the outer rules and some he in fact has to make himself but to give a verbal or any other definition about its inner meaning appears to be impossible.

From my earliest childhood I was aware of some of these aspects. I have discussed earlier the fact that according to the law in Czechoslovakia to be Jewish was a nationality in the ethnic sense just like Czech, German, Hungarian etc. Your citizenship depended entirely on being a member of a local community and only a certificate of domicile entitled you to be a citizen of the Czechoslovak Republic.

Schools were practically all state schools where the tuition of religion was in the hands of the State and all religions had to be treated equally and impartially. In practice, the teachers of religious education were often ministers of the various religions who in this respect were employees of the state. There were mostly two or three hours a week allocated in the curriculum. As far as I remember the tuition in the Hebrew language was fairly minimal but two subjects, namely

INTRODUCTION

'Biblical History' and 'Ethics' were rather important. This basically followed a state directed curriculum, although in practice the Rabbi seemed quite free in the way this was taught, although there were books printed by the state, published in the same way as any other schoolbooks.

The result of this process was that by the time of leaving school I had acquired a very good knowledge of the wanderings and the history of the Children of Israel as well as thorough information on the ethical principles and rules of behaviour. Real religious feeling and understanding however did not come from this source.

Although both my father and my mother had come originally from Orthodox Jewish families, by the time of my education, four generations of assimilation had taken their toll of traditional observance and ritual. My father's outer attitude was almost anti religious but his inner feelings, as I understood much later, were deeply traditional. As a child and young man I only saw his outer opposition to traditional observance and like any good son I revolted against what I saw and therefore ended up with openness towards Jewish principles.

My mother was a follower of Rudolf Steiner's Anthroposophical Society and her influence went towards the rejection of a habitual outer form and towards seeing the wider principles of 'right action'.

A brother of my grandfather, my great uncle Julius, was the only member of the family who had been to a Yeshiva (Jewish religious school). I do not recall that he ever spoke to me about Jewish matters or in fact talked to me about anything other than music. The new invention of the radio and the set his son had built for him, which was enormous in size and sometimes even worked in spite of the dominating crackle, allowed him to listen to the performances of the Vienna Symphony Orchestra. Apart from this he told some trivial stories about various members of the family whom I had hardly known.

He officiated at all religious family occasions, particularly at the Seder evening (Passover), when all his children and their offspring would gather. They mostly came from Austria and Poland. Like most Jewish families the members were spread over the whole Austro-Hungarian Monarchy which was now composed of several independent states and it was not always possible to get exit permits, particularly from Poland. These occasions were therefore emotional not only in a religious sense and brought a feeling towards the extended family. For this there is a Hebrew word *Mishpaḥas* which has a specific emotional meaning for which there is no exact equivalent in any other language I know. It includes all the ideas of family quarrels as well as a sense of insoluble family ties, a sense of responsibility for each other and of common fate and destiny.

The last time I attended this Passover Ceremony was in 1938. In 1939 the Nazis set fire to the Synagogue on the very eve of this festival and very few Jews

JUDAICA OLOMOUCIENSIS

The Synagogue in Olomouc, which had 3,800 members in 1939 (it is believed about 600 survived).

took the risk of being in the street at night. As far as I am aware only one cousin from this side of the family survived the war.

My father and Uncle Julius had seats in the Synagogue next to each other. My father attended only on rare occasions, but I was allowed to go from the age of five and stand next to my uncle who took great care that I followed the service. This way I learned to read Hebrew without knowing the meaning of what I read. As most of the service was chanted or sung the effect was much greater than the words alone would have been. It was only many years later that I realised how much has been transmitted by the combination of melody, sound, and the feeling of the people praying around me.

It was by no means always religious feeling that made me attend the religious service. As the state schools had to be fair to all religions the school authorities and the Rabbinate had laid down exactly which religious holidays we could have off completely, which were half day holidays and on which days we could have time off for the purpose of the service only. All the boys considered it a matter of honour to take all the time off which we were allowed. Some boys sometimes played truant from the Synagogue but as my father's seat was in the first row just opposite the Rabbi's seat on the Bimah (the raised part in the front of the Synagogue near the Torah Scrolls and the table of the Reader), the Rabbi would have known exactly when I was absent.

INTRODUCTION

Having come to England I joined the Synagogue in Bradford but this seemed more important from the point of view of social contact, and because this was the only place where I had a RIGHT to be, as opposed to all other places where I was tolerated as a Jew, a Czech and as a foreigner. Even if nearly all the time I was treated very generously and fairly, I was still aware of the difference between being allowed to be here and the right to exist.

When in 1945, whilst in the British forces in Germany, I received confirmation that my parents had been killed and gassed at the Auschwitz (Osvěčín) concentration camp, probably in 1942. I then resolved that I would try never to deny my Judaism and thus their martyrdom, however passively, for being members of this people and faith.

At the Jewish New Year 1946 whilst still in the British forces I attended a service at the former concentration camp of Bergen-Belsen where several hundred people were still living, about eighteen months after their liberation. As I have said earlier, they were there for no other reason than the fact that they had no other place where they had the RIGHT to be. I understood then how important it was for the Jewish people to have a place where they had the RIGHT to live.

Within two years from this time the State of Israel had been established and a place had come into being where Jews had the RIGHT to live, and that after nearly two thousand years of homelessness. I certainly would not have believed anybody who would then have told me that this could be endangered about fifty years later by Jew killing Jew.

But I had not yet heard of Gurdjieff's idea that man was not 'conscious' but 'asleep' and therefore subject to laws which automatically led him in a direction which would deviate from his original intention.

When I now began to follow Ethel Merston's suggestion that I should read this 'interesting book', the Bible, a new possibility opened up to me. Very gradually it became not only the study of a religion of which I had very little knowledge and still less experience, but a study of myself and another aspect of the question: Who am I?

It soon became obvious that just reading by myself was not going to get me very far, although the ordinary information was also necessary.

It came about that Jean and I formed a very close friendship with an Orthodox Jewish family who had also joined the Gurdjieff group in Bradford. This friendship has continued now for nearly half a century. Even after they had to leave active membership of the group because of circumstances of their lives, this contact gave me the possibility of learning a great deal about the way of life of an orthodox Jewish family and also of asking some questions about traditional views.

I was now very much engaged in establishing my position in day to day life. I had become general manager and later director in a woollen mill in Huddersfield. I doubled its size in a fairly short time but after the death of one of the original partners, this firm as well as other units of this private group who were making various speciality fabrics were all taken over by a public company in an allied field. Because of my knowledge of languages I became export manager in the group which entailed a large amount of travel across Western Europe, thus being away from the family at frequent intervals. Both my wife and I also spent large amounts of time in connection with the group, which had grown to more than sixty members, had purchased a house and could provide an opportunity for meetings, movements (a form of 'sacred dances'), the study of ideas, and practical work activities and crafts. Teachers and group leaders guided all this from London.

By 1968 I began to have the feeling that the textile trade might be approaching one of its periodic cycles of decline which have always existed; archaeologists have discovered letters dating from about 500 BC from carpet weavers in Persia, where they explain to the merchants on the coast in what is now Lebanon that the textile trade is now finished and it is now time to give it up. These difficult periods lasted of course for very different periods of time, but as I was now over fifty years of age I would probably be very near retiring age when the next boom would come and with the advent of new fibres, new methods of manufacturing and changing requirements, the special knowledge I had acquired could prove to be out of date.

So one afternoon I discussed the situation with Jean and explained to her the situation and that I wondered whether this was the moment for us to start something entirely different. Perhaps I should try something in London, although I had not the slightest idea what it could be. If this were possible it could bring the possibility of being at a major centre of Gurdjieff's work instead of one of the outposts. It might also give a wider choice of education for our children, as our eldest son would soon be doing 'O' Level exams. The younger one was facing the exams possibly to enter grammar school, the elder daughter was just ready to start school and the youngest one would benefit from a good kindergarten.

This had been a very general conversation and neither of us contemplated any practical action following from this. We probably would have forgotten our talk had I not received a telephone call about two hours later. A friend of mine who together with another friend owned several hotels in Kensington had called quite out of the blue asking whether I might perhaps be interested in joining them and taking over the commercial administration of that small hotel group.

I agreed to come to London and discuss this matter further. This whole event had an atmosphere which was similar to that of my emigration. It had started apparently quite accidentally and certainly without any action or even considered intention and the events that followed this telephone call had the same kind of sequel which I certainly felt was beyond any control and guided by some force which I did not understand. All that seemed necessary for me to do was to allow things to take place and not to interfere.

The proposal that was made to me was conditional on finding a house in London sufficiently near to the place of work so that I could get to work without difficulty if need be even outside standard working hours. Whilst this was a very reasonable condition house prices in London were more than twice as high as those in Yorkshire; and as our children were reaching the most expensive period in education to take on a large mortgage seemed an undue risk. Some years before we had bought a cottage adjacent to our house which had practically no value because it was under a controlled tenure and rent but we had bought it because the daughters of the tenant were willing to baby-sit which meant that they could live rent free and even have some regular income. The tenant was a widow who at that particular moment decided to get married again and move to the Midlands. So quite unexpectedly we found ourselves with a vacant possession which more than doubled the sale value of our property. My father in law, who then lived in London, on hearing that we might wish to move, visited a number of estate agents and got details.

The first house we looked at seemed to serve all our needs. We then saw a large number of other properties which were either unsuitable or beyond our means. Because mortgages at that particular time were very hard to obtain, the vendors of the first house we had seen had missed a sale as the prospective purchaser could not obtain the mortgage. It was therefore on the market at less than the ruling price. One of the directors of my old firm was a solicitor in Huddersfield and he helped us to find an estate agent with the right connections who could not only secure a good price for our old house but also conclude the sale very quickly. The solicitor used his contact with the building society so that we got the required mortgage for the new house without delay.

Within a remarkably short time we managed to wind up our affairs in Huddersfield, move to London and find suitable colleges and schools for the children.

My hunch about the situation turned out to be right. At the time of our move things in textiles still looked all right but within a year the trade faced quite a lot of redundancies and re-employment for executives over fifty was particularly difficult. Whilst it is unlikely that I would have been made redundant at that time, to be in a shrinking industry is always a great deal more strain. I had now changed to the expanding hotel and tourist industries where life was much easier. My new job was far less interesting and less 'creative' than my previous occupation, but it provided sufficient money to keep the family at more or less the same standard as before. It left me more free to occupy myself to follow the 'work' and it also allowed Jean to participate fully as we did not have such long distances to travel and could avail ourselves of all the opportunities which existed in a major centre of the teaching.

I had already heard whilst still in the North that there was a group of people in the 'work' in London who were studying the Hebrew tradition as part of their search within Gurdjieff's teaching. As soon as I could, I therefore asked to join this search which I have now followed for more than a quarter of a century.

I first had to study the rudiments of Hebrew grammar and learn a basic vocabulary, so that I could take part in reading, translating and interpreting some Bible passages, reading about the various movements of Jewish mysticism throughout history and later reading existing translations and in some cases making attempts to translate some passages myself.

CHAPTER 1

Looking for my Roots

IN THE EARLIER PART of this book I have tried to share with you my subjective impressions of my journey through my life in this world and in the same way I can only offer to share the subjective results of this search which was undertaken because of the need to know the Jewish aspect in myself without which any search would have been incomplete.

The most fundamental prayer in Judaism is the 'Shema' (Deuteronomy 6:4-9). It is said at each service; by a really observant Jew at least three times each day. This prayer includes the following injunction: 'And thou shalt teach them [the commandments] diligently unto thy children, and shalt talk of them when thou sittest in thy house, and when thou walkest by the way, and when thou liest down, and when thou risest up.'

Perhaps this injunction given by Moses to the children of Israel about 3,300 years ago could be the reason why the telling of stories has become so central in Jewish teaching. And as these stories have to be told to children they have to be simple.

When I had the privilege of attending a talk in a big synagogue in Sydney by Rabbi Adin Steinsaltz, the greatest living authority on Talmud and probably the greatest Jewish teacher of our generation, to the assembled Rabbis and dignitaries of the town, he had chosen to explain a passage from Talmud which ran roughly as follows. During the first century CE when Jerusalem was in ruins a Rabbi entered a tumbled down building in order to say his afternoon prayer. His teacher came and told him not to pray there but go into the street to pray. The Rabbi asked: 'Why?' The answer was: 'If you pray in a ruin a piece of masonry may fall on your head!'

Having thus 'deflated' all the assembled dignitaries he proceeded to show how real knowledge can be found from one simple passage, and can be missed in the study of the vast and often obscure esoteric literature.

Perhaps we have now got a clue as to why the telling of jokes is so central in Jewish relationships. The only people who do not tell jokes are the fanatics on each fringe of the spectrum. When I looked up the meaning of the word fanatic, I discovered that it comes from a Latin word *fanum*, which is defined as 'a place *solemnly* consecrated to a God' (the italics are mine). This can be the worship of the golden calf, the opposite of inner life. Even before I joined the 'Hebrew group' of the Gurdjieff Society in London I was aware of the fact that the Bible translations I had read did not give an accurate and unambiguous picture of the Hebrew text. When I started learning Hebrew in the framework of that study group it soon emerged that translation alone could not solve this question. It was necessary to find an understanding of the language, the way of thought and attitude to life, which the people of that period had followed.

Although the language has not remained a spoken language in the ordinary sense, it still remains a vehicle for transmitting ideas in a living way and certain ideas and words have come down to us sometimes as words with Hebrew roots used in the version of the Sephardic language which is spoken by the descendants of Jews who lived in the Iberian peninsula for centuries. For Jews living in Western, Central and Eastern Europe this same process could be seen in the use of Yiddish, a form of Middle High German mixed with Hebrew and Slav words.

It seems to me that this, at least partially, living transmission makes it possible to reach a more complete experience. In most other cultures there is a break between an old culture and today's reconstruction which must, by definition, rely much more on information from the head, based on archaeology, ancient literature, history and so on, not allowing the transmission of feelings, which in the case of the Jewish tradition is still possible.

This does not mean of course that we should not use help from any source and tradition, which can often unexpectedly throw light on ancient customs and laws and bring a new understanding.

An example for us of such an understanding came from the study of the laws and rules of marriage in the legal code of Hamurapi, which is the earliest known written codex of law written in Sumer about 200 years before Abraham emigrated from Ur in Sumer to Ḥaran possibly around 2200 BCE. This law describes two forms of marriage. One was the ordinary marriage in the form of a contract in which a man could enter into as many contracts as were necessary to keep his farm or other business in running order in return for which he undertook the care and welfare of his wives. This contract could be dissolved if either party broke the rules and the law says very little about any 'personal' or feeling relationship between the two parties.

The other type of marriage was called 'the marriage between brother and sister'. This was an arrangement that was entered into for life and could basically not be broken. It had of course nothing to do with incest and the marrying of literal brothers and sisters. It seems to me that it is very much more likely that this form of marriage was referred to when it was said that a Pharaoh married his sister.

It seems that this principle was generally known and understood.

If we look at Genesis 12:10-19 in this light we see a meaning in addition to the ordinary one; a new one which reinforces the higher meanings which are ascribed to this chapter. We hear in the early part of this chapter that Abram was a rich man when he left Ḥaran for Canaan and that he took all the possessions and souls with him. It was a normal right of a more powerful potentate to demand the wives of the one coming with a petition (in this case for food) to demand the wives of his vassal in payment. When Pharaoh hears that Sarai is his 'sister', i.e. in the special relationship, he immediately releases her and rebukes Abram for not having told him before. Is this perhaps nearer to the historic events?

During the study of the early lessons in the Hebrew grammar book it became very clear to us that the way things are expressed and a sentence is constructed can point us in the right direction of the way of thinking of a people. Because the Bible has remained unchanged for about 3,000 years a possibility of coming nearer to the original feeling, thinking and experiencing has remained possible. Throughout the whole period there have always been people who have tried to understand and experience the meaning of these writings and live according to the principles. When the Qumran scrolls were discovered and the Isaiah scroll was read it was shown that it varied only in a small number of letters from the known text and that they had been transmitted exactly for at least 2,000 years. They are written in the same script still in use today, which in addition to the literal meaning has a hieroglyphic meaning. The key to this has been preserved in the oral teaching. Each letter has also a numerical value, which opens up to those who understand this language the possibility of appreciating the knowledge transmitted in this way. As in all sacred writings there is of course also the symbolic meaning which can be approached in fairy tales, legends and myths.

There seems to be therefore in the Hebrew tradition the possibility of corroboration of the literal, symbolic, hieroglyphic and numerical meanings to achieve a living experience as near as possible for modern man. It will of course depend very much on the searcher's ability to open and understand the different levels. For us ordinary enquirers, the possibility is perhaps a vague realisation of the immensity of the task, which gives rise to some humility.

CHAPTER 2

The Connection Between Hebrew Grammar and Thinking

THE FIRST REVELATION for me came perhaps whilst studying exercise ten in our grammar book which describes how to express the English idea 'to have' in Hebrew. Instead of 'I have a son,' you have to say 'There is to me a son.' The idea of possession in our sense did not exist. It was considered that everything that we say we 'have' was only given to us 'on loan' for a period, at best for the time of the sojourn on this earth.

The word translated as 'there is', *Yesh* (יש) and its opposite *Ayin* (אין) were originally nouns denoting existence and non-existence.

There is basically a different attitude to time. There are only two tenses:

(1) The Perfect, which describes a completed action; and

(2) The Imperfect, which describes a process still proceeding without necessarily referring to linear time, i.e. that which can be described as NOW.

Whilst the relationship to time looks mainly at NOW and NOT NOW the HOW seems very much more important and conjugation takes place under seven heads:

1. Simple Active
2. Simple Passive
3. Intensive Active
4. Intensive Passive
5. Causative Active
6. Causative Passive
7. Reflexive

In the Bible the intensive and causative modes are often used to describe the action by God or Higher Energies. Once you have become sensitive to this way of thinking there appears a much greater emphasis on the HOW.

The grammatical sequence of words in a sentence is rather different. The sentence usually begins with a verb, which describes the movement. This is followed by the subject, then the adjective describing it; then the object and its adjective. Thus the sentence flows in order of the relative importance of the statement. Example: The English sentence: 'The good King enters the great city' becomes in Hebrew: 'Enters, the King, the good one, the city, the great one.' A change of this logical sequence is possible and draws your attention to a change of emphasis.

The Structure of a Sentence
1) the Verb gives us the basic MOVEMENT of the idea to be expressed
    1(a) Adverb giving details or colour to the concept expressed in the verb.
2) Subject, the noun which is described in the movement
    2(a) Adjective, further information about the Subject
3) the Object, showing the aim, direction, purpose etc of the movement
    3(a) Adjective, giving further details of the object

This structure is probably extremely old and may predate the period of writing. It could give us a guide to the ways, the feeling and the relationship to the world around them of people in the early Hebrew period.

Certain attitudes to life can be sensed which have persisted through the millennia. One of them is perhaps transmission in the form of stories, told on all possible occasions.

There is perhaps a possibility of seeing the structure of Hebrew and perhaps other ancient languages based on movement as similar to the views of certain modern scientists who hold that patterns can give rise to a structure which leads to a flow of energy 'thus creating the world'. Could it be that by accepting both the traditional and the scientific statements we could find a way of searching without having to judge between the one and the other, but making use of both to help our understanding?

Hebrew is based on roots of usually three letters. Some very ancient roots may be based on two letters only. A root may have a number of different possible translations into English. In some instances the meaning of opposites can be contained in the same root. In order to experience and understand what is said and implied it is often necessary to be aware of at least a number of these different ideas which are joined in the meaning of this root. For example the root *KaBeD* (כבד) can mean:

To be heavy
To be violent, vehement
To honour (used to describe the relationship to parents in the fifth commandment)
To harden (the heart of Pharaoh)

		K	B	D		
The numerical value of this root is 26		20	2	4	=	26
which is the same as the root of the Tetragrammaton		Y	H	V	H	
		10	5	6	5	= 26

This equal numerical value indicates that there is an inner connection between these two concepts which cannot be expressed in words, but only experienced, which implies an understanding on a different level.

In addition each hieroglyph has a specific meaning which will also give some pointers to the idea. Only when all this can be simultaneously brought in touch in me can I begin to grasp the meaning in the Biblical context. It will not be difficult to see that this search will lead to many questions which cannot be answered and must certainly not be expressed in words.

Bible/Torah written and with oral transmission

When we use the word Bible we simply use the Greek word *Biblion* which means a strip of *biblos*, which is the inner bark of the papyrus, hence the more general meaning of scroll or book. The Hebrews use the words *Sepher Torah* (ספר תורה). *Sepher* literally means to write, to count, to number; it can also have the meaning to recount, relate, tell, speak, talk. Hence a book (scroll) writing.

The word *Torah* (תורה) is derived from the root meaning of a word *YaRaH* (ירה) which can have the following meanings:

1) to throw or cast
2) to shoot (as an arrow)
3) to lay foundation
4) to sprinkle (water)
5) to put forth (as a finger)
6) to point out, to show
7) to teach, to instruct

Torah thus has the meaning: instruction, direction, precept, teaching. The hieroglyphic meaning shows a movement that flows from the end or lowest *Tav* (ת) to *Vav* (ו) in this context meaning 'here and now', then *Resh* (ר) describing a movement from the periphery to the centre, *He* (ה) which relates to Life.

If we can bring all these ideas and concepts together as far as this is possible we go in the direction of the experience that will arise and be felt when the word Torah is used.

In a more restricted sense the word Torah can be used to describe all the books of the Scriptures, i.e. the five books of Moses, the Prophets and the Writings. If we restrict the meaning still further it relates to the five books of Moses only. We find the essence of these five books in Chapter 20 of Exodus, the so-called Ten Commandments.

In fact in Hebrew the word Commandment is not used in this chapter but it simply says: 'God spoke ALL these words, saying...'

Each number has symbolical meaning and thus the idea of Ten Commandments stands for something that is complete. The number Ten in this numerical sense is used particularly for something that is complete in a Higher state. Completion in the world of man is often described by the number Twelve (twelve tribes etc.).

The Ten Commandments were given in the revelation on Mount Sinai and we are told:

> 'There was a great and strong wind.
> And the Lord was not in the wind.
> After the wind an earthquake,
> but the Lord was not in the earthquake.
> After the earthquake a fire,
> but the Lord was not in the fire. After the fire a 'still small voice...'

It is said that a more literal translation is 'a sound of thin silence'.

The most important esoteric work in Judaism tells us about this event (Zohar III/82b). 'They all stood [which is a symbol of being aware of one's verticality and thus in contact with a Higher level], they all saw, and they all heard.' A comment on this passage states: 'They heard what they saw and they saw what they heard,' in other words not with their ordinary senses and not in ordinary time.

I have been told a comment on this central event which was used by Rabbi Nachman of Bratzlav who said: 'Only Moses was able to "hear" and "see" all the words that God spoke. All the other people who witnessed this event "died" after each word that God spoke and "came to Life again", so that their memory is disconnected and partial.' This appears to indicate that only Moses was able to hold his attention all the time. For the people it broke off after each 'word' and they had to try and re-establish contact.

Whilst we are told that this was a historic event that took place about 3,300 years ago it is stressed, each time the revelation on Mount Sinai is discussed, that this was not a one time event experienced by the people who were there, but that all Sons of Israel (בני ישראל which means those who struggle with God) have to try and experience this moment again. 'The miracle' is not the earthquake and the fire etc., but that it is an event outside time and is therefore Here and Now. The Rabbis stressed that we ALL stand there each generation NOW. In verse 19 of chapter 20 we are told that the Lord instructed Moses to say to the Children of Israel: 'You have SEEN that I have spoken with you from the Heavens.'

After this follows the whole body of Mishpatim (מִשְׁפָּטִים), the Ordinances of the Book of Exodus.

In my subjective understanding the interpretation of this verse holds the key to the meaning of what we now call Judaism. If we understand this literally and give another human being the right to tell us ultimate truths in words of the level of this world then the result will be strife and misunderstanding. Even in the days when there were priests they could only be intermediaries between the truths taught by the prophets and the understanding of the people. This is why even Aaron, the High Priest, could not prevent the people from worshipping the golden calf, which went against the teaching of the Prophet Moses. The Hebrew word for Prophet *NaBi* (נביא) means somebody who has received real knowledge or inspiration from above. For the last 2,000 years there has not even been a priesthood with an authority to mediate; 'A Son of Israel' has therefore to find his own search and 'sacrifice' in the right way. Mr Gurdjieff always stressed how few so-called Christians are real Christians, and it follows that very few Jews are real 'Sons of Israel'. Perhaps a beginning of understanding of 'Levels' is the key for the beginning of this journey.

Four Worlds

One of the most important influences of this study came for me from the Kabbalistic idea that the universe is composed of four worlds.

The Highest world is the
  World of Emanation (OLAM HA ATZILUTH עולם האאצילות)
then come the
  World of Creation (OLAM HA BRIYAH עולם הבריאה)
  World of Formation (OLAM HA YETZIRAH עולם היצירה)
  World of Action (OLAM HA ASSIYAH עולם העשיה)

The only word in a European language, which seems to come near in meaning to the Hebrew word *Olam*, is the Greek word *aeon*. Both seem to describe a period which in the sense in linear time is endless, but in 'cyclical' time is a very large cycle or, as in this instance, a cycle that leads to a different level.

The Zohar explains the fact that the Bible starts with the words *Bereshit Bara Elohim* בראשית ברא אלהים, in the beginning created God. This phrase starts with the second letter of the alphabet because it describes a second world, i.e. the World of Creation. The first world, the World of Atziluth, which starts with the first letter א is so far from us that it can not be described. The second world of *Briyah* בריא is described in the first three chapters of Genesis which gives the basic principles and ends with the descent from the 'the Garden of delight or bliss' גן עדן.

Chapter four tells us that man's wife becomes Eve [*Chavah* חוה = Life].

One might look at the chapter describing Cain and Abel as dealing with energies and laws and perhaps only from Noah on are we dealing with actual people in this world. Apart from this vague allusion of the early chapters of Genesis and the idea of the four worlds this comparison can not be defined any further.

There is an interpretation of Genesis 2:7 which describes that Lord God

(יהוה אלהים) formed man of the dust of the ground (ADAMAH אדמה). This is the same root as for the word for man, ADAM אדם, 'and man received a living soul'. The word 'formed' *VaYYiTZeR* וייצר is here written with two letters *Yod*, whilst in verse 19 the formation of the animal is described with only one *Yod*. The Rabbis suggest from this that it foreshadows that man will be subject to two impulses, 'YETZER TOV' and the YETZER RA, the good and evil inclination (both words in Hebrew start with the letter Yod).

Sepher Yetzirah

I will always remember the connection between the world of formation (OLAM Ha Yetzirah) and the earliest known Hebrew esoteric writing, the Sepher Yetzirah (Book of Formation). Our study group had decided to translate this work from the Hebrew and I was dispatched to the British Library to get a photocopy of an early printed version. I searched and searched and could not find the reference in the catalogue. In my desperation I remembered suddenly that folklore had it that this was written by Abraham. Now I found the reference under 'Authors': Abraham, the Patriarch.

The attempt at this translation proved extremely useful as it showed us the necessity of trying to learn something of the way of thinking of the people who first conceived these ideas. It is quite a short work, consisting of about 66 verses, on average not more than two or three sentences each. The 'long version' has a total of about 2,500 words and the the 'short version' about 1,800 words.

With the historical, archaeological, linguistic and scientific knowledge that is available today it may very well be that the tradition is correct, namely, that it was composed some 4,000 years ago in the days of Abraham and at first transmitted verbally, and perhaps written down some fifteen hundred years later. We know today, and Gurdjiefff stressed this on more than one occasion, that it was possible to verbally transmit sacred texts accurately over long periods. It seems that written versions existed during the second/first centuries BCE. The earliest complete manuscript is in the Vatican library, possibly dating from the tenth century.

Having established the antiquity of this book (Sepher) and the fact that many sages and teachers refer to it we come to the question 'What is it?' The more we study this question the more we must admit that we cannot find an answer that defines this. Professor Gershom G. Sholem, Professor of Jewish Mysticism at the Hebrew University of Jerusalem and the greatest authority in this field in modern times, hints that the origin of the Sepher Yetzirah may be connected with early Jewish Gnosticism, and he points to a remarkable similarity with early Islamic Gnosticism.

'It represents a theoretical approach to cosmology and cosmogony.' (Sholem).
It describes the inner significance of the 22 letters of the Hebrew alphabet.

It also gives the structure of the world in the form of the 10 Sephirot (the Tree of Life).

The 22 letters plus the 10 Sephirot form the 32 channels which describe the movement of energies in the Tree of Life, both in Man and in the Universe. The numerical value of 32 is equal to the numerical value of *LeB* (לב) meaning heart. The heart in esoteric Hebrew is not the centre of feelings but represents the point of balance between head and body.

This becomes intelligible when you realise that the words for book, letter, number and sound (communication) all come from the root *SaPaR* (ספר).

Very ancient sources say that Malchizedek (King of Righteousness) blessed Abraham, which, so it is said, means that he received the explanation of many ancient mysteries which were known in Mesopotamia.

Abraham is said to have been an expert in astrology. Large parts of Chapter 5 of the Sepher Yezirah can be interpreted astronomically and astrologically. Many of the names of stars, constellation, months etc. can also be words describing human qualities and attributes which makes a translation in the ordinary sense quite impossible. It is also said that this book is a practical instruction for meditation and attaining higher states of consciousness. Some say that it also contains practical instructions for 'forming' (*YATZAR* יצר) a New Man (Golem).

After this long description only one thing is absolutely clear: we do not know what the Sepher Yetzirah is.

It seems to me that the only way out, in this case, is tell a Yiddish story: A blind man asked, 'What is milk like?' Answer: 'Milk is a white liquid.' 'What is white?' asked the blind man. 'White is like a swan,' was the answer. 'What is a swan?' 'It is a bird with a very long neck: we have got one in our pond.' They took the blind man to the pond, caught the swan, brought it to the blind man and let him feel the long neck. He carefully and seriously felt the whole length of the bird's neck, pondered a while and gravely said: 'Now I know what milk is like.'

We are told that the Olam Ha Yetzirah is the world of Laws above the Laws of the world of Assiyah (the World of Action). Our eyes of this world of Assiyah must remain blind to the laws of the higher world. We need the eyes and ears corresponding to the higher worlds.

Each of the four worlds in this tree of life has ten Sephirot, thus 4 x 10 = 40. This number in the Hebrew alphabet is written by the letter מ (*mem*) which signifies the development of any idea or material growth from its conception to its birth, or coming into existence. We are therefore faced here with one of the many ways of describing the complete universe.

Sephirot (plural) singular *Sephirah* comes from the root ספר (Sapar) which we have already met for the root for the word book etc. In addition it is also the root of the word sapphire (brilliant) used for instance in Exodus 24:10 and Ezekiel

1:26 and in many other references in the Zohar and also in the eighteenth century work by Isaac Luria in his main work *ETZ Chayim* (Tree of Life).

These point to the idea that one way of describing the universe and the whole of creation is in the form of the descent from the highest light to the 'thickening' of light in our world. It can also be described as the progressive 'screening' and 'obscuring' of the light. The points of thickening can be described as Sephirah. In the opposite direction they become points of 'Enlightenment'.

These Ten Sephirot and 22 channels or paths corresponding to the 22 letters of the alphabet can be shown in a diagrammatical form.

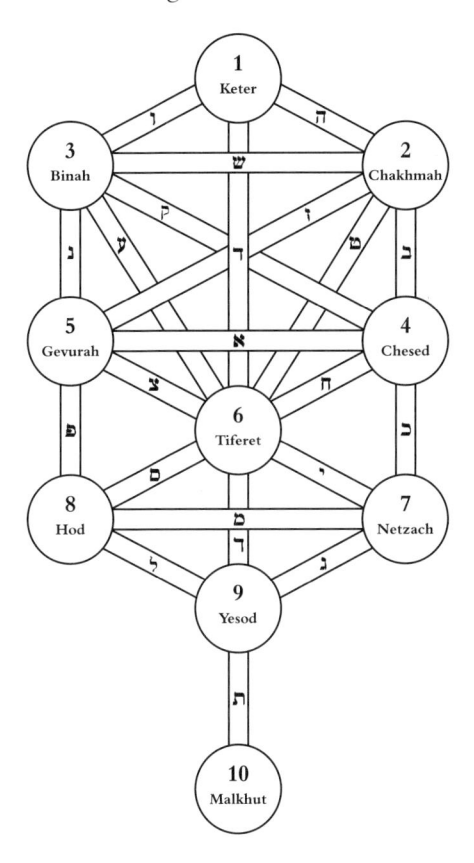

This helps us to become familiar with the information about these ideas. Only when we can experience the meaning, at least momentarily in ourselves in movement, can these ideas help our general understanding.

This diagram can also be shown with the highest point in the centre of concentric circles and the lowest on the periphery; equally the lowest can be in the centre and the highest on the outer surround.

Chapter 3

The Cycle of the Week and the Year

THERE IS ALSO a very different attitude to the calendar and its importance. The week, for instance, is thought of as a cycle of six days and the Shabbat rather than the sequence of seven days. Even now the days of the week have no names and are called day 1, day 2 etc, as in the creation story in the Bible, followed by the Shabbat which is a holy day. The Shabbat prayers ends with a prayer called Havdalah thanking God for the distinction between the holy and the profane. This prayer seems to me to be a recognition of two levels both equally important in their own sphere and not, as it would outwardly appear to be, a sequence of linear time.

Many Hebrew roots have a variety of meanings which in European languages cannot be translated by a single word. A sentence may therefore be translated in a number of different ways which are all equally valid and will shed light on the different aspects of the basic statement. In order to be able to experience the meaning of Hebrew 'thought' one will therefore be aware of these separate meanings, if possible, simultaneously.

The Zohar says that each word or phrase in the Bible has seven meanings. The figure 7 may of course not refer to the arithmetical value but to the type of cycle described by seven. Perhaps we can take the second part of Exodus 31:17 as an example.

כי ששת ימים עשה יהוה את השמים
ואת הארץ וביום השביעי שבת וינפש

Because in six days made the Lord the heavens and the earth and on the seventh day He rested and souled [a verb formed from the word 'soul'].

'The Authorised Version' reads: For in six days the Lord made heaven and earth and on the seventh he rested and was refreshed.

Meaning of words: the Hebrew word *Hashamayim* (Heavens) is always used in the plural and tradition says it is composed of the names of two basic elements: fire (*esh* אש) and water (*MaYiM* מים). *Erez* (ארץ earth) is the third basic element, and the last word of the sentence contains the root *NeFeSH* נפש, which includes the meaning 'breath and soul'. So perhaps the four basic elements are contained in this sentence.

For the understanding of the last two words of this sentence it will help if we know that each Hebrew root is composed of three letters which gives the basic verbal meaning and from this the meaning of the nouns as derived. It follows therefore that each noun has a verbal meaning and this can be used to describe the action of the noun. We can therefore speak of a seeding seed or a wind-ing wind etc.

The root *SHaBaT* as a verb means:	to rest from labour
	to cease, desist
	to keep the Shabbat
As a noun the same root means:	a day of rest
	the Shabbat

The root of the last word of this sentence, *VaYiNaPaSH*, is *NaFaSH* נפש, which means to respire, take breath and refresh oneself. As noun *NeFeSH* means breath, odour, life, principle of life, soul, life force.

Making use of the fact that we can use the same word in translating both the verb and the noun we can now translate the last two words: He ceased from labour and 'souled'. Perhaps this indicates the opposite movement to the first six days forming a balance to the labour of the first six days.

There must of course be further interpretations of this sentence. If we add the Hieroglyphic meaning of the letters and the meaning of the numerical value we can perhaps see that the search for meaning must remain a continuous process.

The Pentateuch is divided into readings for each Shabbat so that all five books are read each year. If this search is alive it will be new each year as a person develops inwardly. But alas, so many commentaries have been written during the many centuries that it appears to be more and more difficult not to drown in the amount of information produced by all the people who 'know'.

Another example of time not really felt as a linear sequence is the rule that the Circumcision (*BRYT MILH* ברית מילה), literally the covenant of the cutting off, is referred to as a circumcision of the flesh. This has to be done on the eighth day. The Zohar says: 'When the child is one week old.' As the week has only seven days this would therefore seem to mean that it is on another level. The ceremony is a symbolism of opening. This opening of the flesh has to foreshadow the opening of the heart. When the child grows up and acquires the possibility of understanding, the circumcision of the heart i.e. the opening of the heart, can follow. As we have already said, the heart is the point of balance of the functions.

Just as the story of creation in the first chapters of Genesis seems to assume a deeper meaning when we take the idea of different levels into account, so also the festivals of the year become more meaningful if we experience them as the cycle of events in nature, at the same time as events of inner development.

New Year of the Trees

Perhaps it is easiest to start the cycle of the year with the 'New Year of the Trees', in Hebrew called *TU B'Shevat*, which means the 15th of the month of Shevat. (*TU* טו is the Hebrew way of writing 15: it is the letter ט *Tet* which has the numerical value 9 plus the letter ו *Vav* which has the numerical value of 6 thus 9 + 6 = 15. It cannot be written 10 + 5 because that would be י *Yod* = 10 and v *He* = 5 which would be a name of God *Jah* יה). The month of Shevat falls somewhere between late January and early February in the Christian calendar.

This festival takes place at the time when the sap starts to flow in the trees and the first blossoms appear on the almond trees. The following story is told about deciding the date for this festival. The early Rabbinical School of Hillel and Shamai were discussing this. Shamai's views were always on the side of the correct law (*Din*) and Hillel's always took into account the other side of Grace (*Chesed*). Shamai said that this date should be the first of Shevat which was the correct date of the almond blossom in the valley, but Hillel, who always had the poor and underprivileged in mind, said that 'Whilst it is true that the blossom starts on the first of the month in the rich valleys, the poorer hill farmers only see the blossom on the 15th.' Hillel's view prevailed.

To care for trees was considered very important and the scriptures hold detailed instructions on how they must be treated and what is forbidden. Leviticus 19:23-25 states that it is forbidden to harvest and eat the products of fruit trees for the first three years. In the fourth year the fruit is to be offered as a sacrifice and from the fifth year it should be eaten. All these instructions end with the words 'I am the Lord your God.' This shows the importance of these instructions.

Deuteronomy 20:19-20 says: 'When thou shalt besiege a city a long time in making war against it to take it, thou shalt not wantonly destroy the trees thereof by wielding an axe against them; for thou mayest eat of them but thou shalt not cut them down. For is the tree of the field man, that it should be besieged of thee? Only the trees of which thou knowest, that are not trees for eating [the fruit], thou mayest destroy and cut them down and thou mayest build bulwarks against the city that makest war with thee until it fall.'

The planting of trees was always considered a very important act, partly because man does not plant trees for himself but for a future generation and therefore is often a man's least selfish act.

There are three times in the day when a man must interrupt what he is doing and say the appropriate prayer. To this there is only one exception: when he is planting a tree he must *first* finish planting and *then* say his prayer.

There are many occasions in life when a blessing is said: for instance before eating and drinking, before eating bread, at the sight of the sea, on seeing a rainbow and many more occasions. The blessing on seeing trees blossoming for the first time in the year is: 'Blessed art thou, Lord our God, King of the universe, who hast made thy world lacking in naught, but has produced therein goodly creatures and goodly trees wherewith to give delight onto the children of man.'

Festival of Purim

A month after the New Year of the Trees on the 14th of the month of Adar is the festival of Purim, so called because lots were thrown to determine the most auspicious time for the extermination of the Jews by Haman, the Grand Vizier of the King Achashverosh. The name Purim comes from an Assyrian word *puru* meaning stone. These 'stones' were used for casting lots.

On this 14th of Adar the Book of Esther is read which is the last of the five Megillot (Scrolls). It is the only one which is still generally read from a parchment scroll. It was traditional for every household to possess a Megillah.

It has always been one of the most popular books of the Bible. Its clear and simple style and the perennial truths have always had great appeal and the fortunate outcome has always been the occasion for great rejoicing and festivities. It is the only book of the Bible where the name of God is never directly mentioned, yet the sense of Divine Providence pervades the book.

It describes events in the reign of the Persian king Achashverosh, who is probably identical with Xerxes I (485-464 BCE). It is assumed that this book was written by a Persian Jew with accurate knowledge of the Persian court. Modern research has confirmed the historical accuracy of the accounts.

Josephus in his *Antiquities* gives elaborate accounts of the stories. There are many Talmudic and Midrashim (exposition and searches from the early post biblical-period). Perhaps the best way is to read the story itself.

In recent years there have been memorial services in many synagogues to commemorate the extermination of six million Jews by Hitler and the Nazis and a comparison between the lucky outcome of a potentially similar situation 2,500 years ago and the Holocaust in our day must impress itself on us.

The New Year of Kings

On the first of the next month we come to the New Year of Kings and the administration. This is the first of Nisan. This is called the first month and the only practical importance of this in my life was that when in the first year of school I had to learn the names of the months by rote, we had always to start reciting with Nisan and that, as well as reciting the Hebrew alphabet, are the only things that I remember of my earliest period of religious education.

The Passover

On the 14th of Nisan is the festival Pesach (Passover), so called because the Lord passed over the houses of the children of Israel at the time of the last plague, the killing of the first-born of the Egyptians. On the first eve of this festival the Haggadah Shel Pesach (the telling of the story of the Passover) is read. This was probably transmitted orally for many centuries and is still told in a form which can be understood and remembered by all, including the children.

Those who are interested in the story of the inner development described in the whole book of Exodus can look at it as a description of an inner search. This is told in an outer form about a historic event experienced by a people. In this the progress from the ordinary level in the direction of the final aim can be traced.

From the historical research about the time of Joseph we know that he came to Egypt when the Hyksos were the rulers of Egypt. They were a Semitic people and therefore kinsmen of the Hebrews. Joseph became Viceroy of Egypt and the descendants of his father Jacob (i.e. Israel) were allowed to inhabit a land Goshen, the eastern part of the country in the delta of the Nile. For this they paid rent in the form of a physical service.

The book of Exodus starts with renumerating the sons of Jacob who are also the sons of Israel, i.e. those who struggle with God or the Angel (Genesis 32:29). We can from here on perhaps experience this book both on the level of Jacob and on the level of Israel. Exodus 1:6 describes the death of Joseph and his generations and the next verse describes the increase in number and influence of the children of Israel and their spreading beyond the borders of the land of Goshen.

Exodus 1:8 says: 'There arose a new King over Egypt, who knew not Joseph.' Historically this refers to the fact that the Hyksos dynasty had been overthrown and a native dynasty had regained power. The Hebrews were foreigners to the new masters who feared that the physical increase as well as the influence of this people was a danger and that they could be swamped by them. The King of Egypt therefore took measures to reduce their influence and numbers.

In the usual translations of the book of Exodus the Hebrew word *EBED* עבד is translated as 'slave' which makes the whole story rather more difficult to understand. Whilst the word *EBED* can mean slave it has also other meanings. In the context of Exodus it never means a person who can be bought or sold (the Latin *manicipium*). The original relationship with Pharaoh was that of a vassal to his lord. In general, this word can mean to work, to labour, to till the ground, to dress a vineyard, to work for another, to serve, to minister etc.

In an esoteric sense the level of 'Egypt' (*Mizrayim* מצרים) is often used to describe the level of the 'body', or the ordinary level of life. A vassal of Pharaoh can become a servant (or vassal) of the 'Higher'.

A very interesting question emerges when we look at the times when the phrase 'King of Egypt' and when the title 'Pharaoh' is used in Exodus. Could it be that the 'King of Egypt' is an ordinary ruler whilst 'Pharaoh' relates to somebody who can be in touch with a different energy that guides him to an action which serves to fulfil the purpose of the Higher, even if it appears 'wicked' in the ordinary sense?

We see that the instructions of the 'King of Egypt' get thwarted by the Hebrew midwives and they report to the Pharaoh (Exodus 1:19) why the instructions of the 'King of Egypt' were not carried out, and verses 20-21 describe the reward the midwives received from God.

Chapter 2 becomes very much more interesting and surprising if we take into account the various legends and stories relating to this chapter: We are first told that the father of Moses as well as his mother were of the tribe of Levi, i.e. from the Priests.

The story is told in chapter 2:4-9, but the legend that I have read about these events somehow rings more true. According to the legend Moses' sister Miriam and the daughter of Pharaoh had met earlier and Pharaoh's daughter knew this Hebrew family. When Miriam produced a wet-nurse so quickly Pharaoh's daughter would have had a good idea to whom she entrusted the child. In verse 10 we learn that the real mother of Moses brought the child to Pharaoh's daughter and he was thus brought up in Pharaoh's house who was of course also the High Priest of Egypt. We could perhaps assume, although we are not told directly, that he acquired the essence of the inner teaching which was alive at Pharaoh's court.

We are then told how he went to Midian, married the daughter of the High Priest Jethro, and was keeping the flock of his father-in-law. This flock could relate to sheep but perhaps also to Midianites. The root meaning of this word includes the meanings to strive, to contend, to make efforts (*Midyan* מדינ). In Exodus 3:1 Moses leads his flock to the 'furthest edge of the wilderness [literally beyond the wilderness] and comes to the mountain of God, onto Horeb.' This is possibly identical with Mount Sinai, where God had chosen to manifest his Glory at a later time.

There follows the account of the Burning Bush, which could be interpreted as the inner ascent of Moses. First the messenger of the Lord appears to him, that is, not yet God himself, and Moses takes a step towards turning in the right direction and SEE. When the Lord notices that he has turned to SEE he calls him by name, a way to describe that Moses's action has made it possible for the Higher energy to turn to him and make contact. Moses answers: 'Here I AM' (*HiNeNJ* הנני). This can be looked at as a code which is used to describe that a man has reached the next Higher level. Moses is now open to hear the voice of the Lord telling him to take off his shoes because he is on Holy Ground. By obeying this it becomes possible to be told and experience that he is in the presence of the God of Abraham, the God of Isaac and the God of Jacob. Moses understands the contact that has now taken place and he covers his face as no man can see the face of God.

In Exodus 3:8 the Lord declares: 'I have come down... to bring them up' [my people]. Can we see again in this the double movement necessary for man's ascent? Now Moses can receive his mission to bring the people out. He realises the gigantic task and asks Who am I (*Mij ANOKI* מי אנוכי)

To help him he is now told the *name* of God: 'I am that I am.' (אהיה אשר אהיה). And God instructs Moses to say to the children of Israel: 'I AM has sent me to you.'

From here until Chapter 15:22 we read how Moses and Aaron were guided to carry out the mission given to them and this is told as mentioned before in the form of the Hagadah Shel Pesach.

The reading of this book starts with an invitation by the master of the house to all who are hungry and in want to enter and join the celebration of the Passover. According to tradition this is said in Aramaic because this part of the Hagadah was written in Babylon during the time of Captivity (seventh-sixth centuries BCE) when Aramaic (also called Chaldaic) was the vernacular and understood by everybody.

This is followed by the youngest child present asking some questions about the meaning of this day which are answered by the master of the house. Thus all are actively involved in the remembrance 'of this day'.

There follows a passage where four sons ask concerning the meaning of this day. Each asks differently and the father gives appropriately different answers: they represent the Wise, the Wicked, the Simple and 'he who does not know how to ask'.

It is always stressed that this 'remembering' is not a recollection of a happening that took place about three and a half thousand years ago. We experience this each year and have to live this event NOW.

Apart from the inner meaning of each festival there is also a meaning relating to the agricultural time of year or events in nature, which we have already seen when we described the New Year of the Trees. The Passover on this level is a festival of the early harvest, which includes the harvest of the barley. Could this be the reason why in the New Testament, in the Gospel of St John, Chapter 6, barley loaves are provided and it is mentioned that this takes place at the period of the Passover?

Pentecost

From Passover starts the counting of Omer (עמר literally sheaf). Leviticus 23:4-22 gives the details of this aspect of the Harvest festival for both these festivals of Passover and Pentecost (this word comes from the Greek *Pentekonta* = fiftieth). It is the counting of seven times seven days from the offering of the sheaf of barley to the offering of the sheaf of wheat and the ripening of fruit. This festival was first called 'The Feast of Harvest' and the day of first fruits. It is now called 'The Feast of Weeks' (חג שבעות). Pentecost was regarded as the concluding festival of Passover. We can therefore look at the period between these two feasts as the period of ripening which takes seven times seven days or seven cycles called weeks.

On another level it shows the period from the crossing over (עבר) from the land of Mitzrayim (מצרים); from the level of ordinary life through the Sea of Reeds (ים סוף) into the Wilderness (מדבר), the Land of Search.

This statement requires some explanation and must be looked at as one of the many possible interpretations and not as a statement of fact: Mitzrayim (Egypt) is sometimes considered the 'body' and sometimes the ordinary level of life. Pharaoh in the story of Exodus becomes thus an 'Energy' in the service of the Higher which serves in the appropriate way to bring the Children of Israel from the attitude of inner servitude, which is slavery, to the possibility of the road to real service and thus freedom. This moment seems to me to be described in Exodus 12:36 and 3:22 which translated with this idea in mind describes a voluntary giving up which links a justified feeling of *joie de vivre* bringing the searcher into the right relationship with his body; and the body is then able to respond.

Such a state cannot last very long and so the Children of Israel are soon persuaded by the powerful army of Mitzrayim (the body). (None of this has of course any connection with the historical people called the Egyptians.)

The Hebrew word for the 'Red Sea' is *Yam Suph* (ים סוף). In the time when the Bible was written vowels were not used. They were introduced very much later. Using two possible positions of the vowel point in connection with the *vav* (ו) it could therefore be read *Yam Suph* meaning the sea of reeds or *Yam Soph* which would become the sea of the end or termination. Could this 'crossing over' therefore refer to the crossing from one level to another; a form of rebirth?

To cross to the Wilderness (*MIDBAR* מדבר) could again have several meanings. The root *MIDBAR* is connected with the root *DAVAR* דבר, This root can be linked to the word Wilderness but also to the root for a word like the Greek *logos*.

From this connection we can perhaps accept a meaning of this 'Wilderness' as the land of search to which the Children of Israel crossed over, from the ordinary land of existence. The time from the Passover to the Feast of Weeks is a period of ripening of seven times seven cycles, from the inner slavery of 'Egypt' to inner freedom and the Giving of the Law as the beginning of the realisation that freedom requires the acceptance of an inner discipline.

Now it seems to make more sense that the ancient teachers considered the Passover and the Feast of Weeks as basically one festival.

The festival itself we have already described when talking about the revelation on Mount Sinai as the centre of the Torah.

The Ninth of Ab

Following the cycle of the year we come to the ninth of the month of Ab when, according to tradition, the Temples were destroyed.

The temple of Soloman, the first temple, was completely destroyed by Nebuchadnezzar, king of Babylon, in the year 586 BCE. The Persian king Cyrus believed that he had been entrusted with a mission by his God Marduk to conquer the world and restore the various gods which the Babylonians had carried away and restore them to their rightful shrines. Following this policy he authorised the rebuilding of the temple in Jerusalem during the first year of his reign, 538 BCE. And the second temple was rebuilt. In the year 70 CE the Romans stormed the temple area and destroyed it. Like the destruction of the first temple this happened on the ninth of Ab. Since that time this day has always been a day of mourning.

A Rabbi once explained to me some of the inner meaning of this day. It takes place at the time when nature is at its strongest and outwardly most magnificent point (late July/August). Fruit is ripening and all the visible world seems at its richest. From now on everything will begin to decay until in the late autumn it will all outwardly die. What however is most important is that at this time something has to come into being, inwardly, which can grow until the religious New Year and the Day of Atonement when it will be tested as to whether it deserves to continue for a further cycle. For this the temple (*Heikal* היכל) is the outer symbol containing the Holy of Holies (משכן), the 'dwelling place' which can not be destroyed by the material world.

Rosh Ha Shanah (literally: Head of the Year)

The New Year is described in Leviticus 23:24 which says: 'In the seventh month, in the first day of the month there shall be on to you a solemn rest, a memorial proclaimed by the sound of a trumpet [horn = *Shofar* שפר], a holy convocation.

Perhaps the concept of the great twelfth century teacher Maimonides gives a clear picture of the meaning of the blowing of the *shofar*: 'Although the blowing of the Shofar on the New Year is a commandment of the Law, there is a further meaning in it of this purport: Awake, ye slumberers from your sleep, and rouse yourselves from your lethargy. Make search into your deeds and turn in repentance. Remember your Creator, ye who forget the truth in the trifles of the hour, who go astray all your years after vain illusions, which can neither profit nor deliver. Look to your souls and mend your ways and actions; let every one of you leave his evil path and his unworthy purpose.' (Maimonides Hilchot Teshubah III/4)

The New Year festival has three aspects. The first one is the blowing of the *shofar*, which we might call the day of inner awakening. The second one refers to the tradition that it is on this day that the world was created. In this respect it is a day for reflection on the universal sovereignty of the deity. Thirdly it is the day of judgement for the deeds of the past year and the day of account and reckoning. In this respect it is the Day of Memorial (Yom Hazikaron יום הזכרון). Perhaps this last view of the day can be best be described by an extract from a meditation composed by the famous Rabbi Meshullam ben Kalonymous of Mainz in about 1000 CE. This is a portion of the service on this day of Ashkenazi (German) Jews. It is always referred to by the opening words (*unesaneh toqef* ונתנה תקף):

'Let us celebrate the mighty holiness of this day. The great trumpet [*shofar*] is sounded, the still small voice is heard; the angels are dismayed; fear and trembling seize hold of them as they proclaim: "Behold, the day of judgement". The host of heaven is to be arraigned in judgement. For in thine eyes they are not pure; and all who enter the world come to pass before thee as a flock of sheep. As a shepherd seeketh out his flock and causes them to pass beneath his crook, so doest thou cause to pass and number, tell and visit every living soul appointing the measure of every creature's life and decreeing their destiny.'

On the first day of the year it is inscribed and on the Day of Atonement the decree is sealed: how many shall pass away, how many shall be born, who shall live, and who shall die, who at the measure of men's days and who before it . . . who shall be brought low and who raised up.'

But Penitence, Prayer and Charity
Avert the severe decree.

These three English words give only a very approximate idea of the Hebrew terms in this context.

Penitence: *teshubah* תשובה comes from the root *Shub* שוב meaning to turn, return, turn back, to be restored. Hieroglyphically we can see it as a movement from ת (the last letter of the alphabet, i.e. the lowest point or the point of start of this movement). *Shin* ש, a triadic relationship, i.e. perhaps in the sense of the three sephirot where the balance of the two opposites allows a movement in the middle column either up or down. U is ו linked to *Beit* ב = the inner house, *hei* ה = life. We could therefore see Teshubah as a turning from the place where I am to Life. The Greek word *metanoia* describes a very similar idea.

Prayer: *tephilah* תפלה comes from the root *PaleL* פלל, meaning to judge, to intercede, to supplicate. Hieroglyphically it starts again with the last letter *Taf* ת which can also represent something that has descended from above and wishes to return from below. *Peh* פ represents the mouth – speech and breath. *Lamed* ל describes an expansive movement and often the link of two levels, and *He* ה Life.

Perhaps one can see in it a movement by man towards the Higher where some help comes from above.

Charity: *tzedaka* צדקה, comes from the root *Tzedek* צדק = righteousness, justice or equity.

The Day of Atonement

The ten days between the New Year and the Day of Atonement are called the Ten Days of Penitence. Ten symbolises completeness. They stand for the complete preparation for the Day of Atonement. The Rabbis apply the passage in Isaiah: 'Seek ye the Lord while he may be found, Call ye upon Him while He is near.' This period of the ten days is also called 'The days of Awe'.

It is the accepted teaching that Yom Kippur atones only for sins committed against God. For offences against his neighbour a man does not find atonement on Yom Kippur until he has pacified those he has offended.

It is a day of complete fast; neither food nor drink can be taken.

The reasons given for this fast are:

a) As a penance: the man who fasts for his sins is saying, 'I do not want to be let off lightly. I deserve to be punished.'

b) As a self discipline.

c) As a means of focusing the mind on the spiritual.

d) As a means of awaking compassion, when we experience the suffering of hunger and thirst.

The fast must be undertaken sincerely. Thus each year the passage from the prophet Isaiah 58:3 is read:

'Wherefore have we fasted, and Thou seest not? Wherefore have we afflicted our soul, and Thou takest no knowledge? Behold in the day of your fast ye pursue your business, And exact all your labours.'

A sick person whose health may suffer from fasting *must* eat. Preservation of life always takes precedence over all other commandments.

For me it has always been a day which is entirely different from all other days of the year. As a child I used to go to the Synagogue in the morning. My great uncle Julius was always there and I used to stand and sit next to him and try to follow what was going on. From the age of six I was taught to read the Hebrew square script, in which the prayer books are printed and the Torah scrolls are written. With the exception of a few words I was however not taught the language, so that on the whole I had little idea what I was reading, and perhaps saying or singing out loud, and yet the whole procedure had a great deal of meaning for me. My uncle always watched that I followed the reading, asking me periodically to show him the place in the prayer book. When I had lost the place he would show me with the little finger of his left hand where it was. I was usually standing on his left. Occasionally he would give some explanation as to the meaning of some prayer or ritual, very often in the form of a story of what happened to him in his youth. The Yiddish for the Greek word Synagogue is *shul* which has the same root as the English word 'school' and is basically a place of learning. It is therefore quite fitting that such teaching is given whilst the service is going on. There are of course also those who engage in idle chatter.

The atmosphere of a Jewish Orthodox service is thus very different from say a service in the Church of England. It must be remembered that the services on Yom Kippur start when the stars become visible on the night before and last about three hours. On the day itself it usually starts about 8 a.m. and lasts till the stars become visible at night. Sometimes there is an interval of about two hours in the early afternoon. At the age of six I did not spend such long hours in the Synagogue, but started with only one hour or so in the morning. This lengthened every year until by the age of eleven or twelve I spent most of the day at the service. My father had the attitude that any outer ritual was of minor importance and had to be followed only voluntarily, without any compulsion from outside. At thirteen years a Jewish child becomes a 'man', is Bar Mitzvah (a son of the Commandments) and takes on all the religious and ritual obligations.

At the time of the interval in the afternoon, on one occasion, my father appeared carrying a ham roll, offered it to me and said: 'You don't need to fast unless you wish.' This would of course have been a double breach, firstly to eat on the day of fast, and secondly to eat a pork product. This presented an important question which resulted in the fact that I have fasted ever since.

I continued to attend services on the High Holidays without knowing the language until I started to learn Hebrew under the influence of Gurdjieff's teaching at the age of fifty-three. This brought me to the question, what had been going on all these years? I knew I had not followed a ritual blindly and just outwardly. Examining this, I realised that by standing next to my uncle during all the years of my youth, I had taken in a great deal of the meaning with other parts than my head. The ancient melodies and cantillations had entered my feelings in a direct way. Perhaps the fact that I did not understand the words had made it possible to experience something that my head would have prevented me from seeing, had I spoken the language.

For me the meaning of this day, which is taken out of ordinary life and entirely devoted to the question of the significance of life, is best illustrated by a Chasidic story which I heard many years ago. In one of the Chasidic communities of Eastern Europe led by one of the important Rabbis of the period, a man whom nobody had ever seen entered the Synagogue at the time of the Neilah (concluding) service. This is the last service of the day, when the emotions are highest. It is the time when, according to tradition, the decision is taken 'on High', as to whether the entry which was made in the book of life at the New Year is to be 'sealed'. The man was dressed very simply, so was possibly of rather humble origin, certainly not a learned man. He proceeded to pray with obvious great devotion, but what he was saying was simply the letters of the alphabet: *aleph, beit, gimel,* and so on. When he came to the end, he would simply begin again. This was all he knew.

Before the end of the Service, the Rabbi rose to speak, and said: 'If the prayers of this community have been heard and accepted today, this is due to the devotion and prayer of this man, whom none of us have ever seen before. He has been able to open the Gate for all of us.'

The emphasis is always on the community and never on the individual. I do not recall ever having heard a discussion as to what this community is, for which there are a number of Hebrew and Yiddish words, except on the level of ordinary administration and money matters. I have of course later read learned explanations. But apart from the fact that this idea can have many different meanings on many different levels, I do not think that I have learnt anything very useful from the words.

Since a man is only a relatively independent concentration of energies and therefore must retain a relationship with other such concentrations of energies, the questions 'Who am I' and 'Who are We?' are part of the same search, which I or We must pursue. No answer can however be given.

Sukkot (Tabernacles)

Five days after Yom Kippur we come to a festival called in Hebrew *Sukkot* סכות meaning 'booths' from a root *Sakak* סכך which has the root meaning to cover, to protect, to place as covering. The noun *sukkah* סכה means booth, tent, a temporary dwelling made from boughs and branches. For reasons which I do not know this is called 'tabernacles' in English, using the Latin word for tent or booth which is the same as the Hebrew word *sukkah*. But the word 'tabernacle' is also used for the translation of an entirely different idea, namely the Hebrew word *Mishkan* משכן which comes from a root 'to dwell' and in this context is the dwelling place of the *Shekinah* שכינה, the female aspect of the immanent form of the Deity. The Sanctuary, which was constructed to contain the Tablets that Moses brought from Mount Sinai and which was carried by the Israelites in the desert, is the *Mishkan*. Some believe that a special tent was constructed to contain the *Mishkan*, the Sanctuary.

The *sukkah* in relation to this festival is a temporary dwelling covered with leaves and branches, where it has to be possible to see the sky through the roof. The idea is that by dwelling for seven days in this hut we are reminded of the kind of dwelling our ancestors lived in during their forty years of wandering through the wilderness. On another level it is to remind us of the impermanence of our existence on this earth which is compared to the journey of our search in the 'wilderness'.

Why these two entirely different aspects of dwelling in movable or impermanent structures should be described in English with an identical Latin word I have never understood. From the questions I have been asked, I must conclude that many people must have been just as confused as me.

The first mention of this festival is in Exodus 23:16, which describes it as the Feast of Ingathering חג האסף *Chag ha Asiph*: 'at the end of the year when thou gatherest in thy labours out of the field.'

Leviticus 23:34 gives details of this festival. 'Speak unto the Children of Israel saying: On the fifteenth day of the seventh month is the feast of Sukkoth for seven days unto the Lord...' Like the early harvest festival, the Pesach (Passover), the late harvest festival is also at the time of the full moon, as the Jewish Calendar each month begins with the new moon and the fourteenth or fifteenth of the month is the full moon. The weather, the tides and the likely amount of cloud cover are influenced by the moon. An agricultural community will be very much more influenced by its cycle, which may also have a bearing on the right time for planting and harvesting.

There was indeed a libation of water which was bound up particularly with the eighth day of the festival. It marked the beginning of the rainy season of the approaching winter.

The Mishnah (codification of the oral law or tradition) says that the world is judged for rain at this festival. Prayers for rain therefore became customary. To this day prayer for rain is retained in the ritual. Whilst it has little meaning in Western countries, in Israel rain is the life blood. (I Samuel 7 and Isaiah 12 seem to refer to this rite.)

As a symbol of rejoicing four gifts of the soil were brought into the Temple: the Palm Branch (*Lulab*), the Citron (*Ethrog*), the Myrtle and the Willow. In later times it became customary to hold these in your hand and 'wave' the *Lulab*. This is done during the 'Hallel' Prayer (Praising) and Psalm 118 verses 1-4 and 25 are recited.

From II Maccabees 10:6-8, we know that the feast of Sukkoth was kept in this way in the second century BCE when the Temple still stood with palms and other branches and psalms were sung with gladness, even in those days of outer oppression.

This is how it is still celebrated in all Synagogues today. These outer rituals have of course deeper meanings on other levels. Although the form is repeated each year it is hoped that understanding has grown by the next cycle and that therefore the meaning is new.

The eighth day of this festival is called *Simchath Torah* שמחת תורה, the rejoicing of the Law. On that day the last portion of the Pentateuch (Chapters 33 and 34 of Deuteronomy) are read, followed immediately by the first chapter of Genesis. In this way the reading of the *Chumash* (the Five Books of Moses) never comes to an end and the cycle continues just as the cycles of nature continue. The meaning however is never quite the same and the more we search the more we open ourselves to the meaning.

Simchath Torah is also very much a children's festival. In many Synagogues the children are called to the *Bimah*, to the reading of the Law. I still remember the excitement of seeing the actual writing in the scroll. It is also customary to take all the scrolls from the Ark and bear them in procession seven times around the Synagogue, singing and dancing. The children are often given sweets and fruit.

Fortunately for me, I was given very few 'learned explanations' of the meaning of this day, so that I was able to enjoy the childish rejoicing together with a feeling of awe for the sacred meaning for what was written on these scrolls. This came to me mainly from the attitude of the grown-ups who were able to transfer this feeling of awe without words and, it seems to me, without sentimentality.

Chanukah

The last of the festivals is Chanukah חנוכה, which starts on the 25th of the month of Kislev. The word means consecration and refers to the re-consecration of the temple after the desecration by the Greek conquerors in the year 164 BCE.

The Apocryphal book of the Maccabees gives us a detailed picture of the times. The movement of assimilation to Greek thoughts and ideas in the wake of the conquests of Alexander the Great and the oppression under his successors sets the scene, Perhaps the destruction of traditional values, a complete change of lifestyle and the arising of a sudden movement against it sound to us today much more familiar than when I first heard them nearly seventy years ago. Then the heroic deeds of some men in a bygone age sounded very different from our time.

In chapter 10 of II Maccabees we have a description of how importantly the continuity of tradition motivated their action. The cleansing of the temple took place exactly two years after the desecration. It was important that this was so near to the feast of Sukkoth (Tabernacles), which they had to celebrate in the mountains, in hiding, away from their holy places. Maccabees 4:36ff gives a description of the cleansing of the Temple (purification).

Flavius Josephus refers to this festival as the Feast of Lights. This name is apparently based on the legend that when Judas Maccabeus was recaptured the only thing they could find which had not been defiled was a small cruse of oil, sufficient for one day's light.

Miraculously the light kindled continued to burn eight days and nights. The festival is therefore celebrated today by lighting a single candle on the first night and then one additional light on each successive night until on the eighth night the eight candles of the Menorah are all ablaze. As in Judaism there has always to be an opposition to each idea, some groups carry this out the opposite way, by lighting eight candles on the first day and diminishing the number each day until there is one candle on the last day. Both groups have equally plausible esoteric explanations for their actions.

This legend seems to be connected with a prophecy of Zechariah, concerning the miracle of the oil.

The Persian King Cyrus had given permission for the rebuilding of the Second Temple in 538 BCE. Partly owing to the opposition of the Samarians the building had not been completed in 520 BCE, in the second year of the reign of Darius, the year when the prophecy of Zechariah began. Zechariah זכריה means 'he remembers the imminent aspect of the Lord'. The root Zakar is also used in the sense of remembering oneself. Here it could mean making contact with the energy called Yah. Zechariah's chronology continues: son of Berachiah ברכיה (which means whom the Lord has blessed), son of Iddo עדו (which means timely or his time). (II Chronicles 12:15 to 13:22). It would appear possible that Iddo was active at the time of the return from exile. The holy oil is a symbol of Spirit as in the process of anointing.

Hagai and Zechariah were both active at the same time, and their aim was to help to bring about the completion of the rebuilding of the Temple. This was indeed successful in 516 BCE.

Zechariah Chapter 4 describes the vision of the Golden Menorah, with seven lights and an olive tree on either side. A bowl in the centre gathers the oil from the two sides and supplies the fuel for the seven lamps, the holy oil being a symbol of spirit as in the process of anointing. The Angel explains the meaning: 'Not by might, nor by power but by My spirit, saith the Lord of Hosts.' This is interpreted as an expression of laws of the universe. This vision is usually quoted as the basis of this festival in connection with the Eternal Light in the temple. It connects with the instruction about the first temple and all subsequent temples. It is thus placing it outside time into the 'now'.

The 25th of Kislev, the date of this Festival of Light, is of course very near to the winter solstice, but because of the variation of the moon calendar and the sun calculations it can vary by three to four weeks. The 'feel' however will correspond and soon we shall begin to think about the rebirth of nature and the new cycle starting with the New Year of the Trees.

CHAPTER 4

The Idea of Covenant in the Hebrew Tradition

THE IDEA OR PERHAPS principle of Covenant is very basic in Hebrew thought and goes back to early periods. The description of a covenant as the relationship between the suzerain and his vassal probably goes back to a very early period of cultures in the Fertile Crescent.

The Hebrew word for covenant ברית comes from a root *barah* ברה meaning to choose, to select. To make a covenant is *karat berit* כרתברית, literally to cut, to engrave in stone a covenant. This term gives me the impression of a description of the same action on two levels: the *karat* referring to the physical engraving or writing and the *barah* to the intended relationship with the Higher.

The earliest covenant in the Bible is in Genesis 9:9. Elohim (God the Creator) says: 'Behold I establish My covenant with you . . .' This establishes first that every animal and green herb is food for man with one exception: 'only flesh with a life thereof, which is the blood thereof ye shall not eat.' The Rabbis interpret this covenant given to Noah as the 'Seven Commandments'. These are:

1. The establishment of courts of justice.
2. The prohibition of blasphemy.
3. The prohibition of idolatry.
4. The prohibition of incest.
5. The prohibition of bloodshed.
6. The prohibition of robbery.
7. The prohibition of eating flesh cut from a living animal.

This is sealed with the 'everlasting covenant of the Rainbow' between Elohim and every living creature of all flesh that is upon the earth (Genesis 9:13-17).

In ancient times non-Jews living among Israelites were only required to obey these Seven Commandments, which was considered to be the Natural Religion, vital to the existence of human society.

There follows the covenant with Abraham (Genesis 17) where God is revealed to Abram in the aspect of El Shadai אל שדי, the Almighty, and he is told that his name will be changed from Abram (Father of Heights אברם) to Father of Multitudes (*AB/HAMON* אבהמון). This foreshadows the fact that as the father of Ishmael he would also be the forefather of the Arab nations. The Arab word for multitude, thus *Raham* רהם was used, thus Abraham אברהם. Verse

17:7 says: 'And I will establish My covenant between Me and thee, and thy seed after thee throughout their generations for an everlasting covenant...' This covenant is sealed by the circumcision of all males.

To this the Zohar in (I/91b) says the following: 'The Lord appeared to Abram', and addressed him without reserve. Thus when Abram was circumcised he emerged from the unripe state and entered into the holy covenant and was crowned with the sacred crown and entered into the covenant on which the world is based, and thus the world was firmly established for his sake. For it is written: 'But for my covenant I had not set the ordinances of heaven and earth' and also 'when they were created'. *Behibaream* (when they were created) can be read anagrammatically both *be-Abraham* (for the sake of Abraham) and *b'he'b'raam* (he created them with *He*) and both come to the same thing.

The letter *He* has a numerical meaning of five which esoterically principally stands for Life, and tells us that Abraham has reached a level of contact with a Higher form of energy. Another commentary indicates that the opening (which is the meaning of circumcision) has enabled him to contact the Shekinah, the immanent, female aspect of the Godhead.

In Exodus chapter 6 God remembers the previous covenant with Abraham, Isaac and Jacob, but now to Moses he reveals his name YHVH יהוה, the Tetragrammaton. The process of the Exodus from Egypt starts with the escape from the slavery of outer oppression and leads to the inner development which can bring inner freedom if a person follows the demands of the Covenant of Sinai. This is the focal point of the Bible, as we have already mentioned.

There is a further covenant which is called the New Covenant (*B'rith Chadasha* ברית חדשה), which relates to the teachings of Jeremiah, Ezekiel and perhaps other prophets in that period. Jeremiah describes this in 31:31-6. In verse 32 the Lord says: 'I will put My Law in their inward parts, and in their hearts I will write it.'

Oral and Written Law
The origin of the Oral Law and its relationship to the Written Law has been described in many different ways and has led to many views and controversies which continue to this day.

Perhaps it is best to adhere to the principle followed in the orthodox prayerbook. Every paragraph with no definite author is introduced with the phrase: 'It is said' (ne-e-mar נאמר).

Thus *it is said* that Moses received the Torah (the teaching) on Mount Sinai, in the form of 'the Tablets of Testimony, tablets of stone written by the finger of God.' (Exodus 31:18.) These contained only 'positive' commandments with no negative ones. When Moses descended from the mountain and saw the Children of Israel worshipping the golden calf, he realised that they were not mature enough to understand these commandments and he broke the Tablets.

He was told by God to hew new tablets, although it says that the words written on them were the same. Nevertheless Exodus 34:10 speaks about a renewal of the covenant and says that 'the Lord will go in the midst of Israel.' (34:9)

It is also said that the second lot of Tablets had both 'positive' and 'negative' commandments, which the Children of Israel were able to understand and follow.

The secret oral teaching which Moses had now received directly from the Lord (Exodus 34:29) says that Moses knew not that horns (*Koran* קרן) radiated from his face and that this new radiation made it possible for him to transmit the secret oral law which he first repeated complete to Aaron and his sons, then an appropriately smaller amount to all the priests, and thirdly that which was suitable for all the people. This knowledge was transmitted for a long time by word of mouth only, to those considered worthy to receive it.

In one way this transmission is described in the 'Ethics of the Fathers' **פרקי אבות**, which is read, one chapter each Sabbath, between the Passover and the New Year. Could this be to indicate the journey from the slavery of the ordinary level to the highest moment of the inner struggle? Again and again it is stressed in the Ethics of the Fathers that most Schools had two teachers, one inclined towards one principle and the other to its opposite. In the struggle of these two principles a balance was achieved which allowed a step in the direction of new understanding.

After at least a thousand years these oral teachings started to be written down, on the one hand in the form of the *Halachah* הלכה, which means practice or usage; on the other hand as *Kabbalah* קבלה from the root *kabal* קבל meaning to receive, thus, the received esoteric knowledge.

The formal codification of the Oral Law, is called Mishna (from the root *shanah* שנה which means to repeat, to do a second time, or do again). The recitation of the scriptural text is *miqra* מקרא, from the root *kara* קרא, to read or engrave. Hence it was said that the Scriptures are read but the Mishna is studied.

When the authoritative version of the Mishna was completed, 'extraneous' commentaries or *baraiatha* (singular *baraitha*) in Aramaic were added. One complete collection was preserved called Tosefta, the other existing only in fragments. *Tosephet* means 'addition' in Hebrew.

From about the second century CE the intellectual centres of Judaism moved to the 'Academies' where two great compilations of the Mishna were recorded: the Babylonian and the Palestinian Talmud, which are quotations and supplements on the Mishna text. The additions and commentaries are called the Gemarah.

A vast literature has grown up, which ranges from comments giving a very deep understanding to purely legal questions, comments on ethical behaviour and practical guidance for life. All this grew up gradually without any central plan. It is therefore extremely difficult for anybody who does not devote his whole life to the study of this literature to get a really clear picture of all these writings. As far as I know only Rabbi Moses Ben Maimon (abbreviated as RAMBAM), known as Maimonides, tried in his commentary on the Mishna (1168) to bring order to all those writings.

In our own time Rabbi Adin Steinsaltz is undertaking the monumental task of a commentary and translation of the Babylonian Talmud, which may make it easier for Western Europeans to approach the meaning of these writings.

The esoteric knowledge and practice, the Kabbalah, continued, on the whole, to be transmitted orally for a much longer period. This knowledge travelled from the Middle East to Europe through Italy, Provence, Catalonia and finally to the rest of Spain. After the expulsion of the Jews from Spain it moved to the countries bordering the coast of the Mediterranean, the so-called Maḥreb countries as well as Egypt, and then especially to Safed (Zefat) in Israel. From there it re-combined with the knowledge in Europe and led to the flourishing of the Hasidic teachings mainly in Eastern and Central Europe.

Outer events from the late eighteenth century CE onwards began to influence happenings in rather unexpected ways. The French Revolution with its ideas of equality and freedom brought about the opening of the ghettos in most European countries which brought Jews into a more intimate contact with the 'outer world' and led to the 'assimilation' of a large number of people, who, up to that time, had continued to live in an almost medieval way.

There was an old Jewish saying: 'There is always a going away and a returning.' So it proved to be this time. The continued pogroms in Eastern Europe and anti-Semitism brought the movement of Zionism which resulted in new interest in the Hebrew language and in Jewish thought in general; so that by the time of the Holocaust, when 90 per cent of the Jews there were annihilated, a new endeavour had been established in Israel, where Hebrew had become a living language. With the help of the surviving Jews in Western Europe it became possible to revive the old knowledge. There were now a number of scholars and researchers who could read and 'feel' in Hebrew and translate it into European languages in a living way. It seems that this enabled me in our Study Group to read and experience some Kabbalistic writings in a live way which would not have been possible previously, and thus avoided the pitfall of 'comparing' with other teachings.

I also wonder whether the occasional guidance and hints given to us by M. Henri Tracol, who lived in the area of Provence and Languedoc where these traditions had been particularly strong, was not a factor of making this study such a strong link with our efforts in general.

Gershom G. Scholem, Professor of Jewish Mysticism at the Hebrew University in Jerusalem, points in his writings to the influence of Gnosticism in the early Kabbalistic works of the eleventh and twelfth centuries which raises many interesting questions, to which of course no factual answers can be given, but which indicate the possibility of an exchange of 'something' when people are open beyond facts and words.

CHAPTER 5

Sacrifices and Offerings

Owing to my upbringing, which very strongly stressed the ideas of 'progress', and the belief of modern 'civilised' man who condemned the idea of animal sacrifice as a barbaric custom, it took me a very long time even to suspect that all these instructions and descriptions about sacrifices could relate to inner experiences and have a symbolic meaning. These practices would therefore be far from primitive or savage rituals.

This possibility occurred to me in the following way. For several years I had been attending a study of Hebrew grammar in connection with an enquiry into ancient teachings, within the framework of Gurdjieff's teaching. The Rabbi who instructed me in this grammar sometimes made remarks about the tradition in general, on which he never elaborated.

One day he made the remark that people who witnessed the sacrifices in the temple shared directly the experience of offerings, which gave them a direct understanding. After the destruction of the temple the Rabbis of the first and second century CE had the very difficult task of replacing this direct understanding with new forms.

Because of Gurdjieff's teaching my ideas of 'progress' and 'ancient savages' had already been very much modified and I set out to find out what the Rabbi might have meant by his remark. The first thing that I discovered is that there is no word in Hebrew that corresponds to our association with the word 'sacrifice', which for us has the connection of giving up or 'making holy' in a moral sense. The Hebrew word nearest to it is *ZaBaCh* (ז ב ח) which has the root meaning of the slaughter or the killing of animals.

The same root also forms the word 'altar'. The word in Hebrew relates to something entirely passive and to whom this 'sacrifice' happens. The action of man is best described by 'offering' in Hebrew *TeRuMah* (ת ר ו מ ה) from a root meaning 'to be high', 'to rise', 'to lift up'.

There is a sequence of grades of offering which can be seen as a movement of energies in the opposite direction from the movement of 'Creation'. For this we have to accept that the movement of 'Creation' is the movement from God to man and the movement of the offerings, the movement from man to God.

The first offering in this direction is *QaRBaN* (קרבן) from the root *QaRaB* (קרב) meaning to draw near. The same root letters can also have the meaning of 'middle' or 'inner'. The idea of the three columns or pillars of the tree of Sephirot, the Tree of Life, can also be applied here. If a man by his endeavour can place himself in the centre between the two opposites such as rigorous law (*DIN* דין) and grace (*CheSeD* חסד) he will be able to be connected to the middle column which allows a move upwards or downwards.

At this stage the Hassidic teachings stress the need for *DeVeKUT* (דבקות), usually translated as cleaving (to God) from the root *DaVaK* (דבק): to be placed or set or planted, and can perhaps best be described as the aim to remain in contact with this higher energy.

This enables man to make the next offering which is called *OLAH* (עלה) a burnt offering from the root meaning to 'go up' *ALaH* (עלה). The symbolic meaning of this process is that man has offered all his ordinary functions to the Higher. It is always stressed that this has to be done 'rightly'. Legends describe that when this is done the correct way the smoke of the offering will rise in a straight line upwards, but if it is done incorrectly and something is held back by the person making the offering the smoke will rise making 'strange' shapes and in this smoke the dog BelAdon will come down and devour the offering.

The third stage is the meal offering, the offering of flour and oil which is symbolic of the offering of all of a man's ordinary existence; all that he has produced. This offering is called *MiNCHaH* (מנחה) from the root *MaNaCH* (מנח) meaning to give.

And finally there are the peace offerings *SHaLaMYM* (שלמים) from the root *ShaLoM* (שלם) which basically means to be complete, whole, at peace. At this stage man would offer everything to the service of the Higher and thus be in the real sense 'a servant of God'.

This is of course only one way of looking at the offerings or sacrifices as they relate to the inner effort of man.

The whole early part of the book of Leviticus deals with the various aspects of offerings and Chapters 11 to 16 give the Laws of Purity leading to the description of the Food Laws; a connection which became even closer after the destruction of the Second Temple when the Rabbis of the first and second centuries tried to incorporate some of the principles of the offerings into the Dietary Laws. The consequence of this was that the importance of the Sabbath and Festival meals in the family greatly increased so that in one way one might say that the centre of worship moved from the temple to the family home. The father led the prayers and the intellectual teaching of the Laws, whilst the mother 'performed the sacrifices' and was in charge of the practical examples, particularly of emotional understanding.

To this day the recital of Proverbs 31:10-31, referred to as *ESHeT ChaYiL* (אשת חיל) 'a woman of worth' is a central part of the Friday night service in a

Jewish home. The Synagogue thus became a place for meeting and study, rather than only a place of worship. As I have said before, even today the Yiddish word for Synagogue is *shul*, the same word as English 'school' and that means its main function, as well as the attitude to this place, is very different to that of a Christian church. It seems to me that there is a connection to the fact that Jewish Synagogues of outer magnificence were mainly built in periods of decay of inner spirituality.

Food Laws
There are certain aspects of the sacrifices which also form part of the food laws. The most important one is probably the prohibition that blood must not be eaten. Blood is part of Life, energy connected with the Higher level, and must not be food for man.

Blood in some form of ceremony is returned to the 'earth' from which it came. The Hebrew word for blood, *DaM* (דם) is also the basic root of the word 'man' (אדם) and the root of the word 'earth' *AdaMaH* (אדמה). Man in this sense is the product of earth containing the vital energy of blood. The first time the returning of blood to the earth is mentioned in the Bible is the spilling of the blood of Abel (*HaBeL* הבל). HaBel means 'breath' or 'spirit'. This is perhaps an indication of why the sacrifice of animals was such a sacred process, which could only be performed by the Priests if they themselves were clean, i.e. had 'sanctity' (קדשה). We have the description in II Chronicles 30:17, where it is explained that many in the congregation had not sanctified themselves. For this reason the Levites took charge of the *SheCHiJTaH* (שחיטה), the ritual killing. This was about 720 BCE and ever since then the ritual killing of animals has been done only by a qualified person, the *ShoCHeT* (שוחט).

It was always stressed that all animals for sacrifices had to be without blemish. Anything which was imperfect could not be offered for 'transformation'.

The system of sacrifices is generally accepted to be the oldest form of communal worship. It has been developed over a very long period and was influenced by all neighbouring civilisations. It must have included many different forms and meaning, and in Biblical times, they seemed to have included simultaneously different levels of meaning and purpose.

The book of Numbers (במדבר) starts with the organisation of the Tribes, their mustering and counting. The Levites were not 'numbered' but appointed to look after the Tabernacle of Testimony and perform all the duties of divine service. When the people came into the 'Land', it was divided and each Tribe received their portion. The Levites however, had no portion and therefore had to be maintained by the Tribes. Some of the offerings constituted a form of tax, which maintained the Levites.

In many of the burnt offerings we find that the parts of the animal which could not be eaten were completely burnt on the Altar and the edible parts were eaten by the priests and Levites. It was thus an economical and practical arrangement, where little was wasted, at the same time 'feeding' the people on the higher levels through the symbolical and experiential.

The various instructions about permitted and forbidden foods were on the whole given in such a way that the inner reason for a prohibition was rarely explained, but only an outer reason given: parting of the hoof, fish with scales etc. Pondering about this, I wonder whether this was done so that people who did not ask questions could simply obey the rules but those who searched could find the reasons by experience, without being misled by explanations in words. When the Second Temple had been destroyed and the Rabbis were faced with the task of how to transmit the principles that had governed the system of the offering and sacrifices, they seemed to have used similar ideas. Again those who did not question could simply carry out 'the Commandments' and those who searched could find out from experience. In all these matters decline brings rigidity and a tendency to fundamentalism. A constant vigilance is therefore necessary in all these situations where 'knowing' replaces 'questioning'.

Because of the increased importance of the food laws after the destruction of the second temple the role of the woman in the religious Jewish household became even more important than it had been before. The religious ceremony on the eve of Sabbath assumed a central role.

This ceremony commences with the kindling of the Sabbath Lights by the mistress of the house, when she says the following blessing: 'Blessed art thou Lord our God, King of the universe who has sanctified us by thy Commandments and commanded us to kindle the Sabbath Light.'

It is important to understand here that the whole of the story of creation, as well as the possible development of the material universe in general and the development of man in particular, can be described and experienced in the form of the movement of light.

The movement from the Highest light downward is called *AwR* (אור), which can be described hieroglyphically as a movement of All Possibilities, Here and Now, from the centre towards the periphery. This is the light of Genesis 1:3 when the creator says: 'Let there BE Light.' A part of this light can reach man from above, and in all languages I know, it is called by a name equivalent to the English expression 'to Enlighten'.

The light that moves upwards from the material world is called *NuR* (נור) which is fire or light and gives the light which is called *NeR* (נר) which means lamp or candle. The same idea and root is the basis of the Arabic word *minaret*, where the call to prayer is a reminder for the 'upward movement'.

The woman by kindling the light and pronouncing the blessing initiates therefore the movement upwards.

The ceremony continues by the parents blessing the children with the words:
'The Lord Bless Thee and keep thee
The Lord make his face shine upon thee and be gracious unto thee
The Lord turn his face unto thee, and give thee peace.'

In Hebrew the first line consists of three words, the second line of five words and the third line of seven words. Apart from the symbolic meanings of 3, 5 and 7 the total adds up to 15 which is the numerical value of *YaH* (יה), a name symbolising the immanent aspect of God. Perhaps this blessing at this time can be seen as the opposite movement to the movement of the lighting of the candles.

There now follows a song which begins with the words: 'Peace be to you ministering Angels, Messengers of the Most High, the supreme King of Kings, the Holy One, blessed be he . . .'. This song is based on the tradition that two Angels accompany each person home from the Synagogue service on Friday evening. Could this be an indication that, although each family celebrates in their own home, there still remains a link with the whole community?

The master of the house now recites Proverbs 31:10-31 which praises the importance and valour of the woman. There follows the recital of the last phrase of Genesis 1:31 and the first three verses of Genesis 2 and the blessing of the fruit of the vine.

The next blessing reminds us that the Sabbath is a memorial of creation and a remembrance of the departure from Egypt. Thus it reminds us again of the movement from the Highest down to our level and the beginning of the opposite inner journey through the 'inner' wilderness 'to the Land of Israel', the land of our aim.

There follows the ritual usually referred to as the 'washing of the hands'. On closer examination we find that the words *NeTiLaT YaDaYiM* (נטילת ידים) really signify 'the purification' of the hands. This appears to me to suggest that an inner purification is indicated here, in addition to the hygienic requirement, so that the person can be worthy and able to receive food.

A special loaf of bread is now broken into small pieces and shared amongst the people present and the blessing is: 'Blessed art thou Lord our God, King of the universe who bringest forth bread out of the Ground.' The word bread, *LeCHeM* (לחם) can also mean food in general and perhaps food of different levels.

The mistress of the house now serves the meal. It is always stressed that it is *her* house and that the woman determines both the outer and the inner level of the household. The man's task is to provide the material means to maintain the household and also to provide learning and mental understanding.

Perhaps a modern Chassidic opinion would clarify the position of woman: All that is sacred to the nation of God and is fundamental to the house of Israel in establishing and rearing an upright generation, was entrusted by God to the women of Israel.

The woman who fulfils her obligation and destiny in the life of the family in conducting the house and in seeing to the education of all members of the household in accordance with the Torah teaching, this woman is the subject of the verse: 'The wisdom of women constructed the Home.'

CHAPTER 6

The Ten Sephirot – The Tree of Life

WHEN LOOKING AT THE Sepher Yetzirah we saw that in a certain way we could make a statement that the 10 Sephirot plus the 22 letters of the alphabet form the 32 mystical (or wonderful) paths which describe the whole creation.

About the ten Sephirot (spheres or classes) we can say that they describe all the laws of the universe. They can be seen as the pattern of Adam *QaDMON* (אדם קדמון) 'Primordial Man', as well as the flow of energies that keeps everything in a kind of balance but with the necessary tensions.

Having made such a grandiose statement which, God forbid, could lead to an impression that all these laws are now understood, this can perhaps best be rectified by a story based on the scriptures:

Genesis 32 tells us that Jacob was returning home from his fourteen years of sojourn with Laban, now his father in law. He was afraid that his brother Esau, who in this situation personifies physical power, might attack him, so he sent his family and all his possessions across the river Yabbok (יבק meaning effusion). Yabbok is a tributary of the river Jordan (ירדן which means to descend), and is halfway between the sea of Galilee (in Hebrew called Yam Kineret ים כנרת which can be translated as sea of vibrations) and the Dead Sea (the sea of salt ים המלח) a level where all movement stops.

'And Jacob was left alone and there wrestled an *Ish* (איש) with him until daybreak...'.

This word *Ish* could be translated as Man, or Angel, or a Higher Being. For four thousand years or longer people speculated about the right meaning and some of the most important Rabbis stated that this ambiguity was there because it was something man was not allowed to investigate in the ordinary way. Because Jacob understood that this was a mystery which he had to accept as such, it was given to him to see the role he had to play from then on. He was given the name Israel (ישראל) which means: he who wrestles or struggles with *EL* (אל). In a loose way *EL* can be translated as God. But since this is only a word for a mystery, which words cannot explain, it means perhaps that it is only to the extent we can 'wrestle' in ourselves and experience the movement or flow of energies in ourselves that we can partake in this search and become 'Children of Israel'.

As there can only be one truth, this search cannot belong to one group of humanity only, but must be universal. On the other hand, as long as we are on this earth and have to use language and outer form for our communication, we have to accept these outer forms of sharing as an aid. It is however essential to remember that all words and diagrams can only be aids, and what matters is the real experience in ourselves.

During the thirty years in which I have studied the Tree of Sephirot and other powerful ideas of Kabbalah I had to remind myself again and again that one does get identified with them and they become graven images (Pesel פֶּסֶל) in the sense of the second commandment. This leads to the worship of other gods (ELoHIM ACHeRIM אלוהים אחרים), that is, of taking the ideas and outer forms for the truth itself.

It is very important never to *compare* ideas from different teachings or religions as this can only be done by an ordinary part of our head and usually takes the form of analytical thinking. This process is comparable to carving up a living body to see how it works. We may see the parts but it is no longer alive. If we study different teachings or methods then, as far as they are understood, the identity of two methods will be experienced in us and often one way can complement the understanding of the other.

After these warnings we can perhaps turn to the diagrammatic description of the Sephirot. The easiest way to approach the meaning of the diagram of 'This Tree' seems to be in the diagrammatic form in three columns.

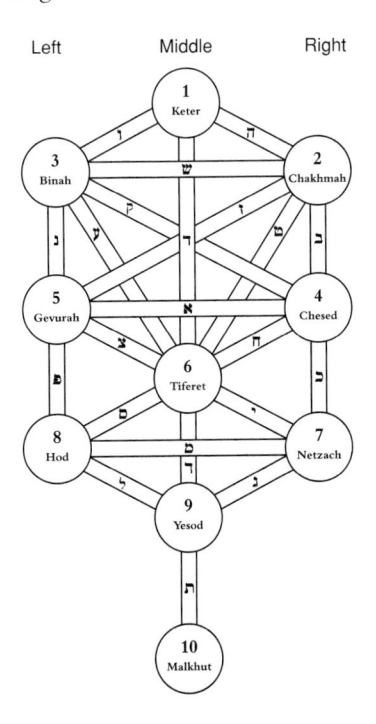

This diagram can only begin to have any meaning if we can experience it as energy in movement. When the two opposites on the 'Right' and the 'Left' are in a form of balance this can allow the energy in the middle column to move up or down. These energies can also flow in both directions simultaneously as the Lower yearns towards the Higher and the Higher has to descend towards the Lower to make the ascent of the Lower possible. I find it helpful to picture this struggle as a need to allow the flow to enable symbiosis to take place, rather than a fight against something, the way our habitual thinking has been programmed.

The Tree of Life can also be seen as a description of Adam Kadmon (אדם קדמון – the Principal Man). The diagram can give an approximate idea and to the extent we can experience these positions, they can be sensed.

The ten Sephirot can be divided into the top triad of Keter-Chokmah-Binah which is called Arikh Anpin, an Aramaic term meaning the Long Face, or by the Greek term Makro-Prosopus; and the remaining seven which form the Zair Anpin (Short Face) or Micro-Prosopus, and are called the seven Sephirot of manifestation.

The descent or ascent through these ten Sephirot and the ascent from our world to the next higher world can also be described in the form of the flow of light.

The light of Ain Soph (Endlessness) flows into Keter (the Crown) and from there into Chokmah (Wisdom). Thence it flows towards Binah (Understanding). The light of Chokmah is like the light of the sun, whilst the light of Binah receives it from Chokmah like the moon receives the light from the sun, and reflects it like a mirror to Chesed (Grace). Here it encounters its opposite: Din (Law). The importance of the balance between the rigour of the Law and the transcendence of this rigour by mercy forms a great deal of the discussions and explanations of this stage of the flow.

From this stage it flows to Tipheret (Beauty) which is often called the heart and can be seen as a point of gravity. All channels from Tipheret connect with every other Sephirah except Malkut (Kingdom).

Malkut is the point which connects with the next lower world and of course simultaneously the point of the meeting from the lower world to the next higher.

This point is also called Shekinah (the Dwelling Place) and represents the female aspects of God. The meeting of the 'Sons' of Israel, those who struggle with or for the Higher, are said to enter into the marriage of Israel with the Shekinah.

Over the last eight centuries a great deal has been written about the principles of the Kabbalah and during the twentieth century good translations into English have appeared. Various schools differ in the details of the interpretation and new ways of formulation are constantly being found.

I was recently very struck by the description of a 'self perpetuating system' in the subatomic world described by Fritjof Capra in his recent book *The Web of Life*. He seems to describe something that has some relationship to the idea of the ten Sephirot, particularly the thought that such a system should never be in absolute balance but as far from equilibrium as can be sustained. When reading Capra's description it seemed to throw some light for me on the idea of the continuous struggle between Chesed and Din, which transcends the absolute 'Justice' of Law.

I also wondered whether the idea expressed by Capra in the same book, that the basic system of nature is based on a symbiosis of its different parts and not the basic need to destroy, as described in Darwin's theory of evolution, gives us a wider view of the meaning of the universe. Perhaps this view has brought us nearer to the tradition of the Kabbalah, the Zohar, and the Gnostic views about our place in the universe.

The Zohar gives us also a Gnostic and simple view of the soul and the framework of creation. Perhaps a mystical hymn written by Moses Ben Nachman, the twelfth century Kabbalist, paints a better picture of the journey of the soul which is a spark of divine life.

> From the beginning of time through eternities
> I was among his hidden treasures.
> From Nothing he called me forth, out of the end of time
> I shall be reclaimed by the King
>
> My life flows from the depths of the Spheres
> Which give order and form to the Soul
> Divine forces build it and nourish it;
> Then it is preserved in the chambers of the King
>
> He radiated light to bring her forth
> In hidden well-springs, right and left
> The soul descended the ladder of heaven
> From the primeval pool of Siloam to the garden of the King.

Epilogue

AFTER TEN YEARS OF struggle and fight against the Nazi regime with all the terrible brutalities and planned cruelty. I returned in 1947 to civilian life. Like me, many of my contemporaries thought that this was the end of a period of injustices and killings, and that we could now look forward to a period of enjoyable peaceful living.

This expectation of peaceful life soon proved to be an illusion. The period of the Cold War between the two superpowers, the USA and the Soviet Union, at least still allowed a balance of power to prevent major catastrophes.

After the collapse of the Soviet Union in 1991 only one superpower now remained. The Soviet Union had supported the former Eastern Republics in a material sense, so that they could lead a relatively normal life. It was not foreseen that with the disappearance of the Soviet superpower these Eastern Republics would lose their economic way of life. The Soviets had tried to replace the old proud local culture with a western-type Soviet outlook, but with the collapse of the Soviet Union this disappeared and the old native system no longer existed.

I recently saw a programme about the famine in Tadzikistan, which showed a young man in an immaculate white business shirt and clean European type trousers, digging for the food local rats had hidden for their future use. The programme explained that this was the only nourishment that they could find.

There appeared before my eyes the picture of the Tadzik prisoners we had interrogated towards the end of 1944. We had to see them immediately on their arrival in the camp. They sometimes still wore their old civilian clothes under their Soviet uniforms; and over this German uniforms. By this time they were usually just three sets of rags covered with lice. They had a cat-like dexterity of movement and their independent attitude could only be admired. They were very different to us but yet human beings one could feel respect for.

What I saw in this film fifty years later were people with many more outer goods, but who had lost the ability to feed themselves and were dependent on other people's charity. What is progress?

I had also, during the last few years, studied the differences between Western and Eastern languages, particularly Semitic ones, which showed me the impossibility of direct translation of such diverse languages and backgrounds. It would go far beyond the aim of this work to explain these difficulties. The only way would be to establish real human relationships, which go beyond mere words and include the understanding of gestures, attitude and even physical relationships. That certainly needs time and direct contact from person to person.

These people, deprived not only of their physical means to live, but also the traditional support of the old values, are now entirely in the hands of ruthless fundamentalist propaganda and enticement to violence.

In order to create the broadest possible coalition and a fight against the fundamentalist violence there seems to have been recent attempts to appease more vulnerable peoples or nations. This to me had the same flavour as the attempts in 1938 to bring peace to Europe by sacrificing the Republic of Czechoslovakia. I have lived through this appeasement as a member of the Czech Forces and I am quite convinced that any appeasement in the present situation would lead to the same catastrophic results as the sell-out and consequent destruction of Czechoslovakia in 1938/9.

After the defeat of these evil forces a way will have to be found to reduce first of all the amount of hate and then forge a new way of life based on mutual respect and tolerance. How to bring this about?

Bibliography

J.G. Bennett, *Gurdjieff: Crisis in Human Affairs* (Turnstone Books)
Fritjof Capra, *The Web of Life* (Harper Collins, 1996)
Gordon Thomas & Max Morgan-Witts, *Voyage of the Damned*, 2nd edition (Dalton Watson, 1994)
G.I. Gurdjieff, *All and Everything* (Routledge & Kegan Paul)
P.D. Ouspensky, *In Search of the Miraculous* (Routledge & Kegan Paul)
Fritz Peters, *Boyhood with Gurdjieff* (Victor Gollancz Ltd., 1964)